WITHDRAWN
SMU LIBRARIES

Yale Historical Publications

Miscellany 87

Published under the direction of the
Department of History

Strasbourg and the Reform

A STUDY IN THE PROCESS OF CHANGE

BY

Miriam Usher Chrisman

NEW HAVEN AND LONDON, YALE UNIVERSITY PRESS, 1967

Copyright © 1967 by Yale University.
Designed by Anne Rajotte,
set in Caledonia type,
and printed in the United States of America by
The Colonial Press Inc.
Distributed in Canada by McGill University Press.
All rights reserved. This book may not be reproduced,
in whole or in part, in any form
(except by reviewers for the public press),
without written permission from the publishers.

Library of Congress catalog card number: 67-13431

Published with assistance from
the foundation established in
memory of Philip Hamilton McMillan
of the Class of 1894, Yale College.

ℒ 106823/87

FOR DONALD

FONDREN LIBRARY
Southern Methodist University
DALLAS, TEXAS

CONTENTS

Preface

Part i. Strasbourg Before the Reformation
1480–1520

Part ii. The Reformation in Strasbourg
1520–1534

Part iii. The Impact of the Reform
1534–1548

CONTENTS

PREFACE

How do the ideas of a philosopher, a scientist, a political or religious reformer move from the realm of theory to the pragmatic world of everyday life? How does the idea communicate itself? How does it become an effective factor in creating social and political change? Who, for instance, first listens to the new idea? Why do some men accept it, others reject it? When it is accepted is it still the same idea? How is it assimilated into the preexisting pattern of thought and by the traditional institutions? Does it maintain its original independence of novelty, or does a certain amount of synthesis inevitably take place?

Intrigued by such general questions, I was initially drawn to the study of intellectual history and intellectual movements. Gradually, in pursuit of answers, I turned to the period of the Reformation. Here was a moment in history where changes occurred very swiftly. A series of new ideas were introduced, clearly and consciously distinguished from the traditional ideology and theology. Preaching and teaching of these ideas led to political change and created new social groups. Old institutions crumbled and new ones were formed. Thus, it was a period in which it was possible to observe with relative clarity the interplay between ideas and institutions. The problem was to limit the study in some way to provide sufficient depth, and I decided to limit myself to a small geographic area. I would use a set of city walls as my boundary, turning inward to examine the people and their institutions, their adaptations to the new movement, making no attempt to describe the Reformation in its broader aspects or even to place the city in these larger events. For the Reformation such a geographic limitation was not entirely artificial since the city-states of Switzerland and Germany were still functioning as autonomous units; they enacted their own laws, and their social and political institutions were often quite highly differentiated from those of their neighbors.

My city is Strasbourg. A free imperial city, it was self-governing and created its own course of action throughout the period. Bordering both Germany and Switzerland, it was influenced not only by Luther but by Zwingli and the Swiss reformers, as well as a constant stream of Anabaptist leaders. Significantly for my purposes, no one reformer totally dominated the scene, controlling events by the sheer weight of his own personality. Thus it is possible to observe the development of the Reform without being overwhelmed by one individual.

Once the initial choices had been made, the study broke into three rather distinct parts. It was essential to examine thoroughly the status of the major institutions of the city—social, political, and economic—before the Reformation to determine their traditional interrelationships. This analysis was aided by the work of German scholars who were interested in the late medieval economic and constitutional development of the city and who had collected and printed the basic documents and written a series of comprehensive monographs. The first part of the book will serve as a summary of their work.

Having established the milieu before the Reform, I could then turn to the primary materials to examine the process of change. Here I first attacked the question of the protagonists of the new ideology and then attempted to discover who listened to them and was influenced by them. Very early, by 1525, the reformers were faced with the question of how far they wished to go in fomenting a social revolution. This opportunity they repudiated: Their goal was spiritual rather than social; they still thought in traditional political terms and gradually found themselves subordinated to the state.

The final step was to determine the impact of the new ideology on the traditional institutions of government, on the old established structure, and on the customary social patterns. Here it was possible to see a reciprocal action—established institutions could adopt and adapt a new idea, modifying it to suit their own ends, as well as being changed by it. Thus the existing institutions played an important role in the development of the ideology and in changing its emphasis and its methods of action.

The book owes many things to many people. It began as a question raised in a graduate seminar with Professor Leonard Krieger, and it was he who suggested the city of Strasbourg. Professors Franklin Baumer and Roland Bainton were also interested in the problem and were always generous with advice and encouragement. Professor Hajo Holborn directed the study when it was a doctoral thesis and then suggested that I pursue it further as a book. Professor Franklin Ford of Harvard generously offered bibliographic aid and his own knowledge of Strasbourg materials. In addition to these men, I owe a very special debt to my father, Abbott Payson Usher. In conversations over a long period of time we pursued the question of the nature of ideological change and the moment of invention, and his work profoundly influenced my own thought and work.

The Yale University Library collections were open to me as a graduate student and Mr. Robert Haynes, librarian of the Harry Elkins Widener Memorial Library, made it possible for me to draw on Harvard's rich collection. The William Allan Neilson Library of Smith College generously permitted me to use its microfilm facilities in the early stages of my research.

The group of scholars at the University of Strasbourg and the Municipal Archives—M. François Wendel, M. Jean Rott, M. Phillippe Dollinger, and the late M. Hans Haug, Curator of the Museums of Strasbourg—welcomed me cordially, encouraged my undertaking and shared with me their knowledge of the period and their familiarity with the sources, directing me to materials that would be fruitful. M. Joseph Fuchs, Archivist of the Municipal Archives, not only graciously corresponded with me with regard to microfilm and materials and the endless final details, but when I was working at the Archives, he was always available to consult, suggest, and encourage. With rare grace he creates a community of scholars of those who work in the Archives.

I wish also to thank Mrs. Alice H. Manning and Mrs. Marjorie Erikson, who tirelessly typed draft after draft from illegible copy.

Finally, the book represents my husband's conviction that one family can support and contain two scholars. Despite the incessant demands of his own research and his surgical practice, he encouraged me to undertake the book, and created the time and opportunity for me to work and to write, always with the genial assurance that these activities did not disrupt the household. In the end, the book became a family project, and our sons, Nicholas and Abbott, contributed their particular aid, assistance, and enthusiasm. For all of us, the book is a token of our special affection for the city and the people of Strasbourg.

Miriam Usher Chrisman

Northampton, Mass.
September 1966

PART I

𝔖trasbourg 𝔅efore the 𝔎eformation

1480–1520

CHAPTER 1

ECONOMIC STRUCTURE

N the year 1480 Strasbourg[1] was one of the leading free imperial cities of the Holy Roman Empire, a position owed in large part to her geographic location. Her walls and cathedral rose dramatically from the flat Alsatian plain that served as a vital granary for the more arid and mountainous areas to the north, east, and south. A contemporary observer was moved to the use of utopian terms: "All things are found in over-abundance in this city, especially wine and grain, for she lies in a noble land, and while the soil is not as good for fruit as it is for wine, . . . some hundred gardeners raise turnips, radishes, onions, and cabbages with such great

1. Strasbourg as a subject presents certain orthographic problems since German historians spell all place names and names of individuals in German, while French historians use the French forms. This means that all individuals have two names, the *Ammeister* Jacob Sturm becomes Jacques Sturm in French, while the French humanist Jean Sturm becomes Johann Sturm in German texts. Since I found this rather confusing when I started to work in Strasbourg, I decided against translating all names into English, which would have created two new people named James and John Sturm. I have translated geographic names into an accepted English equivalent, but names of persons have been left in the native language of the individual concerned, whether German, French, Swiss, or Latin, on the theory that a person does not change his name when traveling. Martin Bucer, as a well-known figure, appears in various languages. While Butzer is the old German form, I have chosen to follow recent German and English scholars in using Bucer.

3

bounty that there is nothing like it to be found in all Germany."[2]

Even more important was the city's position on the Rhine. Lying on a tributary of the great river, Strasbourg dominated not one but two waterways. The Ill, rising just below the Belfort gap, flows parallel to the Rhine through the Alsatian plain. At the city's walls a series of locks diverted it into a network of canals that formed a double ring around the city. Thus, goods coming up the Saone-Rhone waterway from Italy could reach the city with only a short land portage from Belfort to the Ill. In Strasbourg the cargos were unloaded onto the quays which edged the canals, then stored in the warehouses of Strasbourg merchants, ultimately to be transferred to barges and carried out to the Rhine waterway by Strasbourg boatmen, who exercised a firm monopoly over Rhine transport to Mainz and Cologne.[3] In the fourteenth century, with the decline of the great French fairs and the insecurity resulting from the Hundred Years War, this old Rhone route was partially bypassed. The Strasbourg merchants or their agents went to Basel by boat and proceeded thence to Italy, either via the Saint Gotthard pass to Milan or via the Tyrol to Venice and Verona,[4] but the city's function as middleman between Italy and the Rhine Valley was unchanged.

A final economic advantage was the Rhine bridge. Marshy, swampy banks and an exceedingly swift current made it difficult to span the great river below Freiburg im Breisgau, but in 1388 Strasbourg commissioned a series of causeways to be built over the marshes, and pontoon sections were devised for the stream itself. It was an engineering feat, the last bridge over the Rhine before the sea.[5] Since the city

2. Sebastian Munster, *Cosmographia Beschreibung aller Lender* (Basel, 1544), p. 167.

3. Jacques Hatt, *Une Ville du XVe Siècle, Strasbourg* (Strasbourg, 1929), p. 50.

4. Freddy Thiriet, "Sur les relations commerciales entre Strasbourg et l'Italie du Nord à la fin du moyen âge," *Revue d'Alsace, 100* (1961), 122–23.

5. Jacques Ungerer, *Le Pont du Rhin à Strasbourg* (Strasbourg, 1952), p. 8.

controlled two important waterways, the economy focused on brokerage, shipment, and transfer. A few Strasbourg merchants went afield and were active in the great fairs or maintained offices and agents at Venice, Lyon, and Antwerp,[6] but the majority of the city's businessmen stayed at home. The customs records of the period indicate the variety and extent of the import-export trade. Raw materials that came in included coal, wood, exotic woods, building logs from Switzerland, metals, furs, skins, and leather. Textiles were imported from England, the Low Countries, France, and other Rhenish cities. Ribbons from Reims and silks from Paris and Florence are listed on the customs ledgers.[7] Strasbourg herself manufactured and exported a common white and gray cloth; a heavy-duty, black linen and wool mixture; and camelot (loden)—practical, everyday, essential fabrics for sturdy, warm garments.[8] In addition Strasbourg served as the center for the export of Alsatian wines and, in the latter part of the fifteenth century, was beginning to develop a significant activity in paper manufacturing and in printing.[9]

The economy offered, then, a comfortable mixture of activity: the deposit and transshipment of goods for merchants traveling upriver from Flanders to the cities and towns in the Rhone Valley or to the north; the shipping and distribution of goods coming from Italy, France, or Switzerland to proceed down the Rhine;[10] the manufacture of solid articles for everyday use; and the wine trade, which involved both luxury and necessity, depending on the quality. The existence of three or four active printing presses before the turn of the century indicates the level of technological development. Yet Strasbourg did not rank with the great commercial or industrial cities of the time. She did not have a manufac-

6. F. J. Fuchs, "Les Prechter de Strasbourg, une famille de négociants banquiers du XVIᵉ siècle," *Revue d'Alsace*, 95 (1956), 156.
7. Georges Lévy-Mertz, "Le Commerce strasbourgeois au XVᵉ siècle," *Revue d'Alsace*, 97 (1958), 101.
8. Ibid., p. 100.
9. Hatt, *Strasbourg au XVᵉ siècle*, p. 50.
10. Lévy-Mertz, *Revue d'Alsace*, 97 (1958), 101.

turing industry in which she maintained a dominant position, like Cologne or Ulm, or a great fair like Leipzig or Frankfurt.[11] Her trade was regional—within the Rhine Valley.[12] Unlike some of her Rhenish sister cities, she had not made the transition from medieval commerce to a more extensive, wider-ranging trade and industry.[13]

The unit of economic organization was, with a few notable exceptions, the guild. The guild still controlled the training of the labor force, the forms and processes of production, and the distribution of all goods manufactured and sold in Strasbourg.[14] It was no longer, however, the semiautonomous, relatively democratic guild of the High Middle Ages. During the fifteenth century there had been a consistent

11. Willy Andreas, *Deutschland vor der Reformation* (Stuttgart, 1932). In his study Andreas does not even include Strasbourg as one of the important economic centers, although he includes it in his discussion of Rhenish trade.

12. Hans Baron, "Religion and Politics in the German Imperial Cities during the Reformation," *English Historical Review*, 52 (1937), 614–33. Baron emphasizes very strongly the difference between Nuremberg with its large-scale industry and commerce as against Strasbourg, whose trade he feels was far more limited in scope. His figures show that about the year 1500, 232 Nuremberg merchants arrived in Venice, as against 5 from Strasbourg and 62 from Augsburg (p. 616). His feeling is that Strasbourg trade was based on agriculture—the export of corn and wine. The Lévy-Mertz material and Anton Herzog's study, *Die Lebensmittelpolitik der Stadt Strassburg in Mittelalter* (Berlin, 1959), however, do not indicate large grain exports. Indeed there was an attempt to restrict them. Although Baron may somewhat overemphasize the agricultural nature of Strasbourg's trade, his conclusion is nonetheless important, namely, that the scale of Nuremberg's trade made it essential for her to maintain close relations with the emperor and the empire, whereas Strasbourg's more self-sufficient economy gave her a certain amount of independence.

13. The variety and diversification of Strasbourg industrial and commercial activity is represented in the index of trades published by Jacques Hatt in "Les Métiers strasbourgeois du XIIIe au XVIIIe siècle," *Revue d'Alsace*, 101 (1962), 51–78.

14. The guilds covered the most important trades and crafts. Interestingly enough for crafts which employed only a few workmen in each city or town, regional associations were beginning to emerge by the fifteenth century. For an account of these in Alsace see Lucien Sittler, "Les Associations artisanales en Alsace au moyen âge et sous l'ancien regime," *Revue d'Alsace*, 97 (1958).

movement toward consolidation and rationalization of the guilds. They had codified their regulations in a book of guild ordinance. Tasks and duties of apprentices and journeymen had been more rigidly described, qualifications for mastership made more exacting, and the controlling power had been drawn into the hands of the masters. The traditional guild constitutions provided for a general assembly of all the guild members. This group, in turn, elected a court to take care of conflicts within the trade. A guild master, masters for each separate craft, and a treasurer were elected annually.[15] The guild established the terms of apprenticeship and provided guarantees for each apprentice in case he should run away,[16] set the salaries for the different ranks of journeymen, fixed the hours, holidays, and conditions of work,[17] and established the prices to be charged for finished goods. The guild tribunal handled all conflicts between workers and masters and among the masters themselves. In theory, then, the corporations were almost self-governing, but in actual fact this autonomy had been diminished by the end of the fifteenth century, as the municipal government began to extend its regulative authority and assumed broader responsibility for the economic stability of the city.

The process can be seen in the clothmakers guild. As early as 1400 the clothmakers codified their regulations, collecting them together in a great book, the *Buch der Tucher*. Revisions were made during the course of the century, in 1437, 1453, and 1466, and were duly entered.[18] In 1448 they purchased a house which served as a meeting place and a symbol of their independence and prestige. The autonomy was short-lived. Throughout the fifteenth century the clothmakers

15. Jean Rott, "Artisanat et mouvements sociaux à Strasbourg autour de 1525," in *Artisans et Ouvriers d'Alsace* (Strasbourg, 1965), p. 138.
16. Ibid., p. 139.
17. See the Rott article for a detailed discussion of provisions regulating the life of the journeyman apprentices.
18. Gustav Schmoller, *Die Strassburger Tucher und Weberzunft* (Strassburg, 1879), pp. 23–38, 50–69. Hereafter referred to as Schmoller, *Tucher und Weberzunft*.

struggled with their rivals, the weavers, for control of the textile industry. In 1483 the city government, or *Magistrat*, intervened, and decreed that the two guilds were to be considered as one unit for political purposes, and in 1493 they were merged by the city to form a single trade guild.[19] Theoretically the new unit retained the traditional prerogatives, but in fact the Magistrat began to control the relations between the guild and the consumer. From 1480 to 1521 a series of city ordinances was issued, reforming certain aspects of the cloth market and providing for the sealing and labeling of cloth to protect the consumer from poor weight or inferior quality.[20] The task of maintaining discipline within the guild was still left to the masters and the tribunal,[21] but the city felt that it must assume responsibility for the consumer and the public interest and therefore legislated against monopoly, price fixing, and stockpiling.[22]

The original autonomy of the guilds was lost, and so were the traditional democratic forms, for the powers which remained were increasingly concentrated in the hands of the few, the masters, at the expense of the whole body of workers. Regulations were no longer enacted by the *Handwerksgemeinde* but by the master of the guild and his council. By 1551 the assembly of clothmakers and of carpenters and joiners was no longer consulted in the election of guild officers—the outgoing master and the council chose their own successors.[23]

As the guild lost its popular base and became more autocratic, the journeymen suffered most. This was true in other German cities as well. The original concept of brotherhood and equality was lost, and the journeyman found himself no

19. Ibid., p. 476.
20. Ibid., pp. 475–76.
21. Rott, "Artisanat et mouvements sociaux," reviews the regulations of the furriers and tailors with regard to the number of workers permitted to work in each shop, work performed by members of the master's family, work performed by female members of the master's family, etc., pp. 141–42.
22. Ibid., p. 142.
23. Schmoller, *Tucher und Weberzunft*, pp. 488–89.

longer moving up the ladder to mastership. He had become a subordinate, permanently relegated to an inferior status, receiving a money wage that was insufficient to support a wife and family. As a result, the years from 1480 to 1523 saw great unrest among the journeymen,[24] and Alsace and Strasbourg were not exempt from the general disturbance. The cities looked on these men as a nomadic, unstable element and feared they would propagate revolutionary ideas. As early as 1432 and 1436 representatives from various Alsatian cities, including Strasbourg, met to discuss a common policy.[25] After the conference the Strasbourg Magistrat prohibited all masters or journeymen from joining any sort of association without the permission of the city authorities. The journeymen could have neither common meeting place nor group organization nor common treasury for any purpose.[26] The guilds forbade them to drink each other's health, get drunk, swear, or indulge in fist fighting.[27] In 1495, despite all restrictions, the bakery workers of Colmar went on strike, finally leaving the town in a body. They were in touch with journeymen in other communities, including Strasbourg, and the unrest spread to other trades and other cities. It is perhaps significant that the dispute did not involve wages or working conditions, but prestige. The issue was whether the masters or the journeymen were to walk closer to the Holy Sacrament in the Corpus Christi procession.[28]

The period from 1480 to 1525 was, however, the last in which the journeymen tried to mount some opposition to the superior forces that were soon to overwhelm them. They would make common cause with the peasants during the Peasants' War, but that defeat was final. After 1525 the municipal governments adopted a rigid attitude; no attempts to improve the conditions of the workers appear in the docu-

24. Andreas, *Deutschland vor der Reformation*, p. 301.
25. Lucien Sittler, "Les Mouvements sociaux à Colmar du XIVe au XVIe siècle," *Revue d'Alsace*, 95 (1956), 132.
26. Ibid., p. 134.
27. Rott, "Artisanat et mouvements sociaux," p. 141.
28. Sittler, *Revue d'Alsace*, 95 (1956), 138.

ments after this point. The cities were supported by the imperial authorities—a series of mandates directed to the whole empire forbade protest by the workers and prohibited all forms of association.[29] Most interestingly there is no record in the Strasbourg materials of any demand by the workers for an increase in wages after 1525.[30] The workers had submitted.

One novel form of economic organization did appear in Strasbourg at this time. In 1490 the Prechter, Ingolt, Wurmser, and Boecklin families, who were already allied by marriage, created a family society in which funds available from various members were used to carry on extensive trading activities. The society had agents in cities all over Europe, trading and speculating in wax, saffron, silk, wine, lead, and copper. Its extensive financial operations also included loans for business and trading purposes, but the Prechter society eschewed loans to the emperor, to princes, or to municipal authorities.[31] These "societies," which existed in other German cities as well, represented a new form of business organization and an interest in the accumulation and organization of capital for investment purposes. In some cities, Augsburg for example, the societies were important politically as well as economically.[32] There is no indication that this was true in Strasbourg, where neither the Prechters nor the Ingolts were important magistral families. Their capitalization permitted them to reach beyond the local sphere and take advantage of opportunities for investment and profit in Antwerp, Venice, and the Levant. The attitude of these families toward Strasbourg itself is perhaps indicated by their actions in 1548, when the city voted to reject the imperial edict establishing the interim religion—the Prechters, Ingolts, and their associates renounced their burgher rights and left the city rather than hazard the loss of their wealth and property by falling under the imperial ban.[33]

29. Ibid., p. 140.
30. Rott, "Artisanat et mouvements sociaux," p. 141.
31. Fuchs, Revue d'Alsace, 95 (1956), 157–59.
32. Andreas, Deutschland vor der Reformation, p. 338.
33. Fuchs, Revue d'Alsace, 95 (1956), 151.

Strasbourg was a commercial and manufacturing city whose economic life was still regulated along traditional lines. The hard core of the city's business was still carried on by the guilds. Certainly it is evident that in many of the guilds the master was an entrepreneur. His journeymen and apprentices performed their labors for wages, for the Magistrat itself fixed the basic wage for all handworkers in the guilds.[34] If this is to be defined as early capitalism, it was a capitalism that had adjusted itself to the guild system. Similarly, new technology, such as printing, and new techniques of economic organization, like wage labor or the family societies, simply served to modify the prevailing forms. The traditional forms had indeed become more rigid and would continue to become even more rigid in the period of this study.

It is difficult to arrive at a measure of the level of economic activity in the city. One of the chroniclers, Jacob Trausch, provides data on harvests and general agricultural conditions. His figures would indicate that agricultural production and prices in the period from 1480 to 1520 were subject to a relatively regular swing between good years and bad. Conditions would vary from a year like 1480, when there were great frosts and floods and with many deaths from hunger,[35] to a year like 1484, when the vintage was so abundant that there were not enough barrels: Vintners gave away a measure of wine for an egg in order to empty the barrels.[36] The years from 1493 to 1507 were good agricultural years; wine prices dropped to four or five florins a *fuder* for the best, and rye and wheat sold at low prices, the only exception being a bad year in 1497.[37] Then, beginning in 1508, with a cold spring and bad storms, there followed a decade of late

34. Schmoller, *Tucher und Weberzunft*, p. 60; and Rott, "Artisanat et mouvements sociaux," p. 139.

35. Jacques Trausch and Jean Wencker, *Les Chroniques Strasbourgeoises de Jacques Trausch et de Jean Wencker*, Fragments recueillis par l'Abbé L. Dacheux, Fragments des anciennes chroniques d'Alsace (4 vols. Strasbourg, 1892–1901), 3, 58. Referred to hereafter as Trausch and Wencker, *Chroniques*.

36. Ibid., p. 59.

37. Ibid., pp. 59–60.

frosts, drought, and crop failure, resulting in high prices; this pattern was not broken until 1523. The period just before the Reformation was thus marked by high prices and poor agricultural yields.[38] The year that saw the greatest intensity of unrest in Strasbourg, 1524, afforded a good harvest and low prices. In view of the relatively constant shifts it would seem unwise to try to correlate the rise and fall of agricultural prices with the social unrest at this period. For the most part, these variations were accepted as inevitable and natural. The cycle of good years followed by bad and of bad years followed by good was simply a fact of life in the fifteenth century.

The level of commercial and manufacturing activity in Strasbourg from 1480 to 1521 is illusive. There had been a decline in certain activities, but business had returned to a relatively stable level by 1520. The sharpest decline in commerce occurred in 1450, when the Magistrat faced a heavy debt after a war against the bishop and the invasion of the Armagnac. To increase revenues, the Magistrat levied a new tax on all commercial transactions, placed higher taxes on goods in transit, laid a tax on transport across the Rhine, and increased duties for the deposit of goods at the warehouse maintained by the city. Harassed, the merchants turned away from the city, and the Magistrat was forced to revise the tax schedules in 1477. From 1480 to 1521 there was a gradual revival as trade resumed its former pattern.[39]

The textile industry in Germany reached its highest level of production in the last decades of the fifteenth century. After 1500 the industry began to meet stiff competition from English wool and Flemish linen, and there were bitter complaints against the German clothmakers and weavers, who were accused of engaging in monopolistic practices. The Strasbourg Rat responded to this type of criticism by the con-

38. Ibid., pp. 61–62. The figures for Strasbourg compare with figures given for Augsburg in M. S. Elsas, *Umriss eine Geschichte der Preise und Löhne in Deutschland* (Leiden, 1936), p. 186.
39. Lévy-Mertz, *Revue d'Alsace*, 97 (1958), 110–11.

sumer protective measures already described. Perhaps as a result of these edicts the city's textile industry, which experienced a slump from 1514 to 1520, began to revive in the decade of the twenties and was fully restored by the thirties.[40] The recovery may also reflect the general conditions of economic expansion which characterized the period.[41]

Neither the difficulties experienced by the textile trades nor the fluctuations of the agricultural market mean that Strasbourg had suffered a significant economic depression before the Reformation. These were the variations that the medieval businessman accepted as part of the inevitable risk of his trade. The general economic position of the city was unchanged—Strasbourg remained a vital link in the trade flowing north from Italy and France down into the Rhine Valley. Until this trade was undermined by the expansion of coastal trade in the sixteenth century, the city's economic position was unchallenged. From 1480 to 1521 Strasbourg was wealthy and in a position of uncontrovertible commercial leadership on the upper Rhine.

40. Schmoller, *Tucher und Weberzunft*, pp. 514–15.
41. Andreas, *Deutschland vor der Reformation*, p. 312.

CHAPTER 2

SOCIAL AND POLITICAL STRUCTURE

N 1514, after a sojourn in Strasbourg, Erasmus addressed an encomium to Jacob Wimpfeling, his host:

> I saw a monarchy without tyranny, an aristocracy without factions, a democracy without disorder, prosperity without luxury, happiness without insolence. Can anyone imagine greater good fortune than harmony of this order? O divine Plato, that thou shouldst not have had the joy of beholding such a republic.[1]

Erasmus' enthusiasm might tend to give the modern reader the impression of a remarkably advanced republic. The city was actually an oligarchy controlled by a small, self-contained and self-perpetuating group drawn from the commercial patriciate. The political institutions, developed out of the experience of two revolutions and from the practices and procedures of several centuries, were marked by an accumulative tendency. No office, once established, had been abolished, and no committee, once convened, had been dismissed, so that by 1480 there was a congeries of officers and committees wielding political authority.

In the earliest period, the eleventh and twelfth centuries, the city was entirely under the control of the bishop. City officials were appointed either directly by the bishop or by

1. Quoted in Franklin L. Ford, *Strasbourg in Transition, 1648–1789* (Cambridge, Mass., 1958), p. 14.

one of his administrative staff, and the bishop invested with his own hands the most important two judicial officers—a tax collector and the master of the mint. The first municipal statute, a cartulary dating from 1135, indicates that the bishop's rule rested heavily on the individual citizen. Every burgher owed him five days work per month. The mint-workers, twelve of the furriers, four bakers, eight shoe-makers, all the smiths, all the carpenters, and butchers and coopers owed their entire labor and service to the episcopal household, for which they were probably remunerated.[2]

By the year 1200 a second municipal statute vested some political power in a small group of urban nobles and burgh-ers. The nobility, or *Constoffler*, were members of the bishop's administrative staff, endowed through their service with sufficient lands to be able to contribute one or more horses to defend the city. Their position rested on their lands, and they consciously avoided any contact with trade or com-merce. The bishop now provided that twelve *Ratsherren* should be chosen from among the Constoffler and the burgh-ers, one of whom was to be designated chief or *Magister*. This group was to aid the bishop in formulating the law and in governing the city. A larger council, known as the Schöffen and elected by universal suffrage, helped regulate business affairs. Its members served as witnesses to sales and purchases and made arrangements for payments of debt. In addition they were to stand as witnesses before the *Rat* to everything they had seen or heard,[3] and in very grave mat-ters they might be called upon to consult with the Rat. From these two ill-defined groups Strasbourg's municipal institutions would develop, and although the functions changed, the names Rat and Schöffen would remain.

The growth of the city's liberty was considerably abetted by the conflict between the emperors and the popes. As a general rule the city gave its support to the emperors and in return received important prerogatives and immunities.

2. Rodolphe Reuss, *Histoire de Strasbourg* (Paris, 1922), p. 17.
3. Ibid., pp. 22–23.

In 1205 Philip of Swabia gave Strasbourg the privileges of an imperial free city,[4] and these grants were confirmed and broadened by Frederick II in 1219.[5] These imperial charters increased the city's fiscal independence by granting tax exemptions and by authorizing new areas of revenue. In addition the charters extended the judicial powers of the lay administration. By 1260 the city had achieved a degree of independence that irritated the bishop, and civil war broke out between the bishop and his former agents, the Constoffler. The bishop hoped to maintain the allegiance of the burghers and guildsmen and made a direct appeal for their support, writing them in German. The attempt was fruitless. The burghers joined the Constoffler, and the bishop was soundly defeated by their combined forces at the battle of Hausbergen in 1262.[6] This event was an important moment in the history of the city, marking the end of the bishop's political authority. He was not even permitted to reside within the city walls but lived in his castle at Dachstein, ten miles to the west, maintaining only administrative offices inside the gates. The custom of nonresidence was to continue until Louis XIV restored Catholicism in 1681.

In the treaty drawn up between the bishop and the city in 1263 the latter maintained all the privileges previously conferred by the king or emperor, and although the bishop was to continue appointing four traditional judicial and administrative officers, effective political authority was placed firmly in the hands of the Rat, whose membership was drawn from the Constoffler.[7] The arrangement did not, however, bring peace. Relations with the bishop continued to be strained and uneasy, while new social tensions made themselves felt among the citizens. The Constoffler had always been proud and restrictive, but they had in recent years admitted to their ranks high city officials and a few wealthy burghers if the latter could meet the requirement of con-

4. Rodolphe Reuss, *Histoire d'Alsace* (Paris, 1920), p. 23.
5. Reuss, *Histoire de Strasbourg*, pp. 24–25.
6. Ibid., pp. 36–38.
7. Ibid., p. 41.

tributing a horse for the defense of the city. Thus a natural social assimilation had ensued. With political power now firmly in their grasp, they again became rigorously exclusive.[8] A large and clannish group, whose lives centered on their political-social clubs called *Trinkstuben*,[9] they had no intention of sharing their hard won political power nor their clubrooms, with the burghers, whom they regarded as socially, intellectually, and economically inferior. They became arrogant and autocratic. To further disassociate themselves from their urban origin, they cultivated the landed nobility, participating in their tournaments, feasts, and hunts, and were not above using municipal funds to increase their personal display of wealth and power. They adopted the knightly custom of family feuds and took sides in the quarrels of the local nobility.[10]

The burghers, for their part, clung stubbornly to their traditional prerogatives. Each guild had always maintained its own system of courts for internal discipline and had elected its own judicial and administrative officers, and now the guildsmen had no desire to be brought into new, centralized, city-wide courts. Nettled by the increasingly imperious attitude of their governors, the burghers alleged that the Constoffler had used their political position for their own selfish ends. Even the conditions of military service were found galling, for the Constoffler maintained the cavalry, leaving the onerous duty of the night watch and infantry service to the burghers.

An imbalance of this sort could not persist in the face of the increasing economic strength of the guilds. Outright misuse of their political power by the Constoffler only exacerbated the situation, and the revolution that occurred in 1332

8. Gustav Schmoller, *Strassburg zur Zeit der Zunftkämpfe und die Reform seiner Verfassung und Verwaltung,* Quellen und Forschungen zur Sprach und Kulturgeschichte der Germanische Völker (Strassburg, 1875), *11*, 18. Hereafter referred to as Schmoller, *Verfassung und Verwaltung.*

9. Ford, *Strasbourg in Transition,* p. 16. There were eighteen of these units at this time.

10. Schmoller, *Verfassung und Verwaltung,* p. 19.

is a classic example of the class conflict of the period. A quarrel broke out between two of the Constoffler families in one of the Trinkstuben, resulting in the stabbing and death of several noble youths, and the violence spread to the streets. Both burghers and artisans were afraid that the noble families involved would appeal to the landed aristocracy outside and that the city would be dragged, unwillingly, into a family feud. The guildsmen asked the master of the Rat for the keys and seals of the city in order to defend the city against invasion, promising to return them after the emergency was over. When the threat of military action faded, however, they retained these symbols of office until they had appointed a new Rat. This, they stipulated, should be composed of honest citizens, without restrictions of birth or social status. In effect this meant the addition of one representative from each guild. When the new Rat took office in 1334, all the burghers came together before the cathedral, and in a solemn ceremony the officers swore to perform their duties honestly and faithfully, while the citizens swore obedience. This public, mutual oath, or *Schwörbrief*, was to be reenacted every January until the French Revolution destroyed the last remnants of Strasbourg's unique constitution.[11]

The revolution of 1332 secured effective representation to the guilds and provided for the symbolic recognition of the mutual responsibility of the governing officials and burghers. Characteristically there was no attempt to make sweeping changes in the constitution itself. The old Trinkstuben were abolished as political clubs and were replaced by new guild units. The four *Stettmeister* were still to be chosen from the Constoffler and retained their ceremonial duties and their functions of presiding over the Rat, each serving three months of the year. Effective administrative authority was now vested in a new officer, a master of artisans or *Ammeister*. He was the executive arm of the Rat, supervising internal affairs as well as the conduct of foreign

11. Ford, *Strasbourg in Transition*, p. 263.

18

and military policy.[12] After 1349 the Ammeister was always chosen from the guilds, a further indication of their power and prestige.

The Rat now included twenty-five representatives of the guilds and twenty-two men chosen from among the Constoffler and burgher notables (wealthy commercial men of nonnoble stock).[13] A pragmatic division of power was made at this point. The Constoffler were given responsibility for external affairs, while the guild representatives devoted their efforts to the domestic economy. Having revolted because the Constoffler had usurped the public power for private ends, the guildsmen now made the same mistake. Legislation designed to protect the consumer was modified to the guilds' advantage; penalties for infractions and other disciplinary measures were to be administered by the guilds rather than by the city authorities. Taxes were levied by the guilds without consultation with or the assent of the Magistrat, and guildsmen were exempted from the night patrol and the night watch.

The Constoffler did not readily accept this thrust for power, and the citizens themselves reacted against the blatant self-interest of the guilds. The Constoffler regained some of their old political status in 1349, when younger sons of several noble families emerged as demagogues and attacked the guilds for their clannish and exclusive policies. Political office passed back and forth between the two contending parties until the end of the century.[14]

The guilds then attempted to curb the influence of the nobility by attacking the privilege of *Ausbürgertum*. By ancient custom a noble could own extensive lands and maintain his residence outside the city walls while still claiming all rights and privileges of citizens. The city dwellers realized that the city itself could be drawn into a dispute among the

12. Ibid., p. 12.
13. Schmoller, *Verfassung und Verwaltung*, p. 38.
14. The best account of the complex constitutional development of this period is contained in Schmoller, *Verfassung und Verwaltung*, pp. 40–49.

nobles if an *Ausbürger* demanded his rights of protection as a citizen. The special status was therefore abolished, and a new law provided that a noble who claimed citizenship had to live within the walls and assume his public responsibilities. In accordance with this edict, the Magistrat vigorously prosecuted a group of nobles for breach of the peace. Infuriated, twenty-six Constoffler renounced their burgher status and left the city, hoping to force the Magistrat to withdraw the new law. The protest boomeranged. The burghers regarded the flight as irresponsible and as a final indication of the nobles' lack of loyalty. Any claim to leadership the nobility still might have had was destroyed. Actual warfare, however, was averted, and in 1422 the Treaty of Spires finally settled the question of the Constoffler. The nobility were permitted to return or remain only if they accepted the conditions fixed by the Magistrat; all others were free to leave the city. The seats in the Rat were redistributed, giving twenty-eight to the guilds and only fourteen to the Constoffler. For a year or so, feeling was so high that even Stettmeister were chosen from the guilds, but when the immediate mood of mistrust had passed, some of the old noble families returned and resumed their traditional posts.

The revolutionary phase of Strasbourg's political development ended with the Treaty of Spires. The political ascendancy of the burghers was well established before 1450, and it cannot be claimed that the Reformation arose from the desire of the burghers to assert themselves as a political force. After 1422 the tension between Constoffler and burgher gradually disappeared. The Constoffler families who chose to remain in the city were accepted and respected. They retained their traditional social leadership, and individual nobles often took an active role in civic affairs or occupied honorary political offices. The line between the original, pure Constoffler and wealthier members of the commercial patriciate gradually became blurred and difficult to distinguish. By 1500 only eighty-nine of the old Constoffler families were left in the city, and the eighteen powerful Trinkstuben had shrunk to two.[15]

The Constoffler were replaced by a new type of nobility, or patriciate, urban in its values, drawn from the wealthier commercial class and the municipal bureaucracy.[16] Springing from burgher, even from artisan stock, the new nobility were merchants, guild masters, professional men, who had acquired property and with it position.[17] An edict of 1471 provided that any honorable burgher whose father and grandfather had had sufficient means to furnish horses for the city was to be considered a noble. Usually they were educated men, for while the Constoffler had scorned education, the commercial patriciate served as patrons to the humanists who began to gather in Strasbourg and sent their sons to university either in Germany or abroad.[18] It was this patrician group which held the major political, economic, and social power in the period of the Reformation, dominating both the Rat and the permanent committees.[19]

15. Ibid., p. 49.

16. The nomenclature of these social classes is extremely confusing. Each writer tends to develop his own terminology—Schmoller, for instance, rarely refers to the Constoffler but calls them the patricians. The confusion is further confounded because French sources use French counterparts for the German terms, and the Constoffler become *échevins*. I will use the term Constoffler only in its exact sense, meaning a member of one of the two remaining Trinkstube, one of the traditional nobility. I will use the term "commercial patriciate" to describe the group who came to power after the changes of 1405.

It is necessary to preserve the differentiation. Ford, *Strasbourg in Transition*, p. 17, explains the distinction as an important tradition. There was, he says, "a peculiar relationship between the Constoffler and the urban patriciate. The town's ruling class included many powerful commoners, and in terms of political influence there is little excuse to distinguish the Constoffler from the technically non-noble elements within the oligarchy. Nevertheless, since the constitution made specific concessions to the nobility, it is essential to recognize the line which had survived from the Middle Ages."

17. Schmoller, *Verfassung und Verwaltung*, p. 49.

18. Hatt, *Strasbourg au XV siècle*, pp. 47–48.

19. The commercial activities of this group are well described by Philippe Mieg, "Note sur les négociants Strasbourgeois Muege au XV siècle," *Revue d'Alsace*, 98 (1959), 138–45.

The major political development of the fifteenth century was the emergence of the permanent committees, the complex system of interlocking bodies that actually wielded political control. The first of these to emerge was the Council of IX, which probably grew out of a military commission in 1392. When the particular danger was over, the commission was not disbanded. In a sweeping reorganization of the city ordinances in 1405, four members were added to the original nine, and the group of thirteen was made responsible for the conduct of war and military affairs. In 1448 the committee achieved its final form to include the incumbent Ammeister, four former Ammeisters, four Constoffler, and four guild members. Since the Ammeisters were always chosen from the guilds, the guilds had a sturdy preponderance on this committee. The enlarged group was still called the Council of XIII, and the ordinance of 1448 provided for life appointment, reflecting a new concern for permanence and continuity. From 1405 this group assumed the direction of foreign affairs, a function it always retained.

After the Treaty of Spires and the exodus of the Constoffler, a thorough revision of the municipal laws and ordinances was undertaken in 1425. Eighty-four honorable men were assigned to the task, and in 1433 they submitted their revised code to the Rat. Among other items it provided for a Council of XV—five Constoffler and ten guild members—to supervise the application and execution of the new code. Once established, the committee was never disbanded. The group, appointed for life, became a general watchdog committee to prevent corruption, regulate the guilds, supervise public works, and control the city treasury. They were responsible for the execution of existing laws and advised on new legislation.[20]

The third council, the XXI, was closely associated with the legislative function of the Rat. The system of yearly elections meant that half of the Rat changed every year. It became a custom to submit important matters to a small group of ex-

20. Hatt, *Strasbourg au XV siècle*, p. 27.

Social and Political Structure

perienced Ratsherren. Originally, this group may have comprised twenty-one persons, but in 1401 there were nineteen, and in 1403, twenty-five. By 1450 it was stabilized at thirty-two members, twenty-two from the guilds and ten from the Constoffler. Again appointment was for life; vacancies were filled by cooption but essentially the group involved all the members of the XIII and the XV and four other Ratsherren. Thus, by the end of the fifteenth century, there was a permanent body to formulate foreign policy and direct military affairs, and a second group to serve as a permanent executive committee. Together these two groups reviewed and discussed all important legislation, and in this guise they were known as the XXI; indeed, all major legislative edicts were promulgated in the name of "Meister und Rat und XXI," and this combination was referred to as the Magistrat.[21]

The influence of the councils was further magnified because most important official and supervisory posts were filled by members of the XV, XXI, or XIII. Thus in addition to serving on the Rat and on the Council of XV (and consequently automatically a member of the XXI), a member of the XV might also serve as censor, supervisor of construction, supervisor of firemen, butchers, fishermen, or winemakers, or as inspector of the mint or the market. In all, the members of the XV were responsible for some thirty supervisory positions, not to mention four that they held with members of the XIII. Clearly each individual member had to carry at least two inspectorships.[22] All in all, the complex interweaving of legislative and administrative functions meant that by 1480, effective political control lay in the hands of two inter-

21. Ibid., p. 25. I prefer to use the term *Magistrat* instead of trying to translate it. To use the English term "city council" is misleading because, as is clear, it was more than one council and included the governing *Ammeister* as well. Again, these latter officials were neither mayors nor *Burgomeister* and must be called by their particular name. They serve as a reminder of the acquisition of power by the guilds and represent the transfer of authority from noble to non-noble hands.

22. Herzog, *Lebensmittelpolitik der Stadt Strassburg*. Cf. the section in each chapter on controls and inspection.

23

changing groups: the thirty members of the Rat and the thirty-two members of the XXI.

The fifteenth century also saw the rationalization and reorganization of some of the guilds. Once the guilds became a part of the constitutional structure of the city, the original craft system was cumbersome. Representation in the Rat was tied to the guild, and the franchise was restricted to guild members. During the century several of the smaller crafts were joined together to make political units of equal size and strength. From 1462 on there was a movement to combine similar activities; the hucksters and fruitmen were attached to the salt merchants; the boat builders and boatmen were united; the weavers were joined with the drapers.[23] It is always essential to remember, in a discussion of guilds in Strasbourg that they are no longer purely functional economic units. Two of the guilds were simply agglomerations that included all the burghers who did not fit anywhere else. They were named for the inns at which they met, like the old Trinkstuben of the Constoffler. The *Lucern* included surgeons, millers, and grain merchants. The *Möhrin*, meeting at the Moor's Head, included the merchants who sold lenten fare, the merchants of salted foods, the candlemakers, ropemakers, peddlers, and old-clothes men.[24] All guilds—butchers, goldsmiths, carpenters, masons—included some members of the Constoffler who voted with the guild. When a man purchased *Bürgerrecht,* he was simply assigned to a guild either according to his own craft if he was a craftsman or wherever it might be convenient.

By 1480 Strasbourg's constitution had assumed its final form. From that moment there was political stability, indeed, immobility. The government consisted of the Ammeister, the Rat, and the three permanent committees. For extraordinary occasions when wide popular support was essential, the Schöffen, or Three hundred, could be called in. This was

23. Hatt, *Strasbourg au XV siècle,* p. 16.
24. Friedrich Carl Heitz, *Das Zunftwesen in Strassburg* (Strassburg, 1856), passim.

1200	1263	1334	1450
Bishop	No bishop	*Ammeister:* Chosen from the guilds for 1-year term. FUNCTION: Administrative, reception of official emissaries, minor court responsibilities	*Ammeister:* Chosen from the guilds for 1-year term. FUNCTION: As before
Rat 12 Ratsherren drawn from Constoffler, 1 of these designated to be chief of *magister*. FUNCTION: Advisory and consultative	*Rat* 12 Drawn from Constoffler (of whom 4 chosen Stettmeister). FUNCTION: Assumes all legislative and administrative functions	*Rat* 22 Constoffler (of whom 4 chosen Stettmeister) 25 Representatives of guilds	*Rat* assumes final form: *Council of XIII* 10 Constoffler (of whom 4 appointed as Stettmeisters) 20 Guildsmen; *Council of XIII* 4 Constoffler 9 Guildsmen FUNCTION: War and foreign policy; *Council of XV* 5 Constoffler 10 Guildsmen FUNCTION: Watchdog committee for administration; *Council of XXI* Council of XIII + Council of XV plus others FUNCTION: Consultation and formulation of legislation
Schöffen Larger Council, elected by universal suffrage from the craft guilds. FUNCTION: Regulation of business affairs	*Schöffen* Popularly elected from the craft guilds. FUNCTION: Consultative to Rat	*Schöffen* Popularly elected from the craft guilds. FUNCTION: Consultative to Rat	*Schöffen* or Assembly of the 300 (15 from each guild) Popularly elected from the craft guilds. FUNCTION: Consultative to Rat

an ancient group consisting of fifteen representatives from each guild. In many towns it became the primary legislative body, but in Strasbourg the strengthening of the Rat had rendered the Schöffen less important. There they met only when called by the Rat to take action on edicts already formulated. Although originally the Schöffen had constituted a democratic element, with members chosen from the guild Gemeinde, after 1322 the seats were usually occupied by the guild masters, active or retired, and the Schöffen became, in effect, a group of elder statesmen who provided senatorial counsel within their respective guilds.[25]

By the fifteenth century those who served on the permanent committees or in the position of Ammeister came from a small group at the top of the city's social and economic hierarchy. There tended to be a good deal of rotation from one responsibility to another. The Constoffler still occupied a third of the seats in the Rat and were selected by the Ammeister from the eighty-nine patrician families who had maintained their burgher status. The representatives of the guilds who composed the rest of the Rat were not chosen from or by the whole membership of the guild (the Gemeinde). Indeed, although the documents refer to the guild representatives as *"Antwerker"* or *"Antwerk Leute,"* I have avoided the use of the term as being misleading to the modern reader because the artisan, the man who worked with his hands, was no longer a candidate for elective office. Only guild masters were named, and they were chosen by their peers or by the small board which directed the affairs of each guild.

It is important to consider at this point the significance of this concentration of power. With our particular preconceptions with regard to social equality and the virtues of democratic government, there is a temptation to read into such a clearly inegalitarian structure the basis of social and political conflict. The inevitable next step in the development of the Strasbourg constitution would thus be a revolution in

25. Schmoller, *Tucher und Weberzunft,* p. 496.

Social and Political Structure

which the Gemeinde rose up against the guild masters and seized the economic and political power for themselves, but this did not occur, and from 1480 until 1789 Strasbourg's political life was marked by a degree of stability that it had not known in the five preceding centuries. This is significant to the study of the Reformation in Strasbourg because the absence of a desire to change the political status quo must be accepted as a basic postulate. Political, social, and economic inequalities existed, but they did not produce at this time the conflicts that they would produce in later centuries.[26] A moment of equilibrium had been achieved in which the desire for order was greater than the desire for change. The constitutional development of Strasbourg in the fifteenth century reflects this attitude. Consciously and deliberately Strasbourg evolved a system that placed the responsibility for government in the hands of men of solid economic accomplishment and political experience. Wealth, experience, and knowledge possessed positive values for the burghers of Strasbourg.

The acceptance of inequality—indeed, the assumption that political authority should be placed in the hands of the superior classes—was not confined to the city of Strasbourg. Sylvia Thrupp in her study of London discovered much the same attitude. Official civil documents in London had a standard set of terms to indicate the status of the citizen. There were the more sufficient and the abler citizens, who were assumed to be the better people because they would be more honest, wiser, and more discreet. The poorer citizens, on the other hand, were ignorant, could not pay their taxes, and were inexperienced in public affairs.[27] A major corollary of the medieval attitude toward inequality was an

26. Bernd Moeller, *Reichstadt und Reformation*, Schriften des Vereins für Reformationsgeschichte, 180, Jahrgang 69 (Gütersloh, 1962), pp. 16–17. See also Fritz Rörig, *Die europäische Stadt und die Kultur des Bürgertums im Mittelalter* (Göttingen, 1955), and Fritz Hartung, *Deutsche Verfassungsgeschichte* (8 Aufl., Stuttgart, 1964).
27. Sylvia L. Thrupp, *The Merchant Class in Medieval London, 1300–1500* (Chicago, 1948), pp. 14–15.

unquestioning acceptance of authority, not based on rational principles, but on an emotional response:

The obligation to obey seems to have been regarded less as a rational obligation than as a purely personal matter, deep-grounded. The tendency to resent it and repudiate [it] was held in check by recognized irrational sanctions. To disobey a parent, a lord, a master, or to be disrespectful to a magistrate was to commit sin. The bourgeois context did nothing to free the individual from this kind of pressure but seems to have intensified it. Since everyone knew that the preservation of the local civic liberties hung upon the continuance of orderly behavior, all emotional resources were drawn upon to secure this end.[28]

The aim of civil government in the medieval city was to provide for the common defense and to guarantee order. Responsibility for achieving this aim was vested in the group that was most adequately endowed by nature and by fortune for the task. The social and moral code supported the system by granting special values to these particular attributes of leadership. Inequality must not be looked upon as tending to create political and social discord. It was an accepted element of social and political organization.

The final element that must be considered in the discussion of political conditions in Strasbourg is the relationship between city and empire. In the early period of its development, the city used the struggle between the emperors and the popes as a means of increasing its own independence. In general the city supported the Hohenstaufen emperors and received important privileges in return. However, in the struggle between Ludwig of Bavaria and Frederick of Hapsburg in 1314, Strasbourg supported Ludwig against the pope and the Hapsburgs and persisted in this alliance despite a long papal interdict. As a result, its relations with Charles IV and the victorious House of Hapsburg were marked by

28. Ibid., pp. 16.

conflict and tension. There were constant difficulties with the emperor in the ensuing period. Charles' provisions in the Golden Bull, which forbade the free city to accept new burghers, were regarded as a gross invasion of ancient prerogatives, and the city refused to attend the Diet of 1356, using a recent earthquake as an excuse.[29]

The relationship between the emperor and the city hardly improved under the Emperor Wenceslas. The feudal lords of Alsace, whom Wenceslas was eager to please, were jealous of the growing importance of the city. Wenceslas, himself a man of unstable character, regarded the burghers as hereditary enemies of his house. When the four Rhenish electors met in 1400, deposed Wenceslas, and elected Robert of Wittelsbach, Count Palatine of the Rhine, as his successor, Strasbourg quickly recognized the latter.

Not until 1431 did Strasbourg establish a more stable relationship with the imperial authority. At the time of the Council of Basel, the Emperor Sigismund sought the support of the imperial free cities. In 1433 he granted Strasbourg extensive favors, renewing the old privilege to hold an annual fair, granting the city the right to accept fiefs, to levy tolls on the Rhine bridge, and to receive within the city walls persons under the imperial ban. In 1437 he gave to Strasbourg the formal right to mint money. The city had previously preempted this right from the bishop, but it had never been legally confirmed.[30]

This brief improvement in imperial relations was brought to an abrupt end by the invasion of the Armagnacs. These mercenary troops, left at loose ends at the end of the Hundred Years War, were called into Alsace by the Duke of Lorraine and laid claim to Strasbourg as having once belonged to France. Strasbourg turned to the emperor for help, received none, and then called on her urban allies. Eventually the cities realized that the emperor and the nobility of Upper Alsace had welcomed the Armagnacs, hoping

29. Reuss, *Histoire de Strasbourg*, p. 66.
30. Ibid., p. 96.

to use them to combat the rising power of the cities, and the atmosphere of suspicion between the city and the emperor was revived.[31]

In the last decades of the fifteenth century, Strasbourg's position in the empire was significantly changed by an important shift in the balance of power, occasioned by the defeat of the House of Burgundy at the hands of Louis XI of France and his Swiss allies. The Burgundian War terminated in 1480. Charles the Bold was killed on the battlefield in 1477, and with his death, the dream of a Burgundian state —the old Lotharingia—reaching from the Alps to the sea, was shattered. The Burgundian territories were divided between the Hapsburgs and the Valois, and the buffer state which had separated the two powers was removed: there was no longer a third force operating in the Rhine Valley. Imperial territory now lay next to French territory, and the situation of the princely states and the free cities along the Rhine changed. Lorraine, although it was nominally a duchy within the Holy Roman Empire, now fell under French influence, and the French were not slow to extend their interests from there into Alsace. Alsace began to play the pivotal role it would later occupy in Franco-German diplomacy.

The Emperor Maximilian was slow to realize the significance of the change. He still saw the Rhineland as a family holding. Hereditary claims gave him a strong hold on Upper Alsace and the Breisgau, and his marriage to Mary of Burgundy, the daughter of Charles the Bold gave him the Low Countries. He was convinced that the rest of the Rhine would easily fall into his hands and that no special effort was necessary on his part to maintain his feudal rights. He was, however, fond of the city of Strasbourg, and it became a favorite way station on his journeys between the Hapsburg territories in Austria and the Low Countries. He was a friend and patron of many of the literary men of the Strasbourg Renaissance; Geiler preached for him, and he discussed his

31. Ibid., p. 98.

plan for the restoration of the Holy Roman Empire with Wimpfeling and Brant.

The vital factor in Strasbourg's external relations in the period of the Reformation was not, however, this new and friendly relationship with the emperor, but rather that once again she could use two rival parties to further her own particular political ends. Just as her medieval liberties were gained during the conflict between the emperors and the popes, her religious and political independence in the sixteenth century would stem from her skillful manipulation of the Hapsburg-Valois rivalry.

CHAPTER 3

THE CHURCH AND THE CITY

HE clergy formed a separate social and political group with its own particular inner structure. At the apex was the bishop, invariably a member of the nobility, never resident in the city itself, yet holding important powers both within the city and within the church. Below the bishop were the five chapters: the Cathedral, St. Thomas, Young St. Peter, Old St. Peter, and All Saints, each representing different degrees of wealth and importance. The overweening nobility of the cathedral chapter made it a byword among fifteenth-century ecclesiastical writers; Erasmus said that Christ Himself could not have been admitted to the Strasbourg chapter. The other chapters were not as exclusive, but they were still drawn mainly from noble or patrician families and lived separated from the city behind their chapter walls. There were subtle differences in the relations between the chapters and the city. The cathedral chapter, exemplifying the landed nobility to the Magistrat, was treated with suspicion and distrust. The chapter of St. Thomas, drawing many members from the local patrician families, was apt to be given special consideration by the city.

Below the chapters came the nine parishes: St. Martin, St. Aurelie, Old St. Peter, Young St. Peter, St. Laurence, St. Nicholas, St. Thomas, St. Stephen, and St. Andreas. Four of these were dependent on the chapters, that is, the canons made the appointments and paid the salaries of the incumbents. The parish priests were invariably of middle-class origin, educated locally, not necessarily with university degrees. There were only the most formal, administrative relations between these *Leutpriester* and the upper hierarchy of the church.

The city's monasteries and convents represented almost all the major orders. There were nine regular monasteries, with the Dominicans and Franciscans located, typically, in the heart of the town, each having its own large church, vying with its rival in preaching and in hearing confessions. The majority of the monasteries were on the outskirts of town; four of them were actually outside the walls since a city ordinance of 1276 had forbidden new monastic building within the city proper. In addition to the monks there were two noble orders, the Knights of St. John and the Teutonic Knights. These lived in splendid isolation, involved in the affairs of their orders and the empire rather than in the life of the city which they happened to inhabit.

In 1480 there were eight nunneries, the seven separate Dominican cloisters having been reorganized into four. It was to the nuns of these Dominican convents of Strasbourg that Tauler and Susso had preached and had developed the mystical symbolism which came to be such an important element in the German religious spirit. The cloisters were all relatively exclusive, ranging from the proud and noble ladies of the chapter of St. Stephen, wealthy and worldly, always in need of reform, to the Dominican cloisters, reserved for daughters of old Constoffler families and the patriciate. Even the Augustine convent, originally founded for fallen but penitent women, soon limited itself only to the respectable.[1]

The convents and chapters were significant not only for their spiritual function, but for their function in relation to the town's economic life because they held large lands both within and without the walls. Many of the citizens worked

1. The best account of the establishment, organization and history of the different monastic orders is in Luzian Pfleger, *Kirchengeschichte der Stadt Strassburg im Mittelalter* (Colmar, 1941), pp. 75–91.

lands rented from the convents or lived in houses located on chapter lands. The landlord-tenant relationship, with all its implications and problems, was common between clergy and citizens. In addition to this, the convents were important as employers. The needs of the convents were no longer supplied exclusively by the religious, if at all, so that a large body of citizens worked as servants in these institutions.

The church formed a state within a state, having its own lands, its own government, and its own courts within the confines of the city, and in Strasbourg, as in most medieval towns, there was constant conflict between the two entities. It was the same problem that plagued the relations between pope and emperor, but on a lower level, and essentially it was a problem of definition of membership and nonmembership, of rights, privileges, and exemptions.

The status of the burghers themselves was legally clear. In Strasbourg, a man could purchase Bürgerrecht if his principal residence was in the city. He paid a purchase tax, registered with a corporation, swore an oath of obedience to the constitution, and then became a citizen. As a burgher he was protected by the city against attack by a fellow burgher or foreigner; he could not be judged by a foreign court; he could participate in municipal affairs; and he had the right to exercise a trade or transact commerce in the city.[2] In return he had to pay taxes and render military service, chiefly in the form of the guard duty on the walls.

The problem was where the clergy fitted in. They were not required to buy Bürgerrecht (although they could);[3] yet the city was providing protection, and the citizens on the

2. F. J. Fuchs, "Le Droit de bourgeoisie à Strasbourg," *Revue d'Alsace, 101* (1962), 20–22.

3. Clerical assumption of Bürgerrecht went back to the thirteenth century, but the right of the city to accept the clergy as citizens was consistently questioned by the bishop right through to the Reform. The bishops regarded it as an invasion of *their* rights and privileges; the city claimed it as one of *their* most ancient and eminent privileges. In actual fact from 1440 to 1520 only 130 priests took out *Bürgerrecht*, or less than two a year. Ibid., pp. 26–27.

The Church and the City

walls were keeping watch over lay and clergy alike. Thus there was constant ill feeling, only exacerbated by the recurrent jurisdictional competition and conflict between the two sets of law courts. Was the servant of a cleric, living under his roof, subject to ordinary taxation and military duty, or did he assume the privileged status of his master? If a burgher killed a member of the clergy, which court tried the case? Medieval municipal administration was plagued by this problem of dual authority. In Strasbourg from the fourteenth century on, the general direction had been toward a steady expansion of the municipal authority at the expense of the church.

Originally it was the other way around. Before 1200 only one of the city officials was not appointed by the bishop— the judicial officer who pronounced the final sentence of life or death. Since the medieval church conscientiously avoided the shedding of blood, the bishop made the nomination to this post, but left formal appointment to the emperor.[4] The development of the municipal authority began with the charter of 1202, which established the *Rat* and gave it power to participate in the legislative process. By 1263 the Rat had already begun to reach out, assuming powers that had previously belonged exclusively to the church, including the supervision and administration of the city hospital and the right to nominate to certain prebends in the cathedral.

The revolt against the bishop in 1262 resulted in obvious gains for the secular authority, and the Rat next attempted to establish its authority over the monastic clergy. By 1276 the orders formally recognized the jurisdiction of the Stettmeister and Magistrat. Hoping to decrease claims for tax exemption, the Rat provided that no cloister established outside the walls could be transferred within the city proper; it also curbed the right of clerical inheritance. The Rat was forced to respect the piety of fellow citizens who left rich legacies to monastic orders or charities, although it knew

4. Reuss, *Histoire de Strasbourg*, p. 18.

that these gifts meant the withdrawal of substantial properties from the city tax rolls. Furthermore, members of monastic orders in Strasbourg claimed the right to inherit from their own relatives, a right that siphoned more burgher property off into the church treasury. The Rat made strong objections, and finally the Franciscans, to strengthen their own position and place the Dominicans in an unfavorable light, agreed not to accept legacies that interfered with the rights of the natural heirs. This was a compromise, but it represented some limitation of the claims to privilege on the part of the monastic clergy.[5]

In 1290 the Magistrat assumed the right to administer funds granted to the church for ecclesiastical purposes by taking over the direction of the building and maintenance of the cathedral; the Magistrat thereby acquired prestige and authority as well as considerable sums of money. The Magistrat's next step was to extend its juridical power. In 1314 a Rat's mandate provided that a priest who wounded a burgher was to be judged by the civil authority rather than the ecclesiastical court. Furthermore, he was to be imprisoned in the city hall, not in a church prison. The principle of equality was also applied to punishment. A priest judged guilty of committing a misdemeanor against a burgher was to receive the same punishment as a lay person for the same offense. Clerical right of asylum was abridged by a provision that houses occupied by canons could serve as asylum only for three days and three nights.

The city was gradually drawing ecclesiastical institutions under its supervision and direction; rights of jurisdiction had been established over clerical persons in certain cases, and some of the old tension diminished as far as the city was concerned. During the episcopacy of Wilhelm von Diest (1394–1439), however, the traditional conflict between the city and clergy burst out with renewed vigor. Wilhelm, according to a chronicler, was an enemy of the clergy and of

5. The material on the development of the civil authority from 1200–1400 is drawn from Reuss, *Histoire de Strasbourg*, pp. 41–52.

the city throughout his whole life.[6] His lack of loyalty to his
flock was evident in his initial proposal to exchange Strasbourg for the wealthier see of Liège, offering funds to the
cathedral chapter to influence their vote. His efforts having
failed, Wilhelm was left in Strasbourg to administer his
diocese in a way that was both tyrannous and expensive. He
squandered the goods and property of the cathedral chapter
with such profligacy that the chapter turned to the Magistrat
for relief and protection, and in 1405 the canons and the
Magistrat agreed to unite in opposition to the irresponsible
actions of the bishop. Perhaps because of this coalition, the
following year an agreement gave the Rat new authority
over the cathedral chapter properties, which were placed
under a *collegium* of three men—one appointed by the
bishop, one by the chapter, and one by the city.[7] The arrangement was a device to curb the bishop's use of chapter
funds. When it proved ineffective, the deacon of the chapter, speaking for the clergy and canons of Alsace, asked the
Rat to lead an armed force against the bishop. The city
complied. Wilhelm was captured and remained for months
as a prisoner of the chapter in Strasbourg.[8]

Alliances of this type between the chapters and the Rat
proved to be tenuous and transient. Although all the chapters joined in a confederation with the Rat to protect their
interests and were eager to accept assistance against the
bishop, they were unwilling to make concessions for this
succor.

The Magistrat felt it only fair that the chapters should
submit to the municipal jurisdiction in return for the protection they had received. The canons willingly accepted the

6. Daniel Specklin, *Les Collectanées,* Fragment Recueillis par
Rodolphe Reuss, Fragments des anciennes chroniques d'Alsace (4
vols. Strasbourg, 1892–1901), 2, 168. Referred to hereafter as
Specklin, *Collectanées.*
7. Julius Mann, *Die Kirchenpolitik der Stadt Strassburg am Ausgang
des Mittelalters,* Inaugural-Dissertation Kaiser-Wilhelms Universität
Strassburg (Strassburg, 1914), p. 5.
8. Reuss, *Histoire de Strasbourg,* p. 87.

privileges of citizens but claimed complete immunity from all civil responsibilities, finally appealing to the Council of Constance against the taxes levied by the Rat. The council returned judgment against the city, forbade the secular authority to tax the clergy, and ordered restitution of any monies collected. Emboldened, the four major chapters promptly forgot their alliance with the city and formed a league on August 7, 1419 to defend their traditional ecclesiastical immunities against the demands of the Magistrat. They announced that they would refuse to pay civil taxes and would no longer contribute horses for the defense of the city.[9]

The alliance between the two groups had had no basis other than their common hostility to the bishop and in no way represented a growth of mutual understanding. The problems traditionally separating the two remained unsolved, and not until the Treaty of Spires (1422) was a settlement acceptable to both sides achieved. Although the primary purpose of the treaty was to restore peace between burghers and Constoffler, the Magistrat brought before the mediator the question of the civil responsibilities of the clergy. It was decided that the Magistrat should respect the regular jurisdiction of the bishop over the clergy; the clergy, for their part, were to pay the accustomed, moderate taxes levied by the city; lay inheritances received by the clergy were to be dealt with in lay courts;[10] and the powers of the collegium over chapter property were redefined.[11] Although the decisions were not particularly dramatic—or perhaps because they were not—the Treaty of Spires marked a turning point in the relations between the church and the city authorities. The agreement was constantly cited by both parties as definitive, and a new *modus vivendi* was achieved.

The new relation between church and city was evident

9. Charles Schmidt, *Histoire du Chapitre de St. Thomas de Strasbourg* (Strasbourg, 1866), p. 36.
10. Ibid., p. 37.
11. Mann, *Kirchenpolitik der Stadt Strassburg*, p. 7.

in a symbolic gesture made by the chapter of St. Thomas in 1422. The defense of the town against the Armagnacs had necessitated increased military expenditures, and to meet them, the town had decreed a special tax on wine. The canons requested an authorization from the pope to contribute to the tax, "in order not to be reproached by the town as ungrateful when it had protected them." [12] In the same year the chapters of St. Thomas and Young St. Peter agreed to submit to certain city regulations that prohibited the clergy to carry arms, gamble, or enter female convents, on the grounds that these did not conflict with the liberties of the church. The Magistrat, in turn, agreed to take the chapter members under their protection and promised to defend their rights, property, and persons in the same manner as the other burghers of the city.[13]

In 1439 Wilhelm von Diest died, unlamented by either the burghers or the clergy of Strasbourg, and a young canon, Ruprecht, Duke of Bavaria, assumed the episcopacy. Ruprecht was faced with the difficult task of restoring order to financial confusion. The coffers were empty. The best properties of the church had been mortgaged, the silver chalices had been sold. The resources of the diocese were no longer sufficient for the daily needs of the church.[14] Clearly it was necessary for him to move cautiously; indeed, his position was so weak that he was forced to cooperate with the Magistrat.

Torn between his desire to restore order to the diocese and to spend lavishly on his own court, Ruprecht was at first relatively hostile to the city, but by 1442 the bishop and the city had joined in a pact of friendship, pledging that in case of any difference, each party would send mediators to arrange a settlement.[15] The old issue of the city's right to assess the ecclesiastical courts was settled next. The

12. Quoted in Schmidt, *Histoire du Chapitre de St. Thomas*, p. 39.
13. Ibid., p. 40.
14. Ibid., p. 41.
15. Mann, *Kirchenpolitik der Stadt Strassburg*, pp. 10–11.

city had laid a tax of 220 pfund annually on these units, and the courts claimed insufficient funds to pay it. Under an agreement of 1446 they were assigned revenues collected by the city sealer to enable them to pay the tax; thus the city was willing to sign over municipal funds in order to win a point of principle. The city also agreed to advance the bishop 8,000 gulden to repay the debts of the chapter. As collateral he pledged the episcopal towns and the revenues of his cities and fortified places, and his officers were to swear an oath of loyalty to the city as well as to himself.[16] In both these instances the city emerged with newly recognized authority and in the stronger position.

The financial difficulties of the bishop served to strengthen the ties between the chapters and the city authorities. By 1450 Ruprecht was making heavy demands on the chapters. They refused him, and he imprisoned the canons and seized the chapter properties. Several of the chapters sought lay protection and entered into a pact with the city in 1457. The chapters of St. Thomas and Old St. Peter formally declared before the *Ammeister* and Rat that they would always be loyal to the city as faithful burghers, and in return they were guaranteed effective protection. When the arrangement was renewed in 1462, St. Thomas agreed to pay an annual fee of 36 florins, called *Schirmgeld*, as a contribution for the protection received. Old St. Peter and Young St. Peter made similar arrangements.[17] Thus by 1480 the right of the city to collect a fee from an ecclesiastical unit for its protective services had been established de facto. The bishop opposed these argreements between the chapters and the Magistrat from their inception. He felt that the canons should not call on the lay authorities and that the agreements were a flagrant disavowal of his own authority. His remonstrances, however, were always shadowed by his imminent bankruptcy. He could force

16. Ibid., p. 15.
17. Schmidt, *Histoire du Chapitre de St. Thomas*, p. 42.

neither the chapters nor the city beyond a certain point since they were, finally, the source of his funds. Again in 1465 he had had to borrow money from the city; in return, the city was granted the right to appoint the toll collectors at five of the city gates, an appointment and a privilege that had belonged to the bishop since the founding of the city.[18]

The bishop's position had become financially untenable. Shortly after the formal investiture of the new bishop, Albrecht, Duke of Bavaria in 1478, additional sources of revenue were granted by the pope. The bishop of Strasbourg was to receive the income from every vacant benefice for a year, and he could also sell to those who required it the right to use butter and eggs on fast days. With these new revenues Bishop Albrecht was able to redeem some of the territories that had been forfeited, and he finally paid off his debt of 8,000 gulden to the city.[19] The new sources of revenue meant that the bishop was no longer forced to squeeze money from the chapters, and the leagues, associations, or pacts between the chapters and the Magistrat ceased.[20]

The fifteenth century had witnessed the progressive weakening of the position of the bishop and was marked by increasing tension between the chapters and the bishop. The upper hierarchy of the church was by no means united. It was divided by conflicts in financial interests, and bishop and chapters were both willing to go outside the church to ally themselves with the secular authorities when it seemed to their particular advantage. This lack of cohesion would prove almost fatal in the period of the reform.

18. Mann, *Kirchenpolitik der Stadt Strassburg*, p. 14.
19. Ibid., p. 18.
20. For a detailed account of the type of expenses which the bishop faced see the article by Francis Rapp, "Ce qu'il en coûtait d'argent et de démarches pour obtenir de Rome la confirmation d'une élection épiscopale," *Revue d'Alsace*, *101* (1962), 106–15. Based on the report of the emissary himself, the article provides an excellent account of a medieval journey, complete with itinerary.

The group that had gained the most was the Magistrat. It had not demanded sweeping rights or privileges in return for an alliance or protectorship but, bit by bit, had gradually extended itself. By 1480 the civil authority had appropriated important rights of appointment, had forced the chapters to pay a fee in return for the protection of the city, and could tax the ecclesiastical courts.

The aggrandizement of the civil authority is reflected in the expansion of its control in one specific area—the care of the poor—traditionally regarded as a responsibility of the church. The original welfare foundation in medieval Strasbourg was the *Leonardspital*, founded or reorganized by Bishop Kuno between 1105 and 1116. Originally entirely under the direction of the church, by 1200 two lay members appeared as part of the governing board of the hospital. At first these posts were held by *Ministeriales* from the bishop's staff, but the charter of 1250 provided that free burghers and Ratsherren might be appointed. Thus, even before the war against the bishop, the Rat had been given a degree of participation in an important church foundation. In the peace settlement of 1263 the city received as one concession the right to appoint hospital supervisors and the responsibility of administering the hospital property.[21] The Rat thus assumed full authority for this important institution. By 1315 the Leonardspital was too small to provide adequate care for all the sick and needy. It was moved to the Cistercian nunnery and became semiprivate, although it continued to accept a certain number of charity cases. A new city hospital was erected at the south gate for the exclusive care of charity cases. This became the major welfare institution; public funds were provided for its original construction and later for its being rebuilt. With continued additions through the centuries, it stands on the same site today.

Once the city had assumed the direction of the hospitals, church influence in administration or supervision diminished.

21. Martha Goldberg, *Das Armen und Krankenwesen des Mittelalterlichen Strassburg,* Inaugural-Dissertation, Universität Freiburg (Strassburg, 1909), p. 6.

The statutes of the city hospitals and of the leper house distinctly limited the function of the chaplains to pastoral care and spiritual guidance, and the chaplains were appointed by the Rat rather than by the church authorities. Legally the hospitals continued to be classified as spiritual institutions, in this way retaining their traditional immunity from assessment and taxation.[22] They were, in any case, still dependent on charitable gifts, for the city's support stopped with the provision of the physical building. Operating income came from the original foundation, from real estate holdings in the city, and from the bequests of the pious. The church continued to urge endowments to the hospital and after 1400, such a gift received an indulgence.[23] The hospital also had a lucrative insurance business. A burgher could provide for his declining years by making fixed grants to the hospital over a period; in return, he was cared for by the hospital, in the style to which he was accustomed, in his old age. By the end of the fourteenth century a major problem of the hospital supervisors was to provide for these prepaid cases and still have room for the poor.

The Rat not only undertook to supervise and control the hospitals, but during the course of the fourteenth century it extended itself in other directions as well. In 1353 it assumed the right to supervise the distribution of alms by the cathedral and St. Martin; this involved the distribution of bread every Sunday to some sixty or more poor who were organized in a holy brotherhood.[24] In 1358 the Rat appointed a new set of officers to administer the funds and supervise the gifts.[25] The rationale of these changes was the function of surveillance, for medieval charity was carefully limited to respectable persons who could no longer earn their living.[26] The officials were responsible for assessing the needs of the poor.

Not all the welfare institutions fell under the supervision

22. Ibid., pp. 18–19.
23. Pfleger, *Kirchengeschichte der Stadt Strassburg,* p. 148.
24. Ibid., p. 145.
25. Goldberg, *Das Armen und Krankenwesen in Strassburg,* p. 24.
26. Pfleger, *Kirchengeschichte der Stadt Strassburg,* p. 146.

of the city—the *Phynenspital*, the hospital run by the order of St. Anthony, and several houses of refuge remained independent.[27] Nevertheless, well before the Reformation the care of the poor of the city was no longer exclusively in the hands of the church. It was shared by the civil authority, which had established a proliferation of alms supervisors, hospital superintendents, orphan superintendents, and smallpox hospital overseers—a small bureaucracy in itself.

27. Ibid., pp. 148–50.

CHAPTER 4

THE INTELLECTUAL MILIEU

LTHOUGH economic and political forces were stabilized by 1480 and a certain social equilibrium had been achieved, new vigor and energy flowed into intellectual activities. In the brief period from 1480 to 1520 an awakening occurred, and Strasbourg became an important humanist center.

The city had not been a center of learning during the Middle Ages; it had had its poets and mystics, but no convent or chapter had enjoyed a reputation for scholarship and learning; no school had attracted young scholars to the city. In 1480 the only educational establishments consisted of small, informal classes, in which a child could learn to read and write, maintained by lay persons in various sections of the city. Several chapters and convents maintained schools in which a cleric taught the basic trivium, and in a few of the monasteries, particularly the Dominican and Carthusian, there were brothers who followed scholarly pursuits. Three or four libraries completed the educational resources, the most important belonging to the cathedral chapter and the chapter of St. Thomas; these had continued to receive donations and contributions from the pious, but they were neither well maintained nor extensively used.[1]

Yet in 1480 these meager facilities were adequate for the demand. The citizens of Strasbourg still regarded learning

1. Charles Schmidt, *Histoire littéraire de l'Alsace* (2 vols. Paris, 1879), *1*, xii–iv.

as a prerogative of the church. A young burgher needed to know how to read and write—that much was a practical necessity for life in the world of commerce—but boys who went beyond that were destined for the church and could be sent to the grammar school at *Sélestat*, less than thirty miles away, or to one of the boarding schools in the Low Countries maintained by the Brethren of the Common Life. A few boys from the wealthy families went on to the university, with prospects of a career in church administration or a lucrative chapter benefice.

In the last decades of the fifteenth century, however, a new group of young men arrived to take up various positions in the church, in the chapters, and in the administrative offices of the bishop. These men had been exposed to humanism during their university training, and they came to the city imbued with a new attitude toward learning and a sense of mission. They saw the revival of learning as a means of moral and spiritual renewal and had dedicated their lives to this cause.[2]

Seventeen men formed the nucleus of the Strasbourg movement: Sebastian Brant, Johann Geiler, Jacob Wimpfeling, Jacob Han, Sixt Hermann, Jacob Sturm, Nicolaus Gerbel, Thomas Murner, Johann Gallinarius, Peter Schott, Thomas Wolf, Matthias Ringmann, Thomas Vogler, Hieronymus Gebwiler, Otmar Luscinius, Beatus Rhenanus, and Johann Hugonis.[3] Socially, the group represented a variety of classes. Peter Schott and Jacob Sturm were from old families: The Schotts were members of the commercial patriciate and were regarded as patrons of the arts and letters.

2. M. Vansteenberghe, "Influences Rhénanes," in *L'Humanisme en Alsace* (Paris, 1939), p. 21.

3. The major sources for the lives and works of these men are Schmidt, *Histoire littéraire;* and the notes in Johannes Ficker and Otto Winckelmann, *Handschriftproben des Sechzehnten Jahrhunderts nach Strassburger Originalen* (2 vols. Strassburg, 1905). Since Schmidt is very well indexed and since Ficker and Winckelmann is curiously paginated (using the same number for several pages), it seems better not to interrupt the narrative with footnotes on each point. A final source to be checked on biographical material is the *Allgemeine Deutsche Biographie*.

Peter's father had served as Ammeister four times and had undertaken numerous diplomatic missions. The Sturms were of older origin, of Constoffler rank, and Jakob himself was a respected member of the Magistrat. Geiler, Brant, and Murner, too, came from substantial, responsible burgher families, although not of quite the same social level. Brant's grandfather, a winetaster and wine merchant, had served eight terms as a Schöffen; his father was the host of one of the larger inns of the city. Geiler's father was the adjutant to the secretary of the city of Schaffhausen. The Murners had been leaders in the city of Obernai for several generations, serving on the city council and as Stettmeister. Wimpfeling's family were not of the urbman bourgeoisie but seem to have been people of substance. Farmers, they possessed considerable properties and were able to trace their lineage and holdings back through several centuries. As a result Wimpfeling's father had sufficient wealth to give his sons the same education as a burgher's sons.

Two of the humanist circle came from church families, families that had always had one or two members as canons of a chapter or as members of the bishop's administrative staff. Thus, Jacob Han was the legitimate son of one of the canons of Young St. Peter; Thomas Wolf came from a wealthy family with important connections in the hierarchy of the church.

A few came from quite simple circumstances. Little is known of Matthias Ringmann's early life, but he called himself a peasant. Schmidt believed, from descriptions of landscapes and places in his poetry, that Ringmann was probably the son of a farmer from one of the convents in the Upper Vosges.[4] Beatus Rhenanus' father appears in a city register as a butcher; thus the son sprang from the artisan level of society.

No biographical data are available for the other six, but the general impression is that the humanists came from relatively well-established families, representative both of the old nobility and of the new commercial patriciate, with only

4. Schmidt, *Histoire littéraire*, 2, 88.

a small minority coming from the peasant or artisan group. On the other hand, there is the point that if little is known of a man's birth, he may have come from very simple circumstances.

Data on educational backgrounds are more complete since matriculation lists and lists of candidates for degrees make it possible to trace academic careers. The majority of the Strasbourg humanists were educated at German universities, most of them in their native Rhineland; their educational experience was local and parochial rather than international and European. Only three of the seventeen—Schott, Luscinius, and Rhenanus—received all their university training outside of Germany. Wolf, Gebwiler, Ringmann, and Murner had traveled abroad for some of their university work but had also attended German universities.

Five of the humanists had been at Freiburg, five at Heidelberg, and five at Basel; two had journeyed northward to Erfurt. The education they had received in these universities in this period was still relatively conventional. Most of the German universities maintained the traditional curriculum and let the humanist courses operate on the fringes, as additional lectures or as private lessons. Thus at Heidelberg Peter Luder and Rudolph Agricola read the classics, discussed poetry, and gave lectures on Greek and Latin literature, but the university requirements were still in terms of scholastic philosophy and theology.[5] The teaching arrangements of Maternus Pistoris were typical. Officially he was professor of scholastic philosophy at Erfurt, and in this guise lectured to the student body. Unofficially he was recognized as the leader of the humanist movement and offered private lectures in classics and literature to those students who wished to come.[6]

Only at Basel were humanist studies given full official

5. Hans Rupprich, *Humanismus und Renaissance in den deutschen Städten und an den Universitäten,* Deutsche Literatur. Sammlung Literarischer Kunst-und Kulturdenkmäler (Leipzig, 1935), 2, 32.
6. Ibid., p. 34.

recognition and an important place in the regular curriculum. Founded by Aeneas Silvius, himself a humanist, the faculty had always included classicists and poets. Its scholars had developed their own particular school of humanist studies. Having read the works of the classical authors, the scholars at Basel had turned to a study of the works of the medieval theologians. From these they went to the church fathers and finally directly to the Bible.[7] They used the new tools of philology and textual criticism to analyze the roots of Christian doctrine. Basel exerted a major intellectual influence on Strasbourg in this period, and the most important members of the Strasbourg group were trained there.

The young university graduates who came to Strasbourg in the last decades of the century were, then, still grounded in medieval scholasticism, theology, and canon law. In addition they had been introduced to the literature of classical antiquity, to poetry, and to the analysis of poetic form, but these seemed to have interested them only superficially. It was the Christian humanism of Basel that had sharpened their focus and given them a moral intensity. Learning was not merely a means of furthering their own careers. Through languages and literature they would deepen their own religious understanding and create a moral awakening among their fellow Christians.[8] The mystic elements in the German tradition, combined with the new linguistic knowledge, had given humanism a new direction.[9]

The intellectual concerns of the young German graduates also now reflected a new sense of national consciousness.[10] The humanist poets of the universities did not always look to antiquity for their inspiration. They were keenly aware

7. Ernest Staehelin, "Bâle et l'Alsace," in *L'Humanisme en Alsace,* pp. 36–39.

8. Schmidt, *Histoire littéraire, 1,* ix–x.

9. Hans Baron, "Zur Frage des Ursprungs des deutschen Humanismus und seiner religiosen Reformbestrebungen," *Historische Zeitschrift, 82* (1925), 446.

10. Paul Joachimsen, "Der Humanismus und die Entwicklung des Deutschen Geistes," *Deutsche Vierteljahrsschrift für Literaturwissenschaft und Geistesgeschichte, 8* (1930), 443.

that the German past had differed from Rome, and they chose themes from German history; their heroes were the German tribal leaders who had protected German freedom against the Roman Empire. This current of national romanticism suffused the universities of the period. It was not specifically taught, rather it was assimilated from the very atmosphere of these young institutions. Founded by laymen, the universities breathed a new political consciousness.[11]

The humanist group collected in Strasbourg during the decades from 1480 to 1510. The first to arrive was Johann Geiler, for whom the post of preacher for the cathedral was created and endowed with the necessary benefice under a charter of April 1478. Peter Schott, after completing his doctorate at Bologna, returned to his native city in 1482, taking up residence in his father's house, with a benefice as a canon of Young St. Peter. He was the first scholar to arrive with a knowledge of Greek, but in the years directly after his return he had few learned colleagues besides Geiler. Thomas Murner arrived for a brief stay in 1491; in 1492 Jacob Han, a native Strasbourgeois, arrived from Heidelberg to take up residence in his father's house and continue his studies on the Bible. The group was fragmentary and isolated.

It was not until 1500 that scholars began to collect in force. In that year Sebastian Brant resigned his chair in law at the University of Basel and moved back to become syndic of his native city; Symphorius Altbiesser arrived to become the chaplain of the cathedral. The next year they were joined by Wimpfeling, who arrived without an appointment or benefice, partially to be near Brant and Geiler. He was never attached to any one of the churches or chapters but took up residence in the Wilhelmite cloister. He served as a tutor to the sons of the Sturm and Schott families but devoted himself chiefly to his own study and writing. Thomas Wolf received his degree in Italy that same year and returned to Strasbourg to assume a benefice at St. Thomas, to which he had been appointed at the age of seven. Vogler arrived to become almoner of the cathedral chapter.

11. Ibid., p. 437.

The Intellectual Milieu

By 1503 the influence of Wimpfeling and Brant began to be felt. Young humanists turned to Strasbourg in search of appointments or were sought out by the Strasbourg group. Ringmann arrived, hoping to establish a school; Johann Gallinarius was called to teach grammar and rhetoric at the chapter of Young St. Peter; Beatus Rhenanus came in 1507 to be near his friends; and in 1509 Geiler and Wimpfeling pushed through the appointment of Hieronymus Gebwiler as director of the cathedral school. Other men came as late as 1510, but the movement was well under way at the turn of the century. The flowering of Strasbourg humanism occurred between 1500 and 1520.

The group was scattered throughout the city in different posts, with diverse functions, but centered around Wimpfeling and Brant. A loosely organized *sodalitas literaria* was founded, modeled on that of Conrad Celtis, and it gave the humanists an opportunity to pursue their common interests. The group would gather at one place or another to read classical works, present their own poetry, or discuss new editions of classical authors to be brought out by one of the Strasbourg presses.[12] Almost all the humanists served as proofreaders and advisors to the printers in addition to their official duties, and their own literary production was prodigious. Schmidt lists 352 printed works by the Strasbourg humanists in his bibliographical index.[13] Some of the items are only simple poems or songs, but the total is nonetheless indicative of the vigor of the movement and of the humanists' efforts to reach beyond their own group to a larger audience.

The tasks the Strasbourg humanists set for themselves were disparate in nature. They wished to revive a pure classical style, to restore elegance and form so that the language would be a proper vehicle for Christian truth. Their study of the classics was tied ultimately to moral reform, but the one was sometimes in conflict with the other, and the religious objectives were always given precedence. Wimpfeling's

---

12. Schmidt, *Histoire littéraire*, 1, xviii.
13. Ibid., 2, 317–431.

attitude toward the classical poets was typical. He proposed to confine the study of Virgil, Lucian, and Horace to the elementary schools; the students there were young and innocent and would profit from the style without being diverted by the sensuality. It would not be safe to expose adolescents or men of mature years, above all, men studying for the priesthood, to these poets, for their passions would be aroused and their thoughts corrupted.[14] This attitude affected the writing of all the Strasbourg humanists. They used the classics as models, consciously adopting classical forms—the elegy, the ode, the epigram—but used them to convey traditional medieval religious ideas. A tract with a florid classical title and numerous mythological allusions would be written to promote the supremacy of the pope and the absolute authority of the church.[15] Epigrams were based on moral or religious themes, and an ode could be addressed to the relics of a saint.

The combination of classical form and traditional Christian sentiment is exemplified in the poetry of Sebastian Brant. He wrote numerous panegyrics and odes to Emperor Maximilian and exalted the day when the empire would be reestablished, but his favorite themes were religious and moral, expressed in semidevotional poems, hymns, and odes addressed to the saints. He used classical verse forms, purged his vocabulary of medieval corruptions, and attempted to return to the pure Latin of the classical period. But he was bound to traditional themes and conventional piety.[16] A few examples suffice.

THE RELICS AT AIX-LA-CHAPELLE

Stranger stop! This place will show you . . .
The mantle of the mother of Christ.
May I, too, fasten on me the cloth
With which the limbs of God were covered,

14. Ibid., 1, 149.
15. Ibid., 2, 51.
16. William Gilbert, "Sebastian Brant: Conservative Humanist," *Archiv für Reformationsgeschichte, 46, Heft 2* (1955), 149.

Whose death on the cross brought salvation;
And the swaddling clothes with which the omnipotent
  boy
Was wrapped in the manger and protected from the
  cold.
Add to this the cloth of John the Baptist
Who was sainted in death.
Everyone may see these things here once every seven
  years.
Charles has brought them to us from Greece.
And put them in this place. Praise be to the Supreme
  God.[17]

AD SACRAMENTUM EUCHRISTIAE

Thee, O Good Christ Jesus, hanging lifeless on the cross,
  I adore!
You are bearing the crown of thorns—for your servants!
Thou breastplate of faith, thou unconquerable shield!
Thou sacred body dying on the cross, for us, miserable
  sinners, hail!
Behold the food of the pilgrims, the most honored Holy
  Bread
Which formerly was the property only of the heavenly
  spirits!
And thou, too, Blood, flowing from a pierced heart, hail!
Pierced through the glorious sacred parts of the body
  of my creator!
Grant us, O pious, blessed Christ, we pray, to partici-
  pate in your merits.
Make us share in the banquet with Thy saints in
  heaven.[18]

ELEGIA CHRIST; COLLAPHIS CAELI

Look upon Me, O traveler so dear to me
Whose mark you see on my lips and mouth.

17. The selection of poems is from Sister Mary Alvarita Rajewski, *Sebastian Brant* (Washington, D.C., 1944), p. 20. The translations from the Latin are made by Sister Mary Alvarita.
18. Ibid., p. 23.

Look at the wounds made, and inflicted upon my cheeks
By a horrible and envious hand.
I suffered blows and outrages, yet I never murmured.
Like a lamb in the presence of a shearer, I was silent
And as a lamb that is led to the place of its death.
What more could I do for you, my people?[19]

The Latin forms are there, but the quality of religious enthusiasm and sensibility are part of an emotional response to religious symbolism characteristic of France and the Netherlands at the close of the Middle Ages.[20] There is a tendency to embody religious thought in images—Christ as a lamb, Christ as the armor of the faithful, Christ as the banquet; each poem is a collection of symbolism.[21] The emphasis on the theme of the crucifixion, the passion, the cross, the tears, the wounds, and the blood are elements of the same late medieval attitude that led to copious weeping in prayer or in contemplation of religious objects. Brant's Latin may have been classical, but his emotions were medieval.

Another important subject of Brant's religious verse was the Virgin, and his poetry in praise of the purity and sinlessness of Mary drew him into an acrimonious debate with the Dominicans. Brant believed in and defended the Immaculate Conception; the Dominicans rejected it on theological grounds, reasoning that as a doctrine it struck at the roots of the humanity of Christ. The controversy developed into a full-fledged debate that raged in Strasbourg and out into Alsace from 1509 to 1512, nurtured by all the invective that both sides could summon. The intellectual community was divided between those who supported Brant and those who did not, and the humanists in particular rose to his defense with poem after poem in honor of the Virgin.[22]

The religious preoccupations of the humanists were re-

19. Ibid.
20. J. Huizinga, *The Waning of the Middle Ages* (London, 1948), pp. 171–73.
21. Ibid., p. 190.
22. Schmidt, *Histoire littéraire, 1,* 266–69.

flected in two other controversies that absorbed their energies. Wimpfeling, in a treatise published in 1505, undertook to prove that St. Augustine had never been a monk and that he had never worn the cowl of a monk. This involved Wimpfeling and his disciples in a bitter battle with the Augustine order not only in Strasbourg but all over Germany.[23] In the same year Wimpfeling quarreled with Jacob Locher, another German humanist who had trained at Basel and who had been a seemingly devoted disciple of Brant. In his early career Locher had followed rather closely the pattern of the Alsatian humanists by writing religious verse and defending the Immaculate Conception. He had translated Brant's *Narrenschiff* from the vernacular into Latin verse for the use of the scholarly world. After teaching poetry at the University of Ingolstadt for several years, he launched a vicious attack in 1503 against an elderly member of the university —a theologian who had expressed some fears with regard to the humanist's lectures on the classical poets. The matter became a *cause célèbre*, a battle between liberalism and conservatism, and Wimpfeling took it on himself to head the attack against Locher, which meant defending scholasticism against the pagan authors.[24]

It is always easy to suspect that the humanists indulged in their quarrels partially as a means of displaying their erudition since their differences provoked an endless round of tracts, epigrams, letters, and dialogues. Yet the quarrels are significant as an insight into the sensitive intellectual issues of the day. In the decade from 1500 to 1510, only ten years before the Reformation, the major concern of the Strasbourg intelligentsia was to maintain the conventional medieval ideology, in all its purity, against any modern revisionism. Wimpfeling's attack on the Augustines seems the only exception to this, but in fact he was simply continuing an old argument between the Wilhelmite cloister (where he lived) and the Augustine order. So it, too, was a conventional quar-

23. Ibid., *1*, 50.
24. Ibid., *1*, 57–63.

rel. The Strasbourg humanists were conservative in the most literal sense: They wished to conserve the old way and to restore the social order to the purity of an earlier time.

Sebastian Brant's poem *Narrenschiff* reflects this spirit. A collection of verses pointing out the folly of certain types of behavior or the foolishness of certain kinds of people, it has no particular literary form. Brant makes no attempt to create a special order for the separate pieces; the work is most closely analogous to a collection of fables. It would certainly be impossible, and not even fervent apologists of Brant have tried, to define it in terms of any classical literary form.

Nor can the poem be regarded as a form of social protest or social criticism. There is no particular social criterion in Brant's choice of persons. He censured a widely divergent group: old people, the contemptuous, journeymen, beggars, courtesans, the vulgar, gamblers, bad marksmen, knights, clerks, cooks, waiters, peasants, and courtiers—an assortment that could almost have been picked on the basis of personal dislike or pique. His criticisms of the nobility were apologetic, in part because he wished to restore the nobles and the empire to their former height of prestige. Similarly, his criticism of the church was directed at decadent bishops and others who set a bad example and thus weakened the church.[25] Journeymen and the peasants were criticized because they no longer performed the duties set them but wished to be richer; they did not accept discipline; they had forsaken their traditional place;

No trade is honored o'er the land,
They're overcrowded, overmanned,
Every apprentice would be master
For all the trades a great disaster . . .[26]

25. Fred Genschmer, "The Treatment of the Social Classes in the Satires of Brant, Murner and Fischart," An Abstract of a Thesis in the Graduate School of the University of Illinois (Urbana, Ill., 1934), p. 4.
26. Sebastian Brant, *Narrenschiff*, Eng. trans. Edwin Zeydel, *The Ship of Fools* (New York, 1944), p. 172.

or, again:

> The peasant folk had simple ways
> In not extremely distant days . . .
> While now on drinking wine they're set,
> They plunge themselves in heavy debt,
> And though their corn and wine sell well
> They borrow more than I can tell,
> And payments are always belated,
> They must be excommunicated . . .[27]

The major emphasis of the poem is religious. Although Brant was concerned with human foibles and the folly of love affairs, idle talk, dancing, and serenading at night, his criticism focuses on the contemporary lack of faith and the decline of moral standards:

> Fool he who ne'er is much concerned
> In life eternal he has earned
> And utters prayers that he may
> Live like a fool till Judgement Day . . .
> Oh, fool, no pleasures here on earth
> Can ever more give joy on earth . . .
> Has ever greater fool been born
> Than who'd stay here and Heaven scorn?[28]

or

> But ah, the road to high salvation—
> Pure wisdom's only destination—
> Is very narrow hard and steep
> And few the men that to it keep . . .
> Many are called but very few
> Are chosen. In what class are you?[29]

Brant retained the pessimism characteristic of the medieval attitude toward man: man wastes his life on the vanities

27. Ibid., p. 269.
28. Ibid., p. 161.
29. Ibid., p. 176.

of this life, refusing to recognize his kinship to God or to discipline himself for eternal salvation; instead, he devotes himself to sensual pleasures, to lust and gluttony and feasting, and indulges himself in envy and hatred of his fellowmen. This was the usual medieval catalogue of sins, with no indication of a new attitude toward man and society. Man was still, by Adam's sin, doomed to travail and damnation. Alsatian humanism did not attempt to change this image, nor did it create a new ethical or moral code. Reform was simply returning to the old way. Brant's religious concepts and moral attitudes were still medieval; indeed, Erwin Panofsky considers him the archetype of the medieval in contrast to Erasmus, the man of the Renaissance.[30]

At the time, however, the book was widely acclaimed. It went through numerous editions in German and was translated into French and Dutch. Locher rendered it into Latin and compared Brant to Dante and Petrarch; Ulrich von Hutten praised Brant for utilizing the barbaric German tongue in creating a truly poetic work.[31] The popularity of the poem reveals the tenacious traditionalism of the period. Bolstering the orthodox faith and exhibiting the folly of turning away from the old ways, the book received the applause of the intellectual elite, for it reflected their own views.

Although the poetry of the Alsatian humanists never developed beyond a rendering of conventional ideas and attitudes in rather stilted classical form, Wimpfeling's historical works must be regarded as a novel and original contribution and an outgrowth of the new national consciousness. The question of national origins was particularly central to Alsace in this period. With the defeat of the house of Burgundy and the revival of ties with the house of Hapsburg, Alsace felt itself a part of the empire.[32] Because the re-

30. Erwin Panofsky, "Renaissance and Renascences," *Kenyon Review, 6* (1944), 234.
31. Schmidt, *Histoire littéraire, 1,* 312–13.
32. Paul Joachimsen, *Geschichtsauffassung und Geschichtschreibung in Deutschland unter dem Einfluss des Humanismus,* Beiträge zur Kulturgeschichte des Mittelalters und der Renaissance, *6 Teil 1* (Leipzig, 1910), 60.

lationship had been somewhat tenuous in the past, there was a certain overeagerness on the part of the Strasbourg humanists to proclaim their loyalty, and they undertook historical studies to justify and confirm the imperial relationship. Wimpfeling, in particular, turned to the study of the origins of Alsace, the origins of the Germanic people, and the development of the Roman Empire into a German institution. His first historical treatise, a small book entitled *Tutschland,* was written to prove that the German's inherited the imperial power directly from Rome, without any intervening period of French or Gallic domination:

> It is well known by all Germans that from the time of Julius, the first Emperor, until the time of our own King Maximilian, no Frenchman has been at the head of the Roman Empire. The book of names of the Roman Kings shows that all, either from heredity, birth, or fatherly blood were German. The Roman Emperors took their origin from Italy, Thrace, Arabia, or Hungary, or from "Wynschen Land" until Charles the Great, who was German. From then on, all the Roman emperors have been from the noblest German families, Saxony, Bavaria, Austria, Swabia, Hapsburg, Nassau, and not one Frenchman has ever been Roman Emperor.[33]

He then went on to establish the Germanic origin of Alsace: The Rhine was not the real border between France and Germany but was the result of Julius Caesar's pragmatic decision to use navigable waters as boundaries; the true boundary between France and Germany was the Vosges Mountains. He documented the Germanism of the original emperors, stating that Pepin had been born in Germany and that all his descendants were of German origin. Furthermore,

33. [Jacob Wympflinger von Slettstatt,] *Tutschland zu ere der Statt Strassburg* (Strassburg, 1648), unpaginated. The treatise was originally published in 1501, but the copy in the Yale University Library is a reprint made by German patriots in the seventeenth century, when Louis XIV was developing the French claims in the Rhineland —the polemic had continued. Hereafter this will be cited as Wimpfeling, *Tutschland.*

Pepin was German because it was common for a German mother to say to her child that one could not do a certain thing even if one was as wise as King Pepin. "I cannot believe," Wimpfeling concludes from this, "that our people would so commonly use the name of a Frenchman, but that of a German would be on her lips." [34] Proof of Charlemagne's nationality was also based on philological evidence. Charlemagne wrote books in the German language, drew up the German names for the twelve months of the year and for the winds, and named his children Hymeltrut and Hildegart [sic] "which are foreign to other tongues. It follows that he found these names not among French ancestors, but among Germans." [35] The establishment of the Holy Roman Empire was a German phenomenon; it was the Germanic peoples of the upper Rhine who had brought peace and order to western Europe.

The treatise was written for a particular political purpose, and it has a quality of naïveté and freshness. There are, however, certain original elements. The use of philological criteria is indicative of the humanist emphasis on language. Wimpfeling seems to have thought that this evidence would be accepted as conclusive. The most striking element in the treatise is, of course, its national sentiment: Wimpfeling had certainly forsaken the concept of the *res publica Christiana*. He did not view Germany as an integral part of a united Christendom but was only too eager to separate it from France and to state that the difference reached far back into the past.

Wimpfeling's *Epithoma Rerum Germanicum* (1505) was more thorough, more scholarly, and less polemic. It can be considered one of the first important histories of Germany by a German.[36] The book emerges as a careful and methodical

34. Ibid.
35. Ibid.
36. Ernest Bickel in his thesis raises the question of Wimpfeling's authorship of the *Epithoma*. He concludes that although Wimpfeling undoubtedly took over Sebastian Murrho's notes, he also did extensive work on the source materials himself, and the book must be con-

study, in which the naïveté and the polemic of the *Tutsch-land* have disappeared. Wimpfeling began with the earliest allusions to the German in classical literature, noting that from the first they were referred to as great warriors; they had been conquered only by the Romans, and the latter were invincible. He recorded Roman emperors who ruled over German territories, described the invasions of the new tribes, and then launched into an account, emperor by emperor, of the rulers of Germany from Charlemagne to Frederic of Austria. Chapters on the national character included essays on German constancy, German courage, and German liberality. The book concluded with a description of German cultural development.

Germany had contributed new skills to the rest of Europe; the art of printing had been developed in the city of Strasbourg and was carried thence by local artisans to Italy. German builders had achieved unique forms of artistic and architectural expression. No structure in the orb of the universe could equal the cathedral of Strasbourg in symmetry or in the variety of its sculptural detail. Aeneas Silvius had marveled when he saw it; Scopas, Phidias, Clesiphon, and Archimedes would have recognized it as the perfection of architectural form.[37]

It was only in the last section that Wimpfeling allowed himself to be carried away. For the rest, the *Epithoma* is a well-organized, coherent, and unified book. The diffusion that marks many early histories is absent; it is methodical and pithy. Wimpfeling had culled sources ranging from Plutarch, Caesar, and Tacitus to Aeneas Silvius, Ficino, and John Gerson[38] and had reorganized them to create a systematic narrative.

Wimpfeling was not the only humanist to pursue historical

---

sidered his own. See Ernest Bickel, *Wimpfeling als Historiker,* Inaugural-Dissertation, Marburg Universität (Marburg, 1904).

37. [Jacobus Wimpheling,] *Epithoma Rerum Germanicum usque ad nostra tempora* (Strasbourg, 1505).

38. Bickel, *Wimpfeling als Historiker,* pp. 37–38.

studies. Brant published several short treatises on the Emperor Maximilian that must be classified as political literature rather than historical essays since they dealt with the familiar theme of the restoration of the Roman Empire. He hoped, however, to edit with Wimpfeling the chronicles of Alsace with biographical notes, and he collected materials for this purpose.[39] Ringmann brought out one of the first German translations of Caesar's Gallic Wars,[40] adding to the available source materials in German; and Hieronymus Gebwiler published several historical works: *Libertas Germaniae*, on the problem of German origins; a history of Ferdinand, King of Spain; a catalogue of the archdukes of Austria and the ducal family of Hapsburg; and a study of the devolution of the German and Imperial crown to the House of Austria.[41] Although none of these were of the scope of Wimpfeling's work, they do indicate the importance of historical studies and of the constant exploration of source materials to the Strasbourg humanists.

It is evident that there was a sustained interest in the origins of the Germanic peoples as a whole, in their relationship to the Roman Empire, and in the development of the Hapsburg family. The panegyrics to the Hapsburg princes give evidence of strong traditional political loyalties; yet the tenor of the tracts would seem to indicate that this loyalty to the Hapsburgs was as princes of the German nation rather than in their symbolic role as leaders of Christendom. The universal grouping was no longer meaningful. It is possible that the analysis of past political relationships was in part a search for new political formulas. All these men showed an awareness of Strasbourg's need for support from some larger political entity.

The third element in the thought and writing of the Strasbourg humanists was their concern for education. In the long run this interest had the most important influence on

39. Schmidt, *Histoire littéraire*, 1, 250.
40. Ibid., 2, 106.
41. Ibid., 1, 409–11.

the city. The leader of the movement for educational reform was Wimpfeling, who wrote several pedagogical treatises, all practical in nature, suggesting certain methods of teaching, outlining specific courses of study, and advocating a coordinated school system from elementary instruction through to the university.

Wimpfeling approached education as a social reformer. Much of the immorality of the time was due, he felt, to ignorance. Monks and clergy were poorly educated, the nobility were coarse and crude, and the middle class was ignorant.[42] Furthermore, the universities did not fully perform their duties as educational institutions, for they ignored the problems of the impoverished students by permitting them to beg or serve in menial capacities in wealthy families. As a result, the students were demoralized, were exposed to vulgar standards and vicious habits, and became overly concerned with money and position.[43] A good education, Wimpfeling thought, should not be confined merely to intellectual learning, for it was not enough for a young man to write good Latin—he must be virtuous as well, honoring God and his parents and serving as a moral force in society.[44] To achieve this, the universities should be reformed; existing church benefices should be made available to scholars and students, thus relieving them of the necessity of living on charity; and a *Gymnasium* should be established in every German city to provide a secondary education independent of the church schools. The future of the German people rested on these reforms, for without education the people could read neither the Holy Scriptures nor the laws of their own city.[45]

Wimpfeling outlined his proposal for such a Gymnasium as an addendum to his treatise *Tutschland*, addressing his recommendations to the Magistrat of Strasbourg. He asked

42. Ibid., 1, 132–33.
43. [Jacob Wimphelingii,] *Adolescentia* (Strassburg, 1500), unpaginated.
44. Ibid.
45. Wimpfeling, *Tutschland*.

the city authorities to set aside a building for the school, emphasizing that this would constitute the sole expense to the city because the teachers would be paid by the families of the students. The school would admit students who had completed their elementary work in the chapter schools or with tutors, and it would provide an education designed for laymen—prose and verse writing, letter writing, and historical and moral studies. Thus a burgher could send his children to this school without any fear that they would be turned into priests.[46]

Brant, too, saw the need for educational reforms. He was concerned with the poor quality of education available, and one of his "fools" is the man who does not provide an adequate education for his children:

> A fool is he and blind indeed
> Who ne'er to children pays much heed
> That properly they may be reared
> And in the right direction steered . . .
> Our children too'd be better trained
> If they had teachers like the famed
> Phoenix whom Peleus admired
> And for his son Achilles hired,
> And Philip scoured Greece till he'd won
> The ablest teachers for his son . . .
> But fathers, oh, of nowaday
> Engage such teachers for a son
> Who'd make a fool of anyone.
> That, mark you, that's our children's plight
> If once in youth they've been neglected,
> By teachers, never well directed
> From start to finish honor's prize
> Derives alone from precept wise
> A noble mind's a precious stone,
> Your sacred trust, but not your own.[47]

46. Ibid.
47. Zeydel, trans., *Ship of Fools*, pp. 72–73.

Brant took his own admonition to heart and wrote for his own son a series of pedagogical works composed of Latin maxims on good manners and morals, which he translated into German rhyme.[48] One of these was a group of maxims from Cato; another described correct behavior for various walks of life; a third provided general rules of etiquette. Like Wimpfeling, Brant felt that education was more than mere intellectual training—the educated man was a man of moral probity, with good manners.

The novelty in these proposals is their emphasis on lay education, and this emphasis is particularly noteworthy in view of Brant's and Wimpfeling's loyalty to the church. Convinced that education must be made available to a broader social group, they were equally aware that the burghers would not send their children to schools controlled by the church. The answer was secular schools. They did not go on, however, to establish a new image for the educated man. Wimpfeling's ideal of a Christian gentleman was conventional: The well-educated young man would venerate God; refrain from swearing; honor his parents; be courteous to the old; respect church ceremonies; flee bad society; and tell the truth.[49] Although Wimpfeling offered pedagogical ideas well in advance of the rote learning of the medieval schools, it is a far cry from Strasbourg to the school of Vittorino de Feltre at Mantua.

Through their program for educational reform, the humanists became involved in the life of the city. Wimpfeling's proposal for a Gymnasium was only one example. In 1504, after the Magistrat had failed to act on that recommendation, Geiler, Wimpfeling, Brant, and Sturm encouraged Mathius Ringmann to open a Latin school, hoping that from this beginning a Gymnasium might develop.[50] This attempt failed, too, but in 1509 the humanists, undaunted, persuaded the cathedral chapter to appoint Hieronymus Gebwiler as

48. Schmidt, *Histoire littéraire*, 1, 318.
49. Wimpfeling, *Adolescentia*.
50. Schmidt, *Histoire littéraire*, 2, 94.

director of the cathedral school. Since Gebwiler was at the time head of the Sélestat Latin school, the members of the *sodalitas literaria* were convinced that he would be able to bring the cathedral school up to the same standard. In fact, even under Gebwiler it remained a chapter school, and in the end the humanists were able to achieve a measure of educational reform only at a higher level. The *sodalitas* brought scholars in to instruct chapter members and the monastic orders. Otmar Luscinius lectured on Latin literature to the Knights of St. John, and Conrad Mellisopolitanus gave instruction in Greek.[51]

The achievement of the humanists is exemplified in the failure of their educational reforms. They were unable to arouse an interest in learning among the citizens. The Magistrat represented the best educated of the burgher families; yet it turned down Wimpfeling's proposal for a Gymnasium, and none of the other schools, so carefully nurtured by the humanists, secured any sustained support. The humanists remained an intelligentsia, an elite set apart from the city as a whole. To the average citizen these men were simply canons of one chapter or another, and the mere fact that they were more learned than the canons of forty years before meant little. The burghers were proud of Brant's reputation because it brought honor to the city, but few were stirred to new learning or were moved by the cry for moral reform.

The intellectual awakening that Strasbourg experienced in the years just before the Reformation was confined to a small group and a relatively narrow field. There was no significant change in the basic philosophic or theological assumptions of the humanist group. Brant and Wimpfeling were familiar with Plato; Thomas Wolf worked on an edition of the works of Pico della Mirandola; but the Strasbourg scholars made no attempt to incorporate these ideas into their own thought. Their religious beliefs were too strong

51. Ibid., 2, 178.

to permit new philosophical departures. Stylistically their classicism was artificial and stilted. They had learned the forms of classical poetry—they knew all the rules—but were never able to handle the forms freely. Classicism was a façade, a doorway embellished with Doric columns tacked on to the stout half-timbered frame of an Alsatian house.

Only in those areas where they were not bound by convention and tradition did the Strasbourg humanists develop original and novel forms. Historical writing was a comparatively new field; although certain classic sources were highly regarded, there was no one accepted way to write history. Here the humanists felt less restrained and were able to develop a freer and more natural style. Similarly, there were accepted forms of medieval pedagogy, but existing educational institutions were weak, and the humanists felt that they could make proposals for change. By these educational reforms they did not envision a new relationship between man and his society; instead they hoped to create a better medieval man: more pious, more devout, and more honest, for the Strasbourg humanists looked backward in time. They wished to bring about a reformation, but one that would restore and re-create the past. Brant wanted men to return to the old way, old customs, and old values. He thought that each man should accept his traditional place in the world, that peace and unity would prevail, and that reform would come through restoration of the past.

CHAPTER 5

GEILER VON KAYSERSBERG, PREACHER AND REFORMER

HE humanists wrote for a limited audience: a small group of patrician patrons and their fellow scholars; but Geiler von Kaysersberg preached to the whole city of Strasbourg, for the burghers flocked to the cathedral to hear him. In 1486, Peter Schott, adding to the revenues of the cathedral building fund from his own pocket, commissioned a handsome carved pulpit. This was placed in the nave of the cathedral so that Geiler's words could be heard by a large throng.[1] From the pulpit Geiler called upon the citizens of Strasbourg to change their lives, to give up drinking and gambling, and to refrain from blasphemy; he called upon the Magistrat to recast the laws of the city and thus provide a more Christian justice and grant greater freedom to the church; he called upon the clergy to renounce their worldly ways and dedicate themselves to the church. By his sermons he hoped to bring the city to a deeper spirituality and a new mode of life, and the reforms he sought echoed Savonarola.

At the beginning of his ministry, Geiler addressed himself to the state of the church. In 1492 he asked the bishop to undertake a reform of the clergy. A synod was called, and Bishop Albrecht came with many counts and nobles of his staff—all the nobles of the canonical establishments, the

1. Sébald Büheler, *La Chronique Strasbourgeoise*, Fragments recueillis et annotés par l'Abbé L. Dacheux, Fragments des anciennes chroniques d'Alsace (4 vols. Strasbourg, 1892–1901), *1*, 65.

clergy of other foundations and cloisters, and the provincials, abbots, priors, and prelates of the whole diocese—in all, about six hundred clergy.[2] Geiler's opening sermon on this occasion was addressed to the bishop. The young men of the church were happy, he said, because they saw their leaders with them. The bishop must now exert his authority and give the clergy the rules and orders they needed to live disciplined and holy lives. The immorality of the clergy, he continued, was notorious. It was common knowledge that the monks and nuns lived together; five dead children had been found in a secret place in one cloister,[3] while in other cloisters the nuns were more pious and brought up their children. The fault lay in the lack of punishment; the monks might sin, but the only punishment they received was three days on bread and water. That, stated Geiler dramatically, was a long penance! They might as well be given fifteen minutes.[4] As for the canons and the clergy, they walked around the church and talked and laughed so loudly that the priest serving at the altar was constrained to stop.[5]

"O holy bishop," Geiler exclaimed, "Wake up and reform your church according to the Holy Gospel, the Apostles and the teachings of the true Church." [6] The bishop need not wait for the pope's orders to make such reforms, for these changes would not harm the people of the land but would help them, and the pope was not opposed to godly teaching.

The synod enacted several changes, which the chronicler registers with unusual irony: The cloisters were locked, but the doors were opened when one knocked; the nuns no longer had children; the clergy and the concubines gave up their costly apparel; the clergy were quiet in the churches because they never entered them; widows and orphans were

2. Specklin, *Collectanées*, p. 289.
3. It is interesting to see that the five dead children, who appeared frequently in the polemic of the Reformation, were there at an earlier period as well.
4. Specklin, *Collectanées*, p. 289.
5. Ibid., p. 290.
6. Ibid., pp. 290–91.

taken care of, if they wept blood; and the poor were clothed with old stockings.[7]

Geiler deplored the failure. In the presence of the bishop, he preached before King Maximilian and charged that despite his exhortations for reform no effective action had been taken. Christ Himself, Geiler warned, would send better reformers. At lunch the King admonished the bishop to pay heed to the words of the preacher.[8] Again in 1504, Geiler preached before the King and the bishop and warned them that if neither pope, bishop, emperor, nor king would reform the godless life of the people, God would inspire someone to raise up his people. After the sermon, the King conferred earnestly with the bishop; they sought Wimpfeling's advice, but nothing was done.[9]

Geiler made one final attempt sometime after 1508, and this time the bishop's response was an ordinance forbidding clerical persons to keep concubines. The clergy protested, saying that they were only human like other men, and appealed the matter to the pope. Geiler fought the appeal, but the pope ruled that convents should be left as they were even if the nuns and monks sinned.[10]

Church reform, to Geiler, involved a restoration of internal discipline. The clergy should lead sober, dedicated lives which would inspire the laymen. Those members of the clergy who felt no true religious vocation should be dismissed. Ecclesiastical orders should be open only to those who sincerely desired to teach and to preach and should not be used as a means of ensuring a life income for the sons of burghers and noble families.[11] All this could be achieved by vigorous episcopal action and was not particularly grave.

Geiler felt that a more critical threat came from the city authorities who, by their gradual encroachment into the

7. Ibid., p. 291.
8. Ibid., p. 292.
9. Ibid., p. 297.
10. Ibid., p. 300.
11. L. Dacheux, *Un Reformateur Catholique, Jean Geiler* (Paris, 1876), p. 137.

areas of ecclesiastical immunity, had seriously weakened the competence of the church. He pointed to recent enactments: one law of Strasbourg stipulated that no one entering a religious order could take with him more than one hundred pounds, and the rest he was compelled to bequeath to his heirs;[12] another forbade a layman to give or bequeath money or property for religious and charitable purposes. In addition to this, the city authorities exacted taxes, tolls, and revenues from the clergy, even on necessary articles such as wine and grain.[13] By these acts the Magistrat had made itself a rival and an enemy of the church. It did not respect ancient ecclesiastical immunities, and the exercise of the power to tax was clearly usurpation.

In response to this criticism the Rat asked Geiler to appear before its members in 1500. He presented his recommendations in twenty-one articles that reaffirmed the autonomy of the church, the inviolability of wills, and the right of a cleric in orders to inherit a secular estate.[14] All taxes and levies laid on the clergy should be abolished. Instead of embroiling themselves in these matters outside their jurisdiction, the Ratsherren should put their own house in order. They should proceed with greater severity against gambling, drinking, and dance halls and should prevent further vulgarization of church festivals. They should also refrain from transacting secular business in the cathedral during services.[15] As it was, the Ammeister made a practice of holding court in his customary seat during Mass. Witnesses and injured parties were brought before him, pleas heard, and verdicts given.[16]

Geiler also addressed himself to the injustice and inhu-

12. Murray A. and Marian L. Cowie, "Geiler von Kaysersberg and Abuses in Fifteenth–Century Strassburg," *Studies in Philology, 58* (1961), 485. The article includes the full text of a letter from Peter Schott to the papal nuncio describing Geiler's opposition to certain abuses.
13. Ibid., p. 487.
14. Dacheux, *Geiler,* p. 79.
15. Ibid., pp. 74–93.
16. Cowie and Cowie, *Studies in Philology, 58* (1961), 490.

manity of certain city ordinances. He petitioned the authorities in the name of Christ to permit administration of the last sacrament to those who were to be executed for civil crimes. A citizen who killed a foreigner or an outsider was freed from all punishment on payment of thirty pieces of silver; yet, if he stole some trifle from the same person, he would be hanged. Were the makers of laws like these in a state of salvation? [17]

Another target was the celebration of feast days and Sundays. Like Savonarola, Geiler undertook to abolish customs that had become licentious and vulgar and to replace them with processions and pageants that were appropriate to the occasion and religious in spirit. In a letter to the papal nuncio, Peter Schott described one particular festival:

> [The people] erected in former times high up under the organ in the cathedral a crude statue, the *Roraffe*. This they misuse as follows. During the holy feast of Pentecost itself, when it is customary for the people of the whole diocese to enter the cathedral in procession, with relics of the saints, singing in devotion and praise of God and shouting for joy, some rogue or other, hiding behind the statue, and bellowing forth profane and bawdy songs in a raucous voice accompanied by lewd gestures, drowns out the hymns of the people entering and mocks them in derisive pantomime, with the result he not only turns the people's devotion into discord and their lamentation into guffaws, but also hinders even the clerics singing the divine services.[18]

Similarly, the feast of the Holy Innocents had deteriorated from an occasion for the presentation of mystery plays to a farce in which the children chose a mock bishop who was dressed up in bishop's clothes and who mounted the episcopal throne. Geiler, decrying the custom, restored dignity

17. Ibid., p. 489.
18. Ibid., p. 490.

to the ceremony,[19] for which Peter Schott wrote an appropriate play.[20]

Although he was convinced that he lived in a moment of profound moral decline, Geiler was certain that the problems could be solved by appealing to men's better natures. This was the purpose of his sermons. To the modern reader they seem disorganized, discursive, and full of allegorical stories and examples that border on the folk tale. One modern critic has observed that the pre-Reformation sermon was "a mosaic of interesting religious and cultural facts."[21] Geiler included racy tales of clerical immorality, stories of the works of the devil, the lives of the saints and the apostles— all woven into a rich and colorful narrative. But it was all eminently human, and the delivery was stirring and impressive. No chronicler of the period, no visitor to Strasbourg failed to comment on Geiler's preaching, and young men tried to imitate him.

Most significantly, he preached the gospel, and here he revealed his Christian humanism. In Basel, he had edited the works of the great French churchman, Jean Gerson. Gerson had deplored the sterile subtleties of contemporary theology and had proposed a return to the ancient church fathers to rediscover church doctrine in its purity.[22] Geiler undertook this study of the fathers and from there had been drawn on to the study of the scriptures. Although he had by no means the exegetical skill of the reforming preachers or their more profound understanding of the scriptures, he was the first to begin the task of exposing the Bible to the citizens of Strasbourg in a form which was meaningful to them. In familiar and colloquial language and using parables drawn from everyday life, Geiler expounded the scriptural passages ap-

19. Dacheux, *Geiler,* pp. 58–59.
20. Schmidt, *Histoire littéraire, 1,* 29.
21. Elmer Carl Kiessling, *The Early Sermons of Luther and their Relation to the Pre-Reformation Sermon* (Grand Rapids, Mich., 1935), p. 40.
22. Vansteenberghe, in *L'Humanisme en Alsace,* p. 25.

pointed for the day. The first sermon in his *Evangeli Buch,*
for Christmas Day, gives his own justification for preaching
and his method of exposition:

> I have decided to preach from the Gospel, and I will
> clearly state why I have done so. . . .
> You ask, what are you trying to do with this, why do
> you talk on the Gospels? St. Augustine had to make the
> same explanations when he wrote the prologue to St.
> John; so I answer you, the Gospel to be understood must
> be written about, explained and used.
> One preaches the Gospel to men. One can't preach it
> to the winds and the walls—what was it written for, if
> we weren't meant to preach it? We read it out openly
> in church through the ordinances of God the Holy
> Ghost. It is also sung in the third Mass. Furthermore, if
> the *Rat* wishes to make known a letter to the whole
> city, they have it read out openly. Why, therefore,
> shouldn't we preach the Holy Gospel which was sent
> to us by the Holy Ghost? The priest who reads the
> Mass, ends the Mass with the Gospel . . . "In the be-
> ginning was the Word, and the Word was with God."
> There is a great need to hear the Gospel, so says
> Anthony in his *Summa,* and he tells the story of the
> two hunters, and how one day they were out hunting
> together, and a great storm came up over the fields,
> and the sky grew all dark, and there was thunder and
> lightning, and they heard a voice that said, "Clap, Clap,"
> and there was a thunder clap, and one hunter was
> struck, and the other hunter was frightened, you can
> well believe, for his companion had been taken from
> his side. Not long after, there was more lightning and
> a voice came, "Clap, Clap," then another voice which
> said, "I cannot strike. He has heard the Word that the
> Word has become Flesh." They had both heard the
> Mass but the one had gone away before the Gospel of
> St. John was read. The other heard the Gospel in which

74

these words are said, "The Word has become Flesh."
Therefore he was not afraid of the thunder. Thus, where
the Gospel of St. John is and is read, the thunder can
do no harm. Therefore, when it thunders, men say by
custom that it speaks. "In the beginning was the Word
and the Word was with us." If there is one named John
in the house, there also the thunder does not strike.
This is true, What is John? It is one in whom the Grace
of God resides and where the Grace of God is, no thunder strikes, and if it does strike, it does no harm. And
thus I will say of the Gospel, in John there are twelve
thunder claps. Now mark these things, when you know
these three things, then you have understood very well
the twelve thunderclaps of the Gospel.

The first is, what is a Word.

The second is, Whether a Word can be in God as in
us.

The third is, why the Word of God is called the Son
of God.

A word, Geiler continues, can be inward, which means it
is thought but not spoken, or it can be outward, as with
regular words of speech. The inner word is equated with
thought. Having made this differentiation, he goes on to
consider the second point, stating that God is not a remote
phenomenon, living distant from the world in Heaven. He
is a living Being.

You must not think that God is just a block, sitting
in heaven like a stick which understands nothing and
cannot reason. God is a living Thing, an active Thing.
Therefore He must have within Himself an Inner Word,
and thus His Word is. If he did not have this Word, then
God would be just a stick. . . .

A Son is a living part of the same species. I live and
he also lives. . . . Thus with God, God shines forth in
his Godly way, from this there springs forth a radiance
which is called the Word of God, and the Word is called

the Son of God, because it has all the things which be-
long to a son, it is a living Thing from a living thing
and it is His. . . . The Word of God is living and a
part of Him and therefore it is His Son. Then you say,
why is not my own word, my son's? My word is just
an accident, an occurrence. When I think it, I throw
it from me, and it no longer exists. With God it is not
the same. The Word of God is the substance and the
Way of God. . . . Yes, it is the Wisdom of God the
Father, through which he created all things, as the
Gospel says, all things are created by Him. You must
not think that God the Father is a woman who has just
been delivered of a child and lies behind the curtain
and gives forth the Son from his fatherly heart. It is
not that thing which is called the Son of God, [but] the
Word of God, which God Himself understands. . . . St.
John in the Gospel which you have heard put forth
twelve thunder claps, and these are they:[23]

The eternity of birth.
The relationship of persons.
A way.
An eternity.
The creation.
Life.
An opening.
Generation.
Necessity.[24]

23. Although he states he will list twelve, only nine appear.
24. Johann Geiler, *Der Evangeli Buch* (Strasbourg, 1538), ix–Bii.
The *Evangeli Buch,* like most of the Geiler sermons, was published
posthumously by members of the clergy who had heard the originals
or who had taken them down at the time. The *Evangeli Buch* was
the work of one Heinrich Weszmer who stated they were "angesh-
rieben usz seinen [Geilers] mund." Dacheux credits the various published versions as authentic. The sermons published as the *Evangeli
Buch* were delivered in 1507, first printed in 1515. Dacheux, *Jean
Geiler,* pp. 573–83. The Yale University Library copy, which I used,
is a later edition, for Geiler's works continued to be published through
the period of the Reformation.

Geiler von Kaysersberg

Geiler closed the sermon by reading in its entirety the scriptural passage he had discussed. On St. Stephen's Day he resumed the same subject, picking up the thunderclaps that he had listed at the end of the Christmas Day sermon, explaining each one in terms of its reference to the Word. Thus, he said, the fifth thunderclap, creation, means that all things are made by the Word, and nothing is made without it. We know from Moses that God made the world, but St. John includes this in his Gospel because there are some heretics who maintain that God made the heavens and the devil made the earth. And, therefore, "John thunders against them and says that without the Word of God, nothing is made." [25]

The sermon is illustrative of the transitional nature of Geiler's thought and work. In conception, in its attempt to preach the Gospel, it was modern. He was attempting to bring the words of Christ to the people, to show them the wellsprings of Christian thought and teaching. This was the humanist ideal. Yet, in its style—with its anecdotes, its numerous repetitions, and the story of the hunters—it is medieval. The discussion of the Word as accident and as substance shows that Geiler was a disciple of Gerson and the Occamist tradition, but the explanation is fuzzy and difficult to follow, and it must have been confusing to the layman.

Analysis of other sermons indicates that his conceptions were still medieval. He accepted, for example, the traditional view of the devil. The devil's whole purpose was to create as much trouble as he could for people. Thus he burned down the house of one man in the village. The man rebuilt; so the devil burned down the new one. Finally, the devil burned the whole village.[26] Geiler's world was one animated by all sorts of forces—devils, witches, and sorcerers who entered people and bewitched them.

25. Geiler, *Evangeli Buch*, Biiii.
26. Herman Köpcke, *Johannes Geiler von Kaisersberg, Ein Beitrag zur religiösen Volkskunde des Mittelalters,* Inaugural-Dissertation, Universität zu Breslau (Breslau, 1926), p. 10.

The medieval spirit of the sermons hardly needs to be labored. The fact remains that in their own time Geiler's sermons were regarded as novel and original. The scriptures were being discussed and examined; the sources of the Christian faith were being made available. The sermons were collected and published in Geiler's lifetime, and they constituted an early best seller for the printers of Strasbourg. Publication continued after his death with two or three editions a year from 1511 to 1522.[27] Zell, who was to become one of the reformers of Strasbourg, counted these sermons as a definitive influence on his own thought,[28] and Geiler's image as a preacher was an inspiration to the young clergy of Strasbourg and Alsace.

27. Cf. Charles Schmidt, *Répertoire bibliographique strasbourgeois jusqu' à vers 1530* (6 vols. Strasbourg, 1894).
28. Timotheus Wilhelm Röhrich, *Mittheilungen aus der Geschichte der Evangelischen Kirche des Elsasses* (3 vols. Strasbourg, 1855), 3, 89.

PART II

The Reformation in Strasbourg

1520–1534

CHAPTER 6

THE PROTAGONISTS OF REFORM

N 1517 Strasbourg was securely orthodox —not only orthodox but conservatively so. By 1528 the Mass was abolished within the city. The change resulted from the efforts of a dedicated group of men who were convinced that the preaching of the Pure Word of God would open the citizens to newness of life, to a deeper religious understanding, and to a reaffirmation of Christian principles in their daily life. The protagonists included a handful of intellectuals, a significant number of the Magistrat, and, most important, the reformers themselves, drawn, with one exception, from the lower ranks of the clergy.

The intellectuals were the very first to be influenced by the new ideas. Teachers and professional men, they read Lutheran tracts and books and were known to be of Lutheran persuasion before any public preaching had taken place. This was natural. As men of letters they were open to ideas, and books were easily available to them. Nicolaus Gerbel, a lawyer who served as advocate and secretary to the cathedral chapter, supported Luther as early as 1520.[1] A convinced Lutheran, he was later regarded as an opponent by Bucer and Zell but remained in the city throughout the period of the Reformation as a teacher of history and law.[2] Otto Brunfels, a Carthusian monk known for his humanism

---

1. Timotheus Wilhelm Röhrich, *Geschichte der Reformation im Elsass und besonders in Strassburg* (3 vols. Strasbourg, 1830–32), *1,* 126.
2. Ficker und Winckelmann, *Handschriftproben, 2,* 77.

and his scientific studies, was early drawn to Luther. He joined Hutten, served as pastor in a series of Rhenish towns,[3] and returned to Strasbourg after 1524 to become the director of one of the new Latin schools. Independent, increasingly involved in his botanical and medical studies, he never became a part of the inner circle of the reformers. Finally finding the atmosphere too rigid and uncompromising, he left the city in 1533.[4]

Lucas Hackfurt was another early supporter of the Reform. A scholar who had served as a chaplain, from 1522 on he directed a private school in the city. Later he would be attracted to Anabaptism. Johann Schwebel, one of the teachers in Hackfurt's school also accepted the new doctrine.[5] Yet none of these men, in the period from 1520 to 1522, taught or lectured or discussed the new ideas with persons outside their own small circle. Although they accepted the Lutheran teachings for themselves, they were not moved to promulgate the idea to a wider group.

The men who carried the new Word to the populace were neither teachers nor influential members of the clergy. As people's priests in the various parish churches of the city, they represented the lowest and least respected echelon of the church hierarchy. Throughout the Middle Ages the parish priests were regarded as ignorant and inarticulate and had been divorced from the intellectual life of the church community. Yet within a space of a few years these posts had been filled by well-trained, dedicated young men, fresh from the German universities, where they had supplemented traditional scholastic, theological, and philosophical courses with extracurricular studies in Latin and Greek. Versed in

3. *Neue Deutsche Biographie* (5 vols. Berlin, 1952–60), 2, 678.
4. François Wendel, *L'Eglise de Strasbourg, sa constitution et son organization, 1532–1535* (Paris, 1942), p. 39. There is some question about the date of Brunfel's departure. The *Neue Deutsche Biographie* states that he left in 1532. Wendel found evidence that he was still there before the synod of 1533, and indeed his opposition was one of the reasons why it was essential to hold the synod and formulate a unified doctrine.
5. Ficker und Winckelmann, *Handschriftproben*, 2, 78.

these languages and Hebrew, they read the scriptures from old texts. Inspired with a sense of mission and touched by the current of national enthusiasm that permeated the German universities, they began to formulate and direct the religious aspirations of the middle class from which they had sprung.[6]

The four men who were to change the lives and mores of the citizens of Strasbourg were Martin Bucer (1491–1551), Wolfgang Capito (1478–1541), Matthäus Zell (1477–1548), and Caspar Hedio (1494–1552). Their backgrounds were similar in several ways. They came from small towns in the Rhineland (Sélestat, Haguenau, Kaysersberg, and Ettlingen, respectively); they sprang from artisan or middle-class stock (Bucer's father was a shoemaker, Capito's a blacksmith, and Zell and Hedio came from respectable middle-class burgher families);[7] and all four men had received the major part of their education in Germany. Here the similarities ended. Each differed from the other in temperament, in interest, and in experience, and the Strasbourg Reform represented not the work of a single, powerful mind but the combined efforts of a disappointed Dominican, an ecclesiastical courtier, a university professor, and a self-effacing scholar. By this very diversity it drew to itself the major forces of German intellectual and ecclesiastical life.

Of the four major figures, Bucer was the most dynamic and the most vigorous. Even today his handwriting, impossibly illegible, exposes his impatience, his driving energy, and a rather relentless perfectionism in the continual re-

6. For a discussion of the significance of the emergence of the lower clergy see Hajo Holborn, "The Social Basis of the German Reformation," *Church History,* 5 (1938), 335–38.

7. The best sources on the early lives of these men are as follows: For Bucer: Hastings Eells, *Martin Bucer* (New Haven, Conn., 1931). For Capito: Johann Wilhelm Baum, *Capito und Butzer* (Elberfeld, 1860).
For Zell: Röhrich, *Mittheilungen,* 3. This volume includes a series of lives of various figures important in the Strasbourg Reformation.
For Hedio: *Allgemeine Deutsche Biographie* (45 vols. Leipzig, 1875–1900), *11, 223.*

visions and rewritings. The boy grew up in Sélestat, where he was born, but apparently there was no money for him to attend the Latin school. Prompted by an appetite for learning, he joined the Dominican order in 1506, believing he would receive a good education. To his great disappointment he found the teaching within the cloister empty and rigid. Nevertheless, he persevered with the work offered and finally was sent to Heidelberg, the Dominican center for theological studies. There he was able to attend a few courses at the university and pursue the study of Latin and Greek, which had become his major concern. But even in Heidelberg he was dissatisfied. Whether this stemmed from the scholastic emphasis of the theological studies or whether it grew out of his meeting with Luther at the Heidelberg disputations, we can only surmise. He himself testified that the monks denied him the right to continue his studies and finally forbade him to read.[8]

He decided, therefore, to leave the monastery; it is typical of him that he went through the proper canonical procedure for release from his vows. He was a man of exactness and attention to detail. Thus he petitioned for a papal dispensation to leave the order and was duly heard before a properly constituted ecclesiastical court—every effort having been made, as was customary, to assure that it was a sympathetic court.[9] Bucer gave evidence that undue pressure had been brought upon him to join the order, that during his novitiate he was threatened with everlasting damnation if he failed to take the monastic vows. In April 1521 he was formally released from his monastic obligations by the court and became a member of the secular clergy, still ordained and capable of holding any clerical position open to the nonmonastic clergy. He became a preacher, first at Landstuhl, the paternal seat of Franz von Sickingen, who befriended

8. Martin Butzer, *Verantwortung auff das in seine widerwertigen ein theil mit die wahrheit, ein theil mit lügen zum argsten zumessen* (Strasbourg, 1523), unpaginated.
9. Eells, *Martin Bucer*, p. 7.

him, then at Wissembourg, but his position became increasingly difficult. Still under the onus of having left the monastery, he had married, and his sermons were increasingly Lutheran. In early May 1523 he arrived in Strasbourg to seek the protection that the city was bound to offer him as the son of a burgher.[10]

Thirty-two years old at the time, stocky and rather powerfully built, he would shape and direct the Strasbourg Reform and would give it its unique form. Fundamentally he was a moderate man, given to extremes in neither action nor thought but driven by a conviction that the church had ceased to play a meaningful role in the lives of the people. Thus his theology and ecclesiology were pragmatic. Luther focused on the faith of the individual and on man's direct relation with God, whereas Bucer was concerned with the operation of faith in the daily life of the individual Christian and with the role of the church in the process.

Essentially, Bucer's was an evangelical theology based on a concept of the absolute power of the Word of God. Accepting Luther's justification by faith and election, Bucer's God was less arbitrary and more accessible. God chose the just, but He did not keep the decision secret: By the gift of faith He made manifest His selection. Thus, if a man believed, he knew he was a member of the elect.[11] More significantly, faith was obtainable. Through the Word, by hearing the Gospel, the unregenerate could be opened to God and could find the wholeness of faith and join the elect.[12] This concept gave the church a central role, for it was the function of the church to communicate the Word. The church was a redemptive force. This concept also gave Bucer a sense of

10. Although Bucer was born in Sélestat, shortly thereafter his father left and established himself in Strasbourg, purchasing Bürgerrecht. Martin remained with his grandfather in Sélestat, but he was, nevertheless, the son of a burgher of Strasbourg and could claim the rights and privileges of his father's citizenship.

11. Heinrich Bornkamm, *Martin Bucers Bedeutung für die europäische Reformationsgeschichte*, Schriften des Vereins für Reformationsgeschichte, 169, Jahrgang 58, Heft 2 (Gutersloh, 1952), p. 12.

12. Ibid.

urgency, reflected in Strasbourg in his demand that the pulpits must be supplied with men who could convey the Gospel to the populace. The matter could not be left to individual initiative. If the right words were spoken and heard, even the damned could be saved and the Kingdom of God achieved. It was a more optimistic view than Luther's, occupying a middle ground between the medieval concept of free will and Luther's God-centered determinism.

Conciliation, mediation, and the middle position were typical of Bucer as a person, as a theologian, and as a churchman. Although he broke with the Roman church, he never believed that the break was permanent or final but was convinced that Rome, the pope, and the bishops would be opened to the Gospel and that unity would be restored. At the other end of the spectrum he accepted the Anabaptists as friends and colleagues, admitting the plausibility of their arguments with regard to baptism. It was only with difficulty, after prolonged hesitation, that he came to oppose them because he felt that their concept of the gathered church precluded Christian unity. He was catholic in the broadest sense and perhaps the first modern ecumenical churchman.

Among the reformers he played the role of mediator, trying desperately to create harmony between Luther and Zwingli, who were divided on the question of the Eucharist. At first Bucer accepted Luther's views of consubstantiation but later turned to Zwingli's interpretation that Christ's words of institution were to be taken figuratively. Furthermore he was convinced that the two views could be reconciled, and in 1525 he sent a young churchman to Wittenberg to suggest to Luther that the question of the meaning of the Eucharist should be allowed to rest and that the reformers should be satisfied with the fact that the congregation participated in communion.[13] Luther's reply was scathing: There was no point to participation in communion if the communicant did not know what he was receiving. The difference

13. Ibid., p. 19.

was never bridged between Luther and the Swiss, but Bucer never abandoned his middle position. While Lutheranism and, later, Calvinism became increasingly dogmatic and doctrinaire in their particular interpretations, Bucer believed that none of these questions could be solved by learned theologians or by any one exegete but that the truth lay with the whole body of believers, the larger church, which was informed through the operation of the Holy Spirit.[14] The Eucharist must be left a mystery, its true nature veiled. The XVI Articles of the Strasbourg church would simply state that the wine and the wafer contained the body and blood of Christ, but would not attempt to explain the miracle. This position won Bucer only scorn from his fellow reformers, who berated him as vacillating and obscurantist. In an age when doctrines were sharply defined, when men went to the stake for a word, Bucer had the misfortune to see that words, in themselves, were deceptive.

A third component of his doctrine was an element of universality, stemming from the all-encompassing power of the Holy Spirit, and it was here that the influence of humanism was evident in his thought. Essentially Bucer was incapable of believing in a jealous God, offering Himself only to an elite. He believed that the Godly Spirit had manifested itself before and outside Christianity, in Homer, Hesiod, and Plato. The Spirit had then become incarnate in Christ. Christ was not, as He was for Luther, the antithesis of Moses. He was the universal revelation, the personification of all that was divine in human experience. Bucer trembled on the brink of Platonic deism, and his concept could thus weaken the historic reality of Christ.[15] The belief led him to see truth in all Christian canons and contained within it the germ of tolerance. Like his doctrine of the Eucharist, this was not an idea which appealed to his own time. In the moment of breaking with the Roman church it was important for the

14. Franklin H. Littell, "New Light on Butzer's Significance," *Reformation Studies*, ed. F. H. Littell (Richmond, Va., 1962), p. 146.
15. Bornkamm, *Martin Bucers Bedeutung*, p. 28.

Protestants to stress their dissimilarity, to create fine theological distinctions. Bucer maintained a catholic universalism in an age attuned to dogmatism.

Bucer was both practical and pacific. His correspondence with the bishop of Strasbourg at climatic moments of the Reform lacks Luther's rancor and scorn. He worked closely with the conservative Magistrat of Strasbourg, but rarely pushed himself forward. He occupied a mediating position in the politics of the Reformation as a whole, always appearing as the conciliator between Luther and Zwingli, always convinced that it would be possible to discover a doctrine on the sacraments acceptable to all. He was, as one scholar has put it, seduced by the humanist ideal of peace and concord.[16] In essence his moderation seems to have been a psychological trait.

Wolfgang Capito was a more sophisticated, more urbane figure. He arrived in March 1523 from the court of the Archbishop of Mainz, with an established reputation as one of the leading Hebrew scholars of Germany, to become provost of the chapter of St. Thomas. Although he had come from circumstances as humble as his fellow reformers, he had, during the years of his education, ranged further afield. Attending the universities of Ingolstadt and Freiburg, he had earned a degree in theology at the one and in medicine at the other. Later he became a doctor of canon law at Basel and received his doctorate in theology from Mainz. He was primarily an intellectual, with a searching quality of mind that immediately singled him out for notice and preferment.

In 1515 Capito was called from his post as preacher to the chapter of Bruchsal to become preacher to the cathedral and professor of theology at Basel. It was an important move for him. Basel was cosmopolitan and European and had developed a particular and individual Renaissance, which combined the study of classical languages with a deep and devout Christianity. Amerbach, Heynlin von Stein, and Froben

16. See J. V. Pollet, ed., *Martin Bucer, études sur la correspondence* (2 vols. Paris, 1958–62), 2, 148.

were publishing important classical texts and translations of the Bible, based on Greek and Hebrew sources.[17] Beatus Rhenanus was probing the ancient Christian fathers, hoping to find therein a rule of life for the individual layman.[18] And Erasmus was there, the dominant figure in an active group of scholarly men, some working at the University and some at the Froben or Amerbach press rooms.

Capito moved ahead quickly in the university, serving as rector from May to October 1514[19] and as dean of the theological faculty from September 1518 to 1519.[20] Nor was his scholarly work neglected. During the year 1516 Capito published his basic text, *Institutio in Hebraicam Literaturam,* an edition of the psalms in Hebrew, and a summary of Latin grammar. Most important, he became a friend of Erasmus, moving in the intimate inner circle, working on the famous edition of the New Testament, verifying the citations and proper names in the Old Testament—for Erasmus recognized that this young man surpassed him in knowledge of the Old Testament and Hebrew.[21]

His reputation as a humanist brought Capito further preferment, drawing the attention of Albrecht, Archbishop of Mainz, who hoped to make his own court a center of learning to compare favorably with his Italian peers. In 1519 he appointed Capito chancellor to the court and preacher in the cathedral at Mainz. Capito took the latter job seriously, preaching to his congregation on the Epistle to the Romans, on the freedom of a Christian man, and on the Commandments.[22] He preached not as a Lutheran but as an Erasmian, for he opposed Luther as hasty, rude, and bitter in his attacks on the hierarchy. This criticism of Luther brought cen-

17. Rupprich, *Humanismus und Renaissance,* p. 8.
18. Joachimsen, *Geschichtsauffassung und Geschichtschreibung, 1,* 126.
19. Hans Georg Wackernagel, *Die Matrikel der Universität Basel* (2 vols. Basel, 1951), 2, 334.
20. Ibid., 2, 370.
21. Otto Strasser, "Un Chrétien humaniste: Wolfgang Capiton," *Revue d'histoire et de philosophie religieuses, 20* (1940), 2.
22. Johann Baum, *Capito und Butzer,* p. 42.

sure from several of his Basel friends, including Oecolampadius and Hutten, who charged that the comforts of the
chancellorship made him unwilling to consecrate himself to
the new movement.[23] Ignoring these comments, he helped
prepare the case against Luther at the Diet of Worms and,
with other members of the ecclesiastical estate, heard
Luther's moving defense.

The Diet of Worms disturbed Capito's composure. The
disapproval of his close friend Hutten and the strong action
taken against Luther seem to have affected him, and in 1522
he journeyed to Wittenberg in search of a reconciliation between Luther and the archbishop. On his return to Mainz
he was increasingly frustrated and discouraged by the cabals
and intrigues of the court. In 1523 he resigned suddenly, de-
parting for Strasbourg to assume the office of provost at
St. Thomas, bestowed on him by the pope in 1521.[24] Strasbourg seems to have offered him an escape—a chance for
peace and solitude in which to make his decision, an opportunity to return to his scholarly work. Before the year was
out, he mounted the pulpit to preach the Gospel to his congregation.

Like Bucer, Capito was a moderate. A contemporary portrait shows him as a man of grace and dignified mien, square-
bearded, with large, expressive eyes. He remained always
the intellectual, writing his letters in impeccable Latin in a
neat humanist hand; much of his energy would later be directed toward the new schools and the Gymnasium. Unlike
Zwingli he found no conflict between humanism and the
Reform but continued his scholarly work, writing and publishing despite a crush of administrative duties. During the
climactic years from 1526 to 1528 he published a commentary
on Habakkuk and another on Hosea, with a translation of
the latter into German—sound, scholarly work accomplished
alongside his duties as pastor, preacher, and administrator.
Humanism turned him in the direction of ecumenicism

23. Röhrich, *Geschichte der Reformation*, 1, 151.
24. Ibid., p. 152.

and peace, and in the informal division of labor between the four Strasbourg reformers he seems to have assumed the responsibility for working with the assorted Anabaptist preachers who arrived in the city. He received them, invited them to remain as guests in his house, and communicated to them the Strasbourg point of view. The reformers hoped by these means to convert the Anabaptists to their formulations. In one instance the system proved dangerous, for the quiet and scholarly Martin Cellarius nearly converted Capito to his own Anabaptist views. The incident shows that Capito's loyalties ran deep for he was torn between his feelings toward this new friend and his attachment to Bucer. While by nature a scholar slated for high position, he was eminently human, and the pressure of the times distracted him from his work. As a man of conscience he made his decision and, having cast his lot with the Reform, gave it his undivided loyalty without regret and without looking back to the other life he could have had.

Of the group of four, Zell remained closest to the roots from which they had all sprung. He was a popular preacher, beloved by his congregation. The esteem in which he was held is reflected in a contemporary woodcut—one of those single-page flyers that served as a newspaper. He is shown on his deathbed, his head comfortably placed on a gingham pillow, and a pious inscription notes that, having preached so long and conscientiously to his people, he had now departed in peace to join his Master, lamented by those whom he had left behind. A genuine affection is communicated by the artlessness of the woodcut.[25]

Zell's early life cut across a wider variety of experience than either Bucer's or Capito's. Since Zell had been born in Kaysersberg, Geiler took an interest in him and guided his education: school in Mainz and then the University of Erfurt. Before completing the degree, he left to make the customary student journey through Germany and Italy, and

25. The woodcut is in a collection of prints in the Musée Rohan in Strasbourg.

apparently still restless, served in the imperial army during the Swabian War. He resumed his academic career at Freiburg im Breisgau, receiving his master's degree in 1505 and then remained for further study.[26]

Freiburg at this time was still quite provincial, not greatly affected by the movement of humanism that swept down the Rhine Valley from Basel. Glareanus and Zasius taught in the law school; the theological faculty included Georg Northofer from Tübingen and Johannes Brisgoicus, from Paris, but no major humanist movement developed.[27] In spite of the narrow, relatively monastic spirit of his environment, Zell was drawn to biblical scholarship, and studied the scriptures and Geiler's sermons, laying the foundation for his later career as a preacher. Eventually, but very slowly, he achieved scholarly recognition. On October 31, 1517, he was appointed rector. Apparently he was increasingly dissatisfied with the narrow bonds of academic life; it is possible that he was consciously ignored by his conservative colleagues. In 1518 the high choir of the chapter of the cathedral of Strasbourg called him to be priest in the chapel of St. Laurence, the most important pulpit in Strasbourg. At forty-nine years of age, having lived for the last twenty years in a cultural backwater, Zell left the academic world to become the first priest in Strasbourg to preach the Pure Word of God. Less erudite than Capito, less the statesman than Bucer, he spoke directly to the populace, in the tradition of his mentor, Geiler.

Caspar Hedio was the least important member of the group; a protégé of Capito, he remained always in the shadow of the older man from the time he was a student in Basel. It was through Capito that Hedio was introduced to Erasmus and the Basel circle of humanists. From then on he traveled with Capito. When the latter left Basel for Mainz, an appointment in the archbishop's court was also

26. Röhrich, *Mittheilungen*, 3, 87.
27. I am indebted to Thomas Brady, fellow of the Newberry Library, for this information.

arranged for Hedio; when Capito moved to Strasbourg, Hedio followed. The post of preacher in the cathedral was vacant, owing to the expulsion of a succession of reformers, and Hedio accepted the position. Two portraits of him remain: one, by the contemporary Alsatian painter Hans Baldung Grien, shows him as full-faced and heavily jowled, with a side-long glance that is almost a sneer. The other, a contemporary woodcut, depicts him as a patient, scholarly man, somewhat stooped, somewhat bemused, but with a singularly kindly expression. His major scholarly interests lay in ancient and church history, and he labored to translate the Latin classics into German for students at the Gymnasium, stating proudly that the Tiber had overflowed into the Rhine.[28]

These were the men who gave spiritual leadership to the movement. They were joined by other churchmen and by laymen. While it is impossible to document fully the lay group that went over to the Reform, the response of the Magistrat needs to be singled out since its members were the acknowledged leaders of the city and were responsible for the welfare of their fellow citizens.

A significant number of the Magistrat lent their weight and support to the Reform. There is no evidence, however, that these men acted as an organized party, forcing the religious changes on the community as a whole. At first they had neither plan nor systematic program but maintained a laissez-faire attitude, riding with the tide of change, accepting inevitable innovations but leaving the initiative for change in the hands of the reformers. Roughly by 1528 the majority of the Magistrat were supporters of the Reform. A brief description of some of the individual members will help present an image of the group as a whole. They reappear in various functions and capacities throughout the narrative.

Daniel Mueg was an early adherent of the Reform. Elected

28. Johannes Ficker, *Die Anfänge der akademischen Studien in Strassburg* (Strassburg, 1912), p. 8.

to the Rat for the first time in 1520 from the bakers' guild, he served as one of the city's representatives to the Diet of Nuremberg in 1523–24 and to the Diet of Speyer in 1529.[29] Martin Herlin, entering the Rat first in 1519 from the furriers, was Ammeister five times between 1522 and 1540, represented the city at the Diets of Worms, Nuremberg and Speyer,[30] and later worked for an alliance between Strasbourg and the reformed cities of the Swiss confederation. Klaus Kniebis served in the Rat from 1512, representing the smiths' guild. He held the high office of Ammeister four times between 1519 and 1537 and was a member of the first school committee appointed in 1526; his influence was persuasive in the decision to abolish the Mass in 1529. Known to be a very pious man, greatly respected in the Rat and in the city, his opposition to the old service bore special weight.[31]

Mathis Pfarrer and Jacob Sturm were the most eminent members of the Magistrat in this period, and their support of the Reform was especially important. Pfarrer, kindly, good-natured, mild in manner, was the son-in-law of Sebastian Brant. He served as Ammeister seven times from 1527 to 1563 and as a delegate to a succession of Diets and on important diplomatic missions.[32] Jacob Sturm came from one of Strasbourg's most distinguished patrician families. Wimpfeling had been his tutor, and he was thus drawn into the humanist circle of the city at an early age. His political career began with his election to the Rat in 1524, one of the peak moments of the Reformation. Beloved and respected, he served on ninety-one missions for the city.[33] A contemporary portrait shows him as the prototype of the respectable burgher. Large, broad-shouldered, square-bearded, he resembles a middle-class Henry VIII. Traditionally it is be-

29. Ficker and Winckelmann, *Handschriftproben, 1, 1.*
30. Ibid., p. 2.
31. Ibid., p. 4.
32. Ibid., p. 5.
33. Röhrich, *Geschichte der Reformation, 1,* 172.

lieved that he and Bucer became close friends, and that the intimate relationship between the two did much to influence the pace of the Reform in the city. While I could find no evidence of a familiar or personal relationship between them, the personalities and attitudes of the two men were comparable. Sturm was essentially a conservative who felt that the necessary changes could be made slowly and peacefully. Controversy distressed him, and when the break developed between Luther and Zwingli over the meaning of Communion, he was instrumental in developing Strasbourg's role as mediator.[34]

Bernhard Wurmser was yet another patrician who supported the Reformation. In this case it created division within his family, for his brother Nicholas, the deacon of the chapter of St. Thomas, was one of the few canons of that chapter who maintained a bitter opposition.[35] Jacob Meyer, a representative of the masons' guild in 1519, from 1522 to 23, and from 1526 to 27, was a determined and rather radical Protestant who advocated the removal of images from the churches and cathedral as early as 1524.[36] Two years later he became one of the school inspectors, a position that he held until the end of his life.

Although a significant and important number of the Magistrat were adherents of the Reform, it is necessary to emphasize that other Ratsherren opposed the religious changes and yet remained active in the city government throughout the period. Konrad von Duntzenheim, member of a Strasbourg patrician family, was elected first in 1501 and served as Ammeister five times between 1502 to 1529. He did not openly oppose the reformers, but he offered a firm disapproval. Furthermore, he was functioning as Ammeister during the most critical time.[37] Martin Betscholt was elected

34. See Röhrich, *Geschichte der Reformation,* Chapter IV.
35. Ficker and Winckelmann, *Handschriftproben, 1,* 3.
36. Ibid., p. 10.
37. Ibid., p. 2.

to the Rat in 1522 from the butchers' guild. He offered a decided opposition to the reforms in the period from 1522 to 1529, standing firmly against the abolition of the Mass. After 1529 he withdrew from politics "insofar as they concerned religion," but did not resign from the Council of XIII.[38] This meant that there was at least one firm opponent of the new religion in the most important council of the city until 1546, when he died.

There was a small group of Ratsherren who supported the Reform in the early years but turned away when it became politically dangerous with Charles V's establishment of the Interim religion in 1548. Wolfgang Böcklin renounced his Bürgerrecht when the Protestants were defeated in the Schmalkaldic War. He had never had the reputation of standing firmly for his convictions and had always been paired, in any mission for the city, with a more dependable member.[39] Conrad Joham and Friederich von Gottesheim, both members of the Magistrat, surrendered their citizenship in 1548 rather than court the ire of the emperor.[40]

While this inventory of the attitudes of members of the Magistrat toward the Reformation is by no means complete, the sample indicates that the Rat as a body was never entirely persuaded to the Reform. Even after 1529 men who opposed the new religion continued to serve as members of the major councils. Although the leaders of the Rat accepted the Reform, they always had to work with a certain number of colleagues who did not and with an even larger number who accepted the changes only halfheartedly. Possibly because of this in the early years the leaders of the Magistrat were rarely eager to assume direct responsibility for inaugurating change. They supported the reformers, but left the initiative in their hands. Thus the Reform was not initiated automatically, smoothly, by a clique of the Magistrat working hand in glove with the reformers. It went through the

38. Ibid., p. 3.
39. Ibid., p. 9.
40. Ibid., p. 13.

complex channels of the political process, the reformers sometimes pressing for change, the Magistrat hanging back, loath to make a decision. In the end events themselves seemed to force the hand of both groups, and initiative sometimes shifted to the burghers themselves, who made an overt display of their desire for change.

CHAPTER 7

THE PURE WORD OF GOD

HE focus of the Strasbourg Reformation was on preaching. It was the act of preaching that changed a man from priest to reformer, and it was through sermons that the new ideas were communicated to a significant number of the burghers.

Lutheran books were, of course, available, but the number of Lutheran tracts which flowed into Strasbourg from Basel, Augsburg, or Nuremberg cannot be determined. A tabulation of books published in Strasbourg indicates that no Lutheran or Protestant defenses were published in 1518, although one Catholic attack was printed. In 1519 four books by Luther came off the Strasbourg presses, but it was not until 1520 that publication of Luther's sermons and treatises began in earnest. The peak of the publication of Protestant literature came in 1524 and 1525, after the Strasbourg reforms had already been inaugurated.[1] The publishers mirrored the Reform, rather than influenced it, and it is possible to assume that until 1520 it was relatively difficult to obtain Lutheran books, sermons, or tracts in Strasbourg. Those available were probably handed from friend to friend, rather than distributed through commercial channels. By 1520, apparently, the Strasbourg publishers felt that it was no longer too dangerous to publish a Lutheran book, and topical and polemic treatises, German editions of the Gospels, and commentaries on the Gospels and on the Old Testament became increasingly available.

1. See Appendix A.

The Pure Word of God

The written word still reached only the few, but the spoken word could be heard by all, and through preaching, the ideas of the Reformation were conveyed to the citizens of Strasbourg. The earliest incidents are fragmentary. The individuals concerned appear briefly, in a chronicle, in a single document, and then disappear. The first of these is Master Peter Phillips von Rumersberg, who arrived in Strasbourg in 1520. Where he came from is not known, but he was appointed by the chapter of Old St. Peter to preach. "He was a learned man and preached God's Word purely and according to Luther. This did not please everyone, and he was thus accused before the bishop and expelled." [2]

In 1521 Tilman von Lyn, the reader at the Carmelite cloister, was also dismissed by the bishop. He departed, but not before he had submitted a written defense of his actions to the Magistrat justifying his preaching and anticipating the confusion that would arise from the definition of "the Pure Word of God." He stated that although he, like all men, was a poor sinner and fearful of his sins, nevertheless it was not right that he should be blamed for things he had not done. He had not misused his benefice, for he had never believed that he would be forbidden to preach the truth. He had not read from those works of Luther banned by the pope and emperor; indeed, he had properly read the papal bull against Luther. He had only made certain speeches allowed by his prior, and he could not believe that these could have been so grossly misinterpreted. Indeed, he stated, those who oppose Jesus Christ were those who forbade the true Word of God to be preached; the church's regulations against teaching and preaching were in error. The work of God

2. Specklin, *Collectanées*, p. 309. Nine years later, in 1530, a "Master Peter, one time curate at Old St. Peter," turns up as a person who has possibly harbored and protected an Anabaptist. According to the record, Peter then lived behind the old Franciscan cloister and had given aid to an Augsburg locksmith. Manfred Krebs and Hans Georg Rott state that this is probably Peter Phillip Rumersberger. Cf. Krebs and Rott, *Elsass I, Stadt Strassburg 1522–1532, Elsass II, Stadt Strassburg 1533–35*, Quellen zur Geschichte der Täufer, 7–8 (Gütersloh, 1959–60), *1*, 269, n. 3.

99

would not be suppressed by branding the preacher as an ass, a heretic, and a scoundrel. Finally, it was only the bishop who had criticized him. His prior had been well satisfied both with his preaching and with the manner in which he had heard confessions.[3]

Matthäus Zell was the next priest to become involved. In the same year, 1521, he defended Luther from his pulpit in the St. Laurence chapel of the cathedral by reading passages from Luther's works and suggesting that too much of an uproar had been made over the man. The cry of heresy had been raised against him only because some people were frightened—the very same people who wished to defend infamy and vice so that the roguery of the clergy would go unpunished. The pope had not liked being compared to a scoundrel, and for this reason he had rebuked Luther and branded him a heretic.[4]

To defend Luther was one thing, but to preach the Gospel was another; the latter was the more significant of Zell's decisions. In late summer or fall of 1521 he mounted his pulpit to announce that he would preach the pure Gospel of Jesus Christ, starting with the Epistles to the Romans. The innovation met with immediate success. So many burghers poured into the cathedral to hear him that the chapel to which he was assigned was much too small. Zell wanted to move to the great stone pulpit built for Geiler, which dominates the cathedral nave, but the canons refused, keeping the door of the pulpit firmly locked. Some of the carpenters who inhabited one of the small streets near the cathedral square thereupon made a portable wooden pulpit that was borne into the middle of the cathedral for each sermon and then carefully taken back home by a group of burghers.[5]

The bishop took immediate exception to Zell's preaching, regarding it as undisciplined and inflammatory, and requested the cathedral chapter to institute proceedings

3. Archives St. Thomas, 87, Written Defense of Tilman von Lyn, Dec. 28, 1521. Hereafter referred to as A.S.T.
4. Specklin, *Collectanées*, p. 492.
5. Ibid.

against the priest, as required both by papal and imperial mandates. The noble *chapterherren*, always stiff-necked in their relations with the bishop, regarded the request as an invasion of their rights and privileges with regard to their own appointees. They permitted Zell to continue preaching but continued to keep him out of the great pulpit. This policy created a division within the chapter itself because the nonnoble members, the *Deputaten*, vigorously and openly opposed Zell.[6]

The bishop was unable to press the dismissal through ecclesiastical channels. Thus on August 2, 1522, he wrote to the Magistrat to inform the members that he would carry out the provisions of the Diet of Worms and to ask the civil authority not to intervene or offer Zell any protection.[7] The Rat replied that it would not hinder the bishop from carrying out his duties.[8] Zell was then informed through the bishop's administrative officer, the *Fiskal*, Gervais Sopher, that he must come before the Vicar Jacob von Gottesheim on December 22, 1522, to answer charges that Sopher forwarded in writing. Zell prepared a written statement for his defense, addressed to Sopher, which was published the following year.[9] The defense reveals the significance and emphasis that Zell himself placed on his preaching and the intensity of his conviction that he must continue.

He confronted Sopher bluntly. "Hear what Luther says— 'When we, the servants of the Word of God, hear this same Word preached, then we know we have heard Christ himself.' "[10] For Christ was a preacher who sent his apostles out

6. Adolf Baum, *Magistrat und Reformation in Strassburg bis 1529* (Strassburg, 1887), p. 15.

7. Johann Adam, *Evangelische Kirchengeschichte der Stadt Strassburg bis zur Französischen Revolution* (Strassburg, 1922), p. 3.

8. Ibid., p. 31.

9. Matthäus Zell, *Christliche Verantwortung über Artickel in vom Bischofflichen Fiscal dasselbs entgegen gesetzt und in rechten übergeben* (Strasbourg, 1523). Because this is an early book, pagination is by quarto, that is, by letter and Roman numerals up to viii, when a new letter is used.

10. The following paragraphs are all drawn from the *Christliche Verantwortung*, G. ii ff. The translation of this statement, like those that follow, is my own.

to preach to the world, saying "Who hears them, hears Me." Thus when the Kingdom of God is preached, it is Christ who is heard. The Christian knows the Word of God is spoken when the preacher reveals how God rules within each heart, for the preacher should not dwell merely on the evil, sins, and lusts of the world; his task should rather be to lift up the hearts of men to the love of Christ and of God.

The preacher has an apostolic mission since he serves as the direct emissary of Christ and is responsible for conveying the Gospel in its pure form. It is frequently stated in the New Testament that we are to preach the Gospel and the Word as Christ gave it to us, nothing more. Thus even if an angel from heaven (let alone a pope or a bishop) speaks, if he does not speak by the Word of God, he is damned by the disfavor of God and by Peter and Paul.

> "You must confess, and at Easter take the Sacrament, or you are the devil's. If you eat this, if you touch that; if you do not celebrate a certain day; if you do not give this; if you do not believe that—then you are in deadly sin." What kind of Good News is that, one may well ask? Christ did not mean to have commandments and laws preached, for the Gospel is not law, but a fulfillment of the law. If He had wished to have laws and commandments preached, it would have been sufficient to preach the Mosaic Commandments.[11]

So Christ had ordered, and the church had failed by neglecting the task of teaching and preaching. Instead of inspiring their parish clergy by their example, bishops had turned away from the pastoral duties and were more interested in establishing their power and authority as secular princes than in serving as shepherds of their flocks. "Oh woe," wrote Zell, "that man should be ashamed of the Eternal Word of God. It would be a praiseworthy thing if a bishop would preach in his Cathedral city . . . better . . . than that he should occupy himself with birds and dogs." [12]

11. Ibid., G. ii.
12. Ibid., G. iii.

Zell then appealed to the pope to send out able men to preach, for it would not be possible to stop the preaching by episcopal or imperial bans. Even if a thousand bans were promulgated and the whole Black Forest burned for brands for heretics, the movement could not be stopped. He added to this a recommendation that young men should study the scriptures in school, instead of being forbidden to do so, on the ground that if a student could understand heathen poets and difficult philosophers and Sophists, he could certainly understand the Bible and thus become a learned preacher and servant of the Word of God. Preaching, Zell said, was clearly supported by the scriptures. Christ had sent seventy-two young men out to preach in all the cities, wherever they might go. Let this be done once again, and the church would find itself renewed and revived, teaching and preaching would become again the central act of the church, and the sacraments would fall back into the ancillary position that Christ had meant them to occupy.[13]

It was a stirring statement, trenchantly argued, and the bishop's Fiskal, to whom it was addressed, would himself shortly join Zell, but for the moment little transpired as a result of the hearing. There was a restlessness in the city: crudely printed flyers began to appear on both sides of the controversy. Hieronymus Gebwiler, the teacher of the cathedral chapter school, and a man of parts, launched a barbed poem against Zell:

[This] schoolmaster is harmful in his teaching.
He exorcises ghosts in the mirror.
Performing so that he reveals all to his students,

13. Zell's remarks on the sacraments in this treatise are interesting in view of his later position. At this point, 1522, he believed that the seventy-two young men were the forerunners of the parish priest and that Christ had directed them to teach and preach. He spoke of the Last Supper, however, only to the twelve Apostles; thus, Zell concluded, He saw the Sacrament as of lesser importance. Now the whole thing had been turned around, and the preaching that Christ had explicitly commanded was neglected, while the sacrament, which He had revealed only to a few, had become paramount. *Christliche Verantwortung*, D. v.

Reading out to them Paul's Letter to Titus.
He twists the Epistle around so deftly
That "woman" comes to mean "a benefice."
He wants to play a joke on you.[14]

Another poem anonymously baited Zell more directly:

You and your preaching should be drowned
You run around abusing people and talking nonsense
It means as much as worthless Groschen.

But the Leopard and the Bear are quite wild beasts[15]
They will come with all their arts,
Writers, advocates and priests,
They will give you a good going over.

One man, a certain Steffan von Büllheyn, rose in Zell's
defense, publishing a ten-page verse entitled "A Brotherly
warning to Master Matthäus to ward off and protect himself
from his adversaries and to stand fast by Christian teaching
and truly teach the Word of God to the people." [16] Whether
Steffan existed or whether it was a convenient pseudonym
is not known; no von Büllheyn appears in the *Book of the
Burghers* or other register. The verse took the form of a dialogue between father and son, a favorite humanist technique,
and in this instance the father held to the old customs; to
him tradition and authority were the important consideration
in life. The son, in the end, was able to win his father over

14. Röhrich, *Mittheilungen, 3*, 101. Röhrich gives only a modern-
ized version of the original of this text and those which follow. They
bear the earmarks of having been cleaned up to fit the exigencies of
a church historian of the nineteenth century. To render the expur-
gated verses into English removes them yet one step further from
their original pungency. Unfortunately I could no longer find the
printed texts that were available to Röhrich in the Strasbourg Archives or in the Municipal or University libraries, indicating that they
were probably destroyed in the bombardment of the library in 1870.
15. The "Leopard" and "Bear" refer to two lawyers of these names.
The verse is obviously quite topical and may have been written just
before the hearing at the episcopal court.
16. Excerpts from the text appear in Röhrich, *Mittheilungen, 3,*
95–100.

to the new way. The importance of the poem, however, is in the emphasis it places on the act of preaching.

[And now] they drive Matthäus out of the cathedral with lies
And we cannot do a thing.
It will do no good in the end,
For he does them too much damage with the scriptures.
They are really going on slippery ice.

For it is the preacher in the cathedral called Master Matthäus
Who uses nothing but the Holy Scriptures
And with it overcomes all things,
Teaching from Paul and the Evangelists.

. . .

Master Matthäus alone sticks by the text.
So they say at the tavern *Zu Art.*

The last line is particularly revealing of the impact the affair had had on the city, for the *Art* was frequented by carters and wagoners. The three incidental verses together indicate that the preaching in the cathedral had stirred a varied group to action, from the teacher of the cathedral school, to the workers sitting at their heavy oak tables in the tavern. On December 26, four days after his appearance before the Fiskal, Zell preached a vigorous sermon against the persecutors of the Gospel.[17] The bishop was apprehensive. Before Zell's hearing a group of burghers had placarded the door of his vicar; now Bishop Wilhelm wrote to the Magistrat, citing the papal and imperial mandates, requesting them to provide due protection to his administrative officers against the violence of the parishioners.[18]

The Rat itself was now being pressured into taking a position, and the problem was debated at length. What was the responsibility of the Rat towards the citizens, both lay and clerical, in terms of their right to live freely and peacefully?

17. Adam, *Evangelische Kirchengeschichte,* p. 32.
18. Sebastian Brant, *Les Annales,* Fragments recueillis par l'Abbé L. Dacheux, Fragments des anciennes chroniques d'Alsace (4 vols. Strasbourg, 1892–1901), *4,* 53.

Up until now, it was argued, Zell had done nothing more than preach God's Word and the Holy Scripture. The Rat finally decided to send a delegation to the nobles of the high chapter requesting that they instruct the Deputaten to let Matthäus stay in the church, stating that it was the will of the Magistrat to shelter and protect the Word of God and the truth.[19] A delegation was also sent to the Deputaten. They were willing to consider the Rat's proposal because they believed that it assured them protection by the civil authorities. They therefore elected to cooperate with the Magistrat's request, instructing Zell very firmly, however, that he was to preach nothing from the pulpit but God's Word and that of the holy Evangelists and Apostles.[20] The bishop had been deserted both by his ecclesiastical colleagues and by the civil authorities.

It is indicative of the bishop's particular merit and feelings of responsibility for his diocese that he persisted in pressing the case against Zell.[21] He wrote to the Rat on March 10, 1523, stating the particulars of Zell's errors, and the letter is an indication of the conflict that was developing with regard to the function of the priest. Zell had not, Bishop Wilhelm declared, held Mass as he was supposed to do but had set himself up against the authority of the bishop and against the ordinances of the Christian church, enunciating his own beliefs in the open pulpit and on the streets. He should be furloughed, and a learned priest chosen to take his place so that the people of the city of Strasbourg would be taken care of in terms of confession and parish needs and would have no need to complain to their bishop.[22] Clearly Bishop Wilhelm considered that preaching was not part of the function of the priest. The parishioners did not need to be instructed

19. "Dann ein Rhat des willens in by den wort Gottes und der wahrheit zu schützen und zu schirmen." Brant, *Annales*, p. 54.
20. Ibid., p. 54.
21. Adam, *Evangelische Kirchengeschichte*, p. 32.
22. A.S.T., 47, letter of Wilhelm, Bishop of Strasbourg, Mar. 10, 1523.

in the scriptures or in the Pure Word of God. The priest was there to hear confessions, to minister to the needy, the sick, and the dying; with that his responsibilities ended.

The firmness of the letter was weakened by a final paragraph. The bishop had been informed by certain honest and faithful persons that if Zell were furloughed before St. John the Baptist's Day (June 12), there might be an uprising in the city. Since his year's appointment would terminate on that day, he could remain until then, rather than create a threat to the ecclesiastical and civil authorities.[23]

For a few months the affair simmered down. On March 6, 1523, the Nuremberg Mandate had been issued and the city authorities could justify their actions as falling within its provision that until a German council should be called, the Holy Bible should be preached only in accordance with the interpretation approved by the Christian church. Liberally understood this might cover Zell, and it had been the bishop, after all, who had granted him permission to remain in his pulpit until June. The Magistrat was in a particularly sensitive position that spring. The war against Sickingen had finally dragged to a close, and the city had been allied with the defeated knights. It had loaned Sickingen, now dead and discredited, significant sums of money, and it was open to criticism by the burghers for the loss. It was also apprehensive that the imperial troops still present in the Rhineland might turn eastward in a punitive expedition against the city. Thus, when an imperial mandate was received dated March 14, 1524, asking the cooperation of the city in a crusade against the Turk, the Rat not only permitted the crusade to be preached but urged the people to fight the holy war.[24] At the same time they held back from being further involved in the new evangelical movement. Zell requested permission to debate with his opponents in German, but the Rat refused, advising him to drop the matter, with

23. Ibid.
24. A. Baum, *Magistrat und Reformation*, p. 26.

the further comment that he was to respect the decisions of the Rat and the provisions of the imperial mandate.[25]

The Rat saw its responsibility as the maintenance of peace and the administration of the imperial law. In April 1523 Martin Bucer arrived, married. He took up residence in the city and seemed, at first, to desire to remain inconspicuous. He taught from the Gospel in Latin to such laymen as came to his home, but that meant he reached only the educated. Then sometime in May or June, a group of burghers petitioned that he be permitted to expound the scriptures publicly, in German. This was an easy decision for the Ratsherren. Bucer was married and the answer was no. On the other hand they were not willing to expel him. On June 16, 1523, the bishop wrote to the Rat that Bucer fell under the provisions of the ban because of his marriage and should thus be prosecuted. The Rat replied that Bucer had sought the protection of the city as the son of a burgher, and that by law he must be given sanctuary.[26]

The excitement and tension within the city at the time, the revolutionary force contained in the Pure Word of God is reflected in Capito's final conversion and in his decision to join the evangelical movement. In a written statement that he submitted to the bishop's Fiskal, he described his metamorphosis from provost to preacher. In June 1523, shortly after his own arrival in the city, he had called Zell before him, as part of his duty as provost of St. Thomas. A riot had occurred in July 1522, stemming from the preaching of a radical antipapist.[27] Zell had been accused of harboring the man,[28] and Capito was following a routine procedure of

25. A.S.T., 87, Resolution der Evangelischen Gnadigen ertheilt, Mar. 9, 1523.
26. A. Baum, *Magistrat und Reformation*, p. 27.
27. These antipapist figures, known in German as *Kursthans*, were not a phenomenon of the Reform. They were familiar figures on the streets and marketplaces of late medieval cities and villages and are indicative of the strength of anticlericalism before the Reform.
28. Röhrich, *Geschichte der Reformation*, 1, 136.

examination and admonition.[29] He reminded Zell that his duty was to create a peaceful spirit with the Words of Christ, instead of arousing animosity, envy, and hatred. Zell, he charged, had turned everything upside down, overthrowing the good old order, attacking the pope, the bishops, the learned, and unlearned under the guise of interpreting the Holy Scriptures. Furthermore, he had presented the scriptures in a false light, using them not to convey to the people a true knowledge of God and Christian love, but rather to create bitterness and dissension.

Zell's reply to these charges took Capito off guard. Capito had known Matthäus as a fellow student and thought of him as upright and capable, but he was not prepared for the intensity of the preacher's conviction and the bluntness of his reply. For Zell flatly accused Capito of insincerity and pedantry, charging that as a humanist he took only an intellectual interest in the Bible and the Word of God.

> You and your friends wish to create a reputation and to gain favor and approval of the world through the Word. . . . you wish only to establish a reputation for yourselves among each other and so with your brilliance you make the Word of God weak and powerless, in your mouths it becomes a worldly wisdom which is, in truth, greatly removed from God.[30]

Preachers, however, had an entirely different concept of the Word. They were servants of Christ and did not care whether they spoke with elegance or grace, with consistency or scholarly references. Their object was not to talk to each other but "to bring the knowledge of the cross to the com-

29. Wolfgang Capito, *Entschuldigung an der hoch würdigen fürsten unseren herren Wilhelmen Bischoffen zu Strassburg* (Augsburg, 1524), unpaginated. Capito's defense was first published in Strasbourg by Köpfel in 1523, the year in which he appeared before the bishop's Fiskal. The volume now available in the Strasbourg Archives is a later edition printed in Augsburg. The dialogue between Capito and Zell that follows is a loose transcription of the text.
30. Ibid.

mon hordes, . . . [to] speak to the clever and the dull, to the friendly and the unfriendly, to the gentle and the stern as long as it furthers the cause." [31]

Zell drew a sharp line between the world of the humanist and that of the preacher. The humanist lived in a narrow sphere, communicating only with other scholars, cut off from the rest of society. The preacher had broken the bonds of this narrow compass and felt himself a member of the whole community, directly responsible to Christ Himself to be as His messenger to His people.

> We are concerned alone for the common, simple meaning of the [scriptures] which we can communicate to the common people. We wish to put our whole zeal into this, for this was the reason Christ became a man and did all those things which you yourself know about.[32]

Capito was impressed by Zell's honesty and directness. He found himself swayed by his forthrightness, and he stated, "what concerned me as an added difficulty was that perhaps it was true that my heart had been hardened against Christ." [33] The criticism had gone home, and Capito began to wonder whether Zell's opponents were the ones causing the unrest in the city because of their lack of understanding, their personal greed, and their unwillingness to accept and live by the Word of God. The affair then came to an open uprising,[34] and Capito, as a man of conscience, was forced to make a decision.

31. Ibid.
32. Ibid.
33. Ibid.
34. I could find no specific reference to this particular uprising. None of the chronicles report any particular incident after the Kursthans incident, and this was clearly later. Adolf Baum states that there was unrest after the bishop had furloughed Zell in July 1522, but he reports no incident (Baum, *Magistrat und Reformation,* pp. 18–19.) Röhrich states that when Capito arrived in the city to take up his provostship, he found tension and unrest and a division between those who supported Zell and those who did not. (Röhrich, *Geschichte der Reformation, 1,* 153.)

In an uprising of this sort by the common people I felt that for the love of God and for the honorable people it was my responsibility to God to help according to the best of my ability. I felt I must help the cause of peace and unity, create understanding, and propagate the Word of God. Plato censured the burghers who fomented civil division in his city and would embrace neither side. I felt I must be sure then, before God and my own conscience, of my decision and my partisanship. It was a time which required decision. Now who acknowledges Christ before other men will be acknowledged by Him before His Heavenly Father, Who denies Him and does not accept Him will not be received in Heaven. Thus it was that I went into the pulpits of some of the chapter churches and gave three or four sermons for the priest.[35]

Capito's decision to join Zell was a conscious, intellectual act taken with full knowledge of its consequences. By accepting Zell's arguments, he was led to reject his former values. Through Zell he had heard the Pure Word of God and had been opened to a new life, and a new mission. He would never entirely abandon his humanist interests (perhaps the most revealing sentence in his defense is the one that refers to Plato), but his action finally was a matter of belief. If he was to justify his life before God and Christ and if he were to appear before His Heavenly Father, he must follow Zell.

The significance of Capito's conversion cannot be overestimated. After the bishop and the provost of the cathedral chapter he was the third most important clerical figure in the city. He had overthrown the traditions of several hundred years in mounting the pulpit to speak to the congregation. The novelty can best be conveyed by the chronicler:

At this point Dr. Wolff Capito, provost of St. Thomas, stood in the chancel and himself preached. The people crowded around with wonder that a provost should

35. Capito, *Entschuldigung an der Bischoffen.*

preach and concern himself with such trifles. The monks and priests stated openly in their preaching that Capito did dishonor to the clergy and that it was unheard of and heretical that a prelate and provost should preach himself, and there was so much opposition that Dr. Capito along with Matthäus Zell was dismissed from the chapter at St. Thomas. When Dr. Capito was dismissed, the *bürgerschaft* placed themselves with force at Young St. Peter [demanding Capito as their preacher], and the priest had to stay away against the will of all the clergy.[36]

By preaching, Capito lost his position in the upper ranks of the hierarchy. On July 9, 1523, he broke even further with tradition by purchasing Bürgerrecht.[37] This brought more criticism from his former colleagues, who charged that his motive was to gain protection from the bishop. They may have been right, for on June 13, 1523, the Magistrat had issued an article clarifying the rights of priests who purchased Bürgerrecht or who received it through their parents. The city pledged to protect them and to fulfill the obligations as provided in the oath they took before all the burghers. Furthermore, the priests were free to join a guild if they should so desire.[38] Thus, the priests received full political rights. Capito claimed in his defense to the Fiskal that he had assumed Bürgerrect because he felt that the clergy must draw closer to the people. In the past, he claimed, they had abused their privileges insolently and flagrantly; they had all the rights of burghers, and they should now assume the responsibilities as well.[39]

Capito was not the only member of the clergy to decide to preach the Pure Word of God. Faced by the vacancy which Zell's furlough had created, the cathedral chapter appointed

---

36. Specklin, *Collectanées*, p. 498.
37. A. Baum, *Magistrat und Reformation*, p. 56.
38. A.S.T., 87, Artickel der Priester so das Bürgerrecht Kauffen oder ampfahnen, June 13, 1523.
39. Capito, *Entschuldigung an der Bischoffen.*

Peter Wickgram, a nephew of Kaysersberg's, as priest in the St. Laurence chapel. Shortly thereafter Wickgram began to preach the new religion. The chapter furloughed him and then installed Symphorian Altbiesser, the priest at St. Stephen's, to the post in the cathedral as well as to St. Martin's. Soon thereafter Altbiesser, too, began to preach evangelically. The chapter furloughed him, but the burghers at St. Martin's refused to let him go, and he remained there against the will of the canons.[40] The Chapterherren made a last attempt to provide a Catholic preacher for the St. Laurence chapel, assigning Hedio, newly arrived from the archbishop's court at Mainz. Within a few months he followed Capito's example, and the chapter apparently gave up. No attempt was made to remove him. By the following year, 1524, various parish congregations began to assert themselves with regard to the appointments of their priests, choosing men who preached the evangelical Gospel. There was an added difficulty now because some of these men had married, which meant that, by canon law, they could not be appointed by a chapter or by the bishop. Yet the burghers tended to stick firmly by their choices, defending them against the attempts of the hierarchy to unseat them.

The parishioners of St. Aurelie were a particularly vocal and unruly lot. They represented, in large part, the gardeners' guild and, at this time, reflected the dissatisfaction and restlessness of the peasantry within the walls of the city. For a brief period Symphorian Altbiesser preached to them, as well as maintaining his pulpit in St. Martin's.[41] On his death the chapter of St. Thomas, which controlled the parish, appointed an elderly priest who delivered a sermon asserting the authority of the pope. The gardeners complained. They wanted a "learned Christian man."[42] Their choice was Martin Bucer, who had visited the church, but they lacked

40. Büheler, *Chronique*, p. 70.
41. Marie-Joseph Bopp, *Die Evangelischen Geistlichen und Theologen in Elsass und Lothringen von der Reformation bis zur Gegenwart* (3 vols. Neustadt, 1959), *1*, 24.
42. Quoted by A. Baum, *Magistrat und Reformation*, p. 78.

the courage to ask the chapter for such a change. They went, instead, on January 28, 1524, to the Magistrat to ask permission to call Bucer.

The Rat was in a difficult position. The request clearly lay outside its authority, and Bucer's marriage was a problem, but the Ratsherren feared the riotous reputation of the gardeners. Finally they decided to approach the chapter, which replied in short order that it alone had the right to appoint priests. The Rat finally managed to arrange that the chapter propose two or three men from whom the people could make a choice. The gardeners affirmed that what they wanted was "a preacher who preached like others in the city. If the chapter was going to give them one who fiddled on the same old note, they wished to install a preacher at their own expense." [43] The chapter remained obdurate, and the parishioners took Bucer on without any authorization. He gave his first sermon on February 21, 1524. In March the old priest fell ill, and the parishioners proceeded to name Bucer their preacher. The chapter continued to assert its authority by assigning another priest who followed the old way for confession and communion.[44] The chapter had given up none of its rights, but the parish had established a precedent. The parishioners of Old St. Peter also petitioned their chapter for an evangelical preacher, and when the matter seemed to drag out, they chose Diebold Schwartz, a reformer who had said the first German Mass in the cathedral.[45]

The problem was that these actions were illegal. The parishioners of these churches now turned to the Rat, asking it to confirm those already chosen or to appoint preachers for them. This was the first petition concerning the Reformation written by the burghers themselves, and it reflected their particular concerns at this early stage. It was essential to have preachers because otherwise they, their wives, and

43. Quoted, Ibid., p. 79.
44. Ibid., p. 80.
45. Ibid., p. 84.

their children could not come to God's Word. The parishes had been richly endowed by the forefathers of the Rat, and now unworthy incumbents occupied these positions and did not fulfill their obligations. The city should therefore take over the administration of these benefices. There was also a problem with regard to the services on holidays. The burghers were dutiful men, they averred, and supported themselves by the work of their hands. On holy days they needed peace and quiet, but this had been destroyed by church pageantry and the unnecessary singing [literally howling] of the choir. If the effeminate words of the choir were replaced by preachers and godly Christian officials, then peace, unity, and *bürgerlich* tranquility would be established. The burghers noted that they felt that all this could be accomplished by careful municipal administration of the old endowments; it would not be necessary to resort to new taxes for the support of the preachers. Pledging their obedience and loyalty to the Rat, five parishes signed the petition: St. Laurence, Young St. Peter, St. Martin, St. Aurelie, and St. Stephen[46]—all of which had already taken on evangelical preachers.

The Rat discussed the petition and decided to bring the matter to the Schöffen. On August 24, 1524, the latter voted that the Magistrat should take the appointments of parish priests into its own hands. The action was necessary, the edict stated, because the Chapterherren had not fulfilled their obligations, the city had been thrown into confusion and unrest, and parishioners had resorted to force to appoint their preachers. It would be better and safer for the Rat to assume responsibility for the parishes. Since the preachers would thus become subject to the civil authorities, they were to take the burgher oath, swearing their loyalty to the city and the Rat.[47] The omissions in the edict are interesting:

46. A.S.T., 87, Supplication an den Rat um Versehung allen Pfarren mit Evangelischen Predigern, Spring? 1524.
47. A.S.T., 87, Der Rat ist gesonnen die Pfarren zu seinen Händen zu nehmen, end of August 1524.

It was a straightforward legal document, which stayed clear of any doctrinal statement. There was nothing about the Pure Word of God or about preaching; it was an administrative matter on which, owing to the default of the canons, the Magistrat was forced to act.

A major change had occurred against the will of the ecclesiastical authorities and with only the grudging acquiescence of the Rat. The introduction of preaching was in a sense, the work of one man, Matthäus Zell, who possessed the initial advantage of the revolutionary—singleness of purpose. He believed that he had been called by Christ to manifest His Word to the world and was thus freed from customary restrictions of function and office. He could initiate change because he operated outside traditional institutions and relationships.

The Magistrat and the bishop could move neither as quickly nor as surely. In these first three years the civil authority did not develop a conscious policy toward the Reform. It was thrown off guard, it compromised, it shifted tactics, not because its members changed their attitude toward the Reform or the reformers, but because they were still thinking on traditional lines. The object of the Magistrat was to keep the peace within the city and to maintain its freedom vis-à-vis the emperor and the empire. Its policy toward Zell and toward the other reformers had to be fitted into the context of these broader purposes.

The bishop's position was different. Wilhelm von Hohnstein was sufficiently farsighted to realize the significance of Zell's preaching. He was convinced that if he moved quickly and effectively in this one case, he could prevent further disorder. His tragedy was that the church was no longer capable of united and effective action. The Chapterherren and the Deputaten of the cathedral did not think in terms of the church as a whole. They were prisoners of their own particular objectives, their ancient feuds, and their prejudices. It was more important to them to maintain their independence of the bishop and each other than to join in concerted action.

The Pure Word of God

The reformer or revolutionist may possess the initial advantage precisely because he has, consciously or unconsciously, rejected the traditional structure in order to pursue his particular intellectual, religious, or political daemon. His force depends on a certain blindness. He sees the far-off goal —in Zell's case it was the Kingdom of God—and his vision blinds him to everyday reality. The conventional authorities are left behind while the reformer and his supporters are able to move very quickly, achieving significant changes in a very short time. This stage of growth existed in Strasbourg from 1521 to 1524. Before either the political or ecclesiastical authorities were prepared, evangelical preaching had been established in five of the city's churches.

CHAPTER 8

THE SERMONS

HE Pure Word of God had gone forth with great effect. What was said in these sermons that people pressed into the cathedral to hear? Unfortunately we cannot know precisely, because despite the presence of three important reformers no volume of sermons of even one of these men exists. It is a peculiar lacuna. Sermons had been one of the stock items of the publishing trade. As early as 1480 to 1484 eight volumes of sermons were printed by the Strasbourg presses, the largest amount for any category of religious literature. The number increased in the following decades until between 1515 and 1519, twenty-five volumes of sermons came off the presses.[1] Then there was a significant change. From 1520 to 1524 only eight volumes of Catholic sermons appeared. While twenty-one Protestant sermons were published, many of these represented only single sermons preached by Luther. After 1524 the decline in the publication of sermons was rapid and definitive. No Catholic sermons were published in Strasbourg after 1524; only ten Protestant sermons in all were printed from 1525 to 1548, and most of these were Luther's.

The lack of publication is all the more curious since sermons were such a vital part of the movement for reform. The preachers hoped not only to awaken the hearts of their auditors but to inspire young men to follow them. Sermons could certainly have played an essential role in educating

1. See Appendix A.

and training these young men. Perhaps in this early stage of the Reform the emphasis was so literally on the spoken word that neither the reformers nor their disciples saw the need for transcription. No sermon, preached in the city of Strasbourg itself, exists for Zell, Bucer, or Capito. Their words must be reconstructed by other means.

One chronicler reported on Zell's sermons of 1522–23 in his discussion of the twenty-four articles drawn up by the bishop's Fiskal. Obviously these articles dwelt on the most inflammatory passages, for the notaries who went to the cathedral to take down Zell's words were assigned by the chapter to find damaging evidence.[2] Recognizing this bias, the reports do provide some indication of the subject matter of these first evangelical sermons.

Zell, the chronicler wrote, had openly stated that popes, bishops, or priests who neither preached nor taught were the same as laymen. He criticized the seven daily services of prayer observed by the clergy as meaningless since they were performed without devotion, and he recommended that they be omitted. He had preached against the Holy Sacraments, saying that neither the Mass nor the sacrifice of the Body of Christ could have any effect on the souls of the departed. Frequently during the course of his preaching he had defended Luther, stating that he could not bring himself to oppose the monk who had brought the truth to the light of day.[3]

From the pulpit, the notaries reported, Zell had said that he did not know where purgatory was, that no one could rightly know whether Saint James and Saint Anne were really the parents of the Virgin Mary, and that neither the Virgin Mary nor the Apostles could make remission of sins, since that could be accomplished only by Christ Himself.[4]

From these fragments it is clear that the Pure Word of God, as Zell understood it, had led him to repudiate essential

2. Specklin, *Collectanées,* p. 494.
3. Ibid., p. 495.
4. Ibid., p. 496.

and fundamental doctrines of the church. He based his sermons on scripture and used the texts to reveal a gap between the words of God and the ways of man, and scripture became a standard against which the church could be measured. Thus, the evangelical Word provided not only a revelation of Christ but a formula to guide man's earthly life. For five hundred years this holy, immortal Gospel had been crushed; human, mortal doctrines had been substituted; but now the Word would be released from bondage by preaching the laws of God instead of the laws of the pope and the bishop.[5]

In his defense addressed to the Fiskal, Zell himself answered the charges brought against him, summarizing the contents of his sermons. The statement could hardly have helped his cause. He opened by repeating the statement that the Word of God had been suppressed for more than five hundred years, that as soon as men had begun to rule Christendom by their own laws, they had started to reject and crush the Word of God. This, he said, was clear from the preachers' manuals, which did not go back to the Gospels in search of a code of law and ethics but to Aristotle and other pagan philosophers. Furthermore these manuals concerned themselves with totally inconsequential matters, such as whether angels could talk or where each angel sat in heaven, instead of helping the preacher to convey God's message to his people.[6] The result was preaching and a level of instruction which duped the poor citizen and misled him, for the innocent burgher believed that all the mishmash[7] he heard from the priest was the Gospel. Now, said Zell:

We know well what the Gospel is—Good News from God brought to us by Christ to bring us to the Grace and Mercy of God, as is promised us by the writings of

5. Ibid.
6. Zell, *Christliche Verantwortung*, pp. Q. iii–iv.
7. The phrase Zell used is really untranslatable but should appear because of its sheer euphony—"die stempery uñ gremplerey," meaning on the one hand pre-prepared materials, and on the other, trash.

the Holy Evangelists and the Apostles. And it reveals to us that we will obtain the Grace of God through faith and trust in Jesus Christ.[8]

Anything which does not lead to belief in Christ and love of one's neighbor is not Gospel preaching. Thus you can easily see that it is not evangelical preaching to teach human rules and regulations . . . and the preacher should stay by the text and not be carried off into his own interpretation.[9]

For let it be understood that there are three ways in which the Gospel can be preached. First, using Christ's life and teaching as an example, which is good but not really the right point. Second, as a statute book, which is false because Christ did not come to reveal the Commandments of Moses but to reveal the Truth and Grace of God. And it is this Grace obtained through Christ that is the third and right way to expound the New Testament.[10]

However conscientiously Zell may have tried to follow his own instructions, it is clear that he himself went beyond the revelation of Christ through the text. For example, he censured the practice of tithing, stating that it had not been demanded by Christ or by the Apostles but had been established by the pope under the influence of the devil himself.[11] He freely criticized the clergy. They were learned, yes, but in the subtleties of theology rather than in the scriptures,[12] and they flaunted their immorality and corruption. Zell's manner of presenting the Gospel also went well beyond the requirements of scholarly exegesis. In many instances the texts were used simply as a point of departure from which he could launch a strong attack against the clergy, the usages of the church, and the hierarchy.

8. Zell, *Christliche Verantwortung*, p. Q. vi.
9. Ibid., p. R.
10. Ibid., p. R. ii.
11. Ibid., p. R. v.
12. Ibid., p. R. iii.

Bucer's preaching in Strasbourg itself was not recorded by the chroniclers, nor did he present a written defense there.[13] His report of his preaching activities in Wissembourg, just before his arrival in Strasbourg, must serve as an example of the style and content of his preaching.[14] His *Summary Seiner Predig* was, like Zell's *Verantwortung*, a justification of his pastorship in Wissembourg, an attempt to prove that he had not abrogated the terms of the imperial mandate but preached only the pure Gospel as stipulated by the edict. In fact he, like Zell, used the Gospel as a point of departure for a blistering attack on the church.

All the law and the prophets are based on two commandments: Thou shalt love the Lord thy God with all thy heart and thou shalt love thy neighbor as thyself. That which is in accordance with these commandments is Godly, while that which does not conform to them is without any doubt of the devil. But how does the love of God come to mean that people should have to build churches, provide for Masses, endow brotherhoods, pur-

13. Three Bucer sermons are extant, but only one dates from this period.
(1) *Martin Butzers an ein christlichen Rath uñ Gemeyn der Statt Weissenburg Summary seiner Predig daselbst gethon* (Strassburg, 1523).
(2) *Die Predigen so von dem frömbden Predicanten, die allenthalb här, zu Bernn uff dem Gesprach oder disputation gewesen, beschehen sind* (Zurich, 1528).
(3) *Drei predige aus dem Evangelio: Komet her zu mir alle die ir muhselig und beladen seind etc. Matt. XI. Der Kirchen zu Benfeld zur letzte gethon* (Strassburg, 1538).
Bucer wrote prolifically, but his publications were commentaries—liturgical and political treatises rather than sermons. Cf. F. Mentz, "Bibliographische Zusammenstellung der gedruckten Schriften Butzers," in *Zur 400 jahrigen Geburtsfeier Martin Butzers* (Strassburg, 1891).
14. Martin Butzer, *An ein christlichen Rath uñ Gemeyn der Statt Weissenburg Summary seiner Predig daselbst gethon* (Strassburg, 1523). Since the original edition is paginated by letter and Roman numeral, and in any case not easily available, all reference will be made to the text as it appears in Robert Stupperich, ed., *Martin Bucers Deutsche Schriften* (2 vols. Gütersloh, 1960–62), *1*, 69 ff. Hereafter referred to as Stupperich, *Bucers Deutsche Schriften*.

chase good works, burn candles, and all sorts of absurdities, and all at great expense? These things are not commanded by God, for no one can buy himself for money.

If you wish to help your neighbor, to help Christ through helping your neighbor, [the church requires that] you must support, provide for, and make sacrifices for the wandering infantry of priests. Why? Because they are the anointed ones, the kingly priesthood, to whom everyone should give, but from whom no one should take, whom everyone should serve, but no one control.

And where is all this written? John XVI, [12]. "I have still much to say, but you cannot yet bear it." But who then said it applies to you, you ghouls? Certainly not the spirit of Truth, because in the Spirit of Truth Christ said to his disciples "Any of you who will not deny all that he has, cannot be my disciple. And the oldest of you shall be like the youngest, and the most important shall be like a servant." It is this . . . that the Holy Scripture teaches.[15]

The pattern of the sermons becomes clear. They contained a direct, frontal attack on the clergy and the abuses of the church, a doubly effective assault because it clothed itself in the words and in the righteousness of the Gospel. Bucer's "Pure Word" revealed a world divided between black and white—the works of the pope and the hierarchy were black and of the devil, whereas the works of the preachers would lead to Christ. The style of the sermons was direct and simple, and Bucer significantly identified himself with his hearers, rather than with his clerical brethren, sharing his parishioners' problems and their concerns. He provided an alternative to the old customs and the old evils.

You can rely on that which is preached to you and taught. . . . Let God's commandment, God's writings

15. Ibid., p. 88.

be your guide. "Seek and ye shall find." If you do this
. . . you will find that all truth and learning are in
Christ, that we have in Him a sure faith and trust in the
Father. He will protect us from all evil and forgive all
our sins. This is the faith by which the just live, and it
is this justification which is valid before God. Thus it
was that Paul wrote in Romans V [1], "When then we
are justified by faith, so we have peace with God
through Jesus Christ." [16]

The evils Bucer attacked were hardly novel, for they had
provoked the criticism of clergy and laity alike all through
the late Middle Ages in sermons, in ribald verse, and in lay
writings like the *Canterbury Tales*. Geiler von Kaysersberg
had preached consistently against the vain, frivolous behavior of the Strasbourg clerics, but in comparison to Bucer
and Zell, his words sound like a paternal admonition. For
the young preachers hurled the Wrath of God Himself
against the clergy, using the scriptures as a measuring rod,
as a plumb line to reveal the vanity and iniquity of clerical
life. To anyone who heard the sermons it must have been
clear that if Christ had returned to earth, he would have
found the money changers back in the temple. The task was
clear. The church must be cleansed as Christ Himself had
cleansed it.

At the same time Bucer offered a program of reform, he
also proposed a new support, a new relationship with Christ.
God was not to be thought of only as a judge, sitting eter-
nally in Heaven and weighing out the souls of the saved and
the damned, but God was the Father, eagerly waiting to
welcome the sinner and forgive the sin. He found no con-
tradiction in an emphasis on the commandment of love and
an attack on the church. He returned again and again to the
fact that the true message of Christ lay in the love of one's
neighbor, "For that is His command, that we believe in His
Son and love one another." [17] Bucer reduced "love of one

16. Ibid., p. 89.
17. Ibid., pp. 90–91.

another" to everyday terms. It did not mean supporting churches, Masses, altars, and chapters, but feeding the hungry, giving drink to the thirsty, sheltering the wayfarer, and visiting the sick and the prisoner. These acts were to be done freely, not to secure salvation, but to carry out God's commandment.

It is difficult in these passages to recognize the later Bucer, who would try to bring Zwingli and Luther together and who would never entirely despair of a reunion with the Roman church. For the most part in this early sermon he assumed a bitter and uncompromising attitude toward his opponents and was quick to hold them up to scorn and ridicule. Discipline through work, vigils, and fasting, he wrote, was essential to the Christian, but not as it was observed by monks and nuns. They claimed their singing and muttering, which they did not even understand, to be work; sleeping half the day was a vigil, and filling themselves up with fish was to fast.[18] In fact God had commanded that by the sweat of his brow, man should eat his bread, and true discipline should be based on such effort. To love one's neighbor did not mean saying Mass, singing, and such acts of charity:

> A Christian must make his vigil not as a monk says Matins, getting up in the middle of the night and howling away for an hour or two . . . but the Christian must really break his sleep and spend the time in prayer or other useful exertion.[19]

The sermons, whatever the text, bristled with righteous wrath against the church which had mocked the true words of God and misled and betrayed the people.

In November 1523 or 1524 Caspar Hedio preached two sermons in the cathedral on tithing.[20] He was a disciple rather than a leader, and his sermons lack the style and

18. Ibid., p. 97.
19. Ibid., p. 98.
20. Caspar Hedio, *Von Den zehenden zwo trefflicher predig Beschehen im Munster zü Strassburg* (Strassburg, ca. 1524).

dynamism of Bucer's and Zell's written statements, yet they are significant because of their subject matter and their form and because they are the only sermons we have that were actually preached in Strasbourg.

Hedio's scholarly attitude and his habit of analysis are clearly evident. He started by stating that the first book of Moses (Genesis) and Abraham's grant of the tithe to Melchisedich might seem to provide an unbreakable precedent for tithing. Yet, said Hedio, scripture was a two-edged sword which could cut through such a knot, even if it had been tied by Hercules himself.[21] While the scriptures might be understood to permit tithing for God's purposes, certainly no text provided that money could be collected by man-made ordinances and used for secular purposes. Money collected through tithes should not be thrown away in a dice game or spent for luxury and an Epicurean life, leaving women and children to suffer hunger and want.[22] In practice, the collection of the tithe was ruthless and unjust, for the clergy did not come to ask payment in brotherly love, with an understanding of the needs of the people, but they appeared whether it had been a good year or bad, whether the crops had done well or poorly. Even if there had been thunder, hail, and lightening, they insisted on full payments; furthermore they snatched away small legacies with the excuse that otherwise a poor working man might become covetous.[23]

Hedio then returned to the scriptural sources, quoting a series of texts, beginning with the Old Testament and following through to the New, to prove that God had placed a special emphasis on work—had, indeed, consecrated it.

As the bird is made to fly thus man is created to work and it is a holy thing. Psalm 128. You must support yourself by the work of your hands; if you do this,

21. Hedio's reference to Hercules provides an interesting contrast to Bucer's feelings about Aristotle, which were cited above. The difference in attitude reflects the humanistic training that Hedio had enjoyed and Bucer lacked.
22. Hedio, *Zwo Predig*, p. 2.
23. Ibid., p. 3.

you have done well. For on the contrary, leisure is an unholy thing and forbidden by Paul, 2 Thessalonians 3, and by the prophet Ezekiel and the good-for-nothing Sodome it is shown as an abomination. . . . Then man must hoe, plough, sow, and plant. Hieronymus I. God gives prosperity. I Cor. 3. Wake and maintain the watch. Esa. 6. Beware the false prophets, the dogs and sows who work evil. Math. VII. . . . For the worker is worthy of his pay, Math. X, and who understands this will be doubly honored, especially he who works by words and by teaching. Tim. V, I Thess.[24]

Having set forth this string of quotations with no exterpolation, Hedio went on to conclude that since God had thus consecrated work and made it worthy, the fruits of man's labor should be devoted to Godly purposes, not wasted by indulgences or tithes, particularly if the latter denied the worker the rewards of his labor.

Hedio's sermons were closely argued, and they seem to have stayed closer to the text than Zell's or Bucer's, although this can only be surmised. The end result was the same. By a careful review of all the biblical texts on both tithing and work he was able to present incontrovertible proof that the collections made by the church were not within the scriptural meaning and were thus unlawful. Hedio's sermon was almost a lawyer's brief, in which text after text was marshalled to support his conclusion. It must be remembered that the burghers who heard the sermons despised the idleness of the clergy and looked on their labors in the church not as sanctified but as malingering.

Capito's sermons, as he described them in his *Entschuldigung* to the bishop's Fiskal, struck a different note. Capito had himself borne ecclesiastical responsibility and was not ready to lash out so sharply against his clerical colleagues. Indeed, he was careful to say that he had no desire to abandon the church of the ancient fathers, but on the other

24. Ibid., p. 4.

hand, he did not wish to forsake the pure, inward church of the pious prophets, apostles, and martyrs. Thus he found himself torn between the authority of the bishop and that other authority, the rock of the Gospel. The result was a tragic division, doubly tragic because Christians should be united in Christ, but now one group hated the name of Christ and the Gospels, the other hated the pope, the bishops, and the monks, and on both sides the great mass of people had turned uncharitably against their opponents. For this reason, Capito said, he had decided to appeal for Christian unity to the Godly papists and Lutherans, who alone were sincere in their beliefs.[25]

The solution was for the pious, believing Christians from the two sides to come together for mutual discussion. If such a conference were held, the bishop would find that the Lutherans would not oppose the ancient usages of the church, which were not against God's commandments, and the worthy persons on the two sides would easily come to an agreement. The Lutherans would not press the scriptures offensively, the papists would gladly reform annoying abuses.[26] A major difficulty, however, would still remain. This was the crux of the problem and the justification for Capito's preaching.

> One would [still] be bound hand and foot. For the worthless masses on both sides would want none of it. But if one tries to eradicate one group or the other, or lashes out with strict edicts in an attempt to force them to understand, then nothing will be accomplished but bloodshed, misery and distress. But God, Who is the Heart of all hearts, alone can change this. The more you attempt to put this down by force, the more it will spring up. . . .
>
> And [thus] I have tried to accomplish [this understanding] by certain councils from my own mouth . . .

25. Capito, *Entschuldigung an der Bischoffen*, D. i.
26. Ibid., D. ii.

indeed it was this which I sought to accomplish by my sermons, to quell the uprisings on both sides, and I have thus preached in terms of a basis on which an understanding could be reached by both sides. Without this both sides will be stirred to violence.[27]

According to his statement Capito was the only one of the evangelical preachers who, at this time, counseled caution. We have no way of knowing whether the sermons themselves maintained the same tone of mildness and rapprochement. At Mainz, however, he had attempted to maintain a middle position, and it is not implausible that even after he had mounted the pulpit and identified himself with the Lutherans (whom he referred to as "we"), he could not entirely cast himself off from his former loyalties. Unlike Zell he did not divide the world between evil papists and good Lutherans. He saw, instead, a small group from each side that was genuinely devout and concerned about the church. The masses, on both sides, were driven by hatred and malice.

Fragmentary as the evidence is, it indicates that the early Reformation sermons did not merely open up the scriptures to the masses. More significantly, they justified the traditional complaints against the clergy. The growth of the ecclesiastical bureaucracy in the fifteenth century had greatly increased the administrative costs of the church. A vicious circle had developed in which the papal officials made increasingly heavy demands on the bishops, who in turn laid increasingly onerous burdens on the chapters and parishes. At the bottom of the pile was the individual Christian, beset by eternal levies on earnings which, caught in the general price rise, purchased less and less. Now, for the first time, not just one individual cleric, like Geiler, had risen in protest, but a whole group of young, evangelical preachers, coming from the masses themselves, voiced the pent-up rage and frustration of their class.

27. Ibid.

The significant innovation of this group lay in its appeal to the scriptures. The burghers had long been convinced that the ecclesiastical estate was in need of reform and that their existence as a separate entity created injustice. Now they were told that the system went against the laws of Christ Himself and that the obligations and duties laid by the clergy on the people were not only oppressive but illegal and unsanctified. When Bucer preached from his favorite text, "Come unto Me all ye who are heavy laden," the burghers thought not so much of the gentle shepherd forgiving their sins, as of freedom from ecclesiastical dues.

CHAPTER 9

REFORMATION OR REVOLUTION?

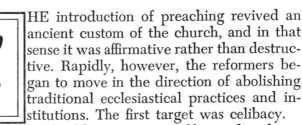

HE introduction of preaching revived an ancient custom of the church, and in that sense it was affirmative rather than destructive. Rapidly, however, the reformers began to move in the direction of abolishing traditional ecclesiastical practices and institutions. The first target was celibacy. Criticism of clerical celibacy was in itself a medieval tradition; poets and story tellers reveled in the details of the amorous feats of monks, nuns, and canons, and indeed the rule seemed more honored in the breach than in observance. Before the Reformation, attitudes toward marriage had begun to change. Nicholas de Blony and Geiler von Kaysersberg preaching in Strasbourg around 1500 and Gabriel Biel in Tübingen had taught that marriage was a natural and favorable state for man and more important, sanctified by God.[1] The reformers developed the theme further and rejected the concept that clerical celibacy was sacrosanct. It was merely a custom, they charged, and it had led not to reverence and respect but had degraded the clergy in the eyes of the people. Living in open sin with their mistresses and fathering illegitimate children, the priests could not attempt to offer moral instruction, nor did they provide an example worthy of emulation for their flock. Furthermore, celibacy had not been commanded by God but had developed out of the monastic rules of the early centuries of

1. François Wendel, *Le Mariage à Strasbourg à l'époque de la réforme, 1520–1692* (Strasbourg, 1928), pp. 22–23.

the church. As a witness to the sanctity of marriage the evangelical preachers broke with the established tradition of the church, took wives, and attempted to set an example of family love and solidarity. Bucer had married before he reached the city.[2] Anton Firn, preacher at St. Thomas, was the first resident cleric to renounce the celibate life. His act resulted in a complex interplay between the evangelical preachers and the church, between the preachers and the Magistrat, and between the Magistrat and the church.

Although clerical marriage was one means of breaking down the barrier between laymen and cleric and although the married clergy placed themselves under the jurisdiction of the civil authorities and assumed Bürgerrecht, the Ratsherren were by no means eager to accept the change and did everything they could to discourage Firn because they were convinced that married clergy would simply draw the wrath of ecclesiastical and imperial officers. They hesitated. They compromised, and they lost by default. This is significant because it indicates that the Magistrat did not snatch at the Reform, seize the initiative, and set about to bring the church under its jurisdiction. Policy was made from crisis to crisis, from incident to incident, and the *Rat* accepted new responsibilities and functions irresolutely and with reluctance.

Anton Firn was the parish priest of the church of St. Thomas. On October 18, 1523, he had announced his marriage from the pulpit, stating that he would bring his wife to church the following Sunday. This presented a rather complex moral issue because his new wife was his housekeeper, who had been his mistress for years. The canons of the chap-

2. The bishop did not let Bucer's marriage go unchallenged. He wrote the Rat on June 21, 1523, asking to be allowed to take action against Bucer. (A.S.T., 47, Letter Wilhelm Bischoff zu Strassburg, Samstag nach Viti und Modesti, 1523.) The Rat replied that since Bucer was a burgher's son, it could not set aside the protection it had granted him, but it was also careful at this time to deny him the right to preach publicly. (A. Baum, *Magistrat und Reformation*, p. 35.)

ter of St. Thomas immediately informed the Magistrat that they would discipline Firn. The Ratsherren affirmed the move, noting that for their part they intended to enforce the Nuremberg mandate, which forbade clerical marriage and placed a married cleric under imperial ban. The chapter should take precedence over the lay authority in the matter, but the Rat would provide protection for the canons if there was any threat of civil disturbance.[3]

The chapter formally deposed Firn, but on November 15 he took his customary position in the chancel as ordained priest. This provided a nice legal problem. Technically, having been deposed, he was not a priest and no longer fell under the jurisdiction of the chapter. Furthermore, he had assumed Bürgerrecht in June and thus was a burgher. The chapter, respecting the legalities, turned to the Ratsherren, who recommended to Firn that he accept his deposition. Even as a burgher they could not protect him from the spiritual authority or from the imperial mandate. Firn, refusing to listen, continued to mount the chancel as a duly ordained priest. Whether the Rat was influenced by his stubbornness or whether it feared a possible disturbance, it proposed to the canons that the matter be dropped. The chapter did not agree and again formally deposed Firn on November 29, reconfirming this on December 7.[4] To complicate matters further, Matthäus Zell married on December 3.

Tension now ran high. Firn's parishioners were apprehensive that he would be removed. On December 12 they petitioned the Rat that he be allowed to remain as their priest, despite the chapter. The Rat feared a riot and requested the chapter to withhold its action. The chapter, also fearing violence, acquiesced. Its fears were justified, for the burghers arrived armed in church the following Sunday, gathering in the cross-aisles. The threat had the desired effect. The chapter relented and gave Firn permission to preach and to

3. A. Baum, *Magistrat und Reformation*, pp. 34–35.
4. Ibid., p. 36.

mount the chancel, but protested to the Rat, stating that it would take no responsibility for the evil consequences which might follow.[5]

The Rat immediately sent an envoy to the bishop with five pages of instructions which were carefully phrased so that there would seem to be no hindrance to the bishop's execution of his duties. The Ratsherren agreed with him; they were especially of the opinion that the clergy of the city needed firmer discipline. Through the new preaching, the masses were being aroused against the priests and clerics, who in many cases presented a bad example. They hoped, therefore, that he would enforce the mandate not only against the married clergy but against all those who needed discipline. They also asked the bishop to provide men learned in the scriptures to supervise the priests. This latter could be interpreted to mean that the Rat hoped for some further control of what was said from the pulpit. The envoy concluded that the Ratsherren were convinced that everything would be well ordered and that life would proceed in a godly way once the bishop was aware of the problems.[6] The bishop replied with a letter to the Rat on December 14. Although the Rat had not shown itself too cooperative before (undoubtedly referring to Bucer), nonetheless he was requesting them once again not to impede him, but to let him take stern measures against Firn. He closed by reminding them of his responsibilities under the imperial mandate.[7]

The Rat was still hopeful that it could remove Firn. Intimidated by the mob, it hoped that a few concessions would alleviate the immediate crisis. Basically desiring to support the Nuremberg mandate and to stand with the bishop rather than assuming full authority and placing themselves in a dangerous position against the emperor, the Rat planned to bring the matter before the Schöffen and have

5. Ibid.
6. A.S.T., 47, Instruktion zu Episcop. der priesterhalb so weiber nemen. Dec. 7, 1523.
7. A.S.T., 47, Episc. Antwort, Dec. 14, 1523.

this larger body of burghers place Firn under the ban.[8] Their
due deliberation had precisely the effect that the chapter
feared. In January 1524, before any meeting of the Schöffen
had been called, five more clerics took wives.[9]

The anxiety of the Rat with regard to the whole matter
is reflected in the length and tone of the instructions that
they gave to Bernhard Wurmser and Daniel Mueg on January 3, 1524, on the eve of their departure for Nuremberg.
Significantly, both men were favorable to the Reform. Their
seven pages of instructions dealt mostly with the issues
raised by preaching and the clerical marriages, and included
a summary of Zell's and Capito's sermons which justified
the marriages on the ground that since priests lived with
concubines, it was permissible for priests to marry. The Rat
averred that both these practices went against the teaching
of ancient councils and were thus illegal.

The emphasis of the instruction was on the need for immediate action. The delegates were to make it clear that
the common people were being stirred up by the preachers,
who were constantly implying that for the first time in
centuries the truth was being revealed to the people. Meanwhile the bishop had threatened to punish the married
priests severely, but nothing had been done about the scan-
dalous lives of the priests and their concubines. The delegates were to make it abundantly clear that the Rat feared
violence. They were to press for an open hearing or council
so that the matter could be discussed, a decision arrived at,
and the division and tumult would come to an end in a truly
Christian peace. The Rat pledged to support any decision
made by such a council.[10]

Toward the end of the month, probably on January 20,[11]

8. A. Baum, *Magistrat und Reformation*, p. 37.
9. Ibid.
10. A.S.T., *Varia Ecclesiastica*, Instruction Aller Handlung, Jan. 3,
1524.
11. Zell's and Firn's citations were apparently drawn up early in
January but were not issued until the end of the month. See A. Baum,
Magistrat und Reformation, p. 42 n.

the bishop issued his citation against the married clergy. The men were to appear before him at Saverne within five days, two delays of five days each being permitted. In the meantime they were suspended from their benefices and from all clerical privileges. It was a sharp and stringent blow. Five of the men—Zell, Firn, Hackfurt, Spatzinger, and Schultheiss—turned to the Magistrat on that same day (January 20) for protection. They charged that the bishop had denied them the freedom of the clergy, for he had shorn them of their offices and robbed them of their benefices when, indeed, they had only carried out Christ's commandments. Thus they petitioned for the help and advice of the Rat.[12] The Rat was not willing to shelter them under the provision that a citizen of the city could not be arraigned before a foreign court as this privilege had never been fully recognized by the ecclesiastical courts. Furthermore, the Ratsherren were still convinced that they should not attempt to settle the matter independently but that the cities should act as a body at the Diet of Nuremberg.

They therefore dispatched two Ratsherren, Mathis Pfarrer and Hans Bock, to the bishop on February 10, requesting him to defer the case against Firn and the others until after the Diet. The Rat reaffirmed its essential agreement with his policy. The married priests should be firmly dealt with, and the other clergy, high in the church, who had lived so disgracefully for years, should also be disciplined. But the matter involved not only Strasbourg but all other cities in the empire as well; so it should be decided by the estates of the Holy Roman Empire at Nuremberg. Thus they asked that the bishop seal up the citation until the Diet had been prorogued.[13]

The city had consistently associated punishment of the married priests with the broader problem of the discipline of

12. A.S.T., 87, Verheirateten Priester und assitantz gegen Episcopi Vorhandlung, Jan. 20, 1524.
13. A.S.T., 47, Auff den Hans Bock und Mathis Pfarrer zu Episcopi von der Rat, Feb. 10, 1524.

Reformation or Revolution?

the clergy. They planned to use the one as a bargaining point
to achieve the other. The bishop now postponed the proceedings against the married men until March 14 and, perhaps struck by the logic of the Rat's argument, on February
19 issued a proclamation to the clergy of the diocese with
regard to their concubines and immoral and profligate habits.
It was his duty as shepherd of his flock to watch over the
morals of the clergy. Instead of setting a good example, they
had lived in luxury and lust, stirring up the people against
them. He therefore required and ordered all clergy of his
city and diocese, whatever their grade, order, or condition,
to live according to the rules of the church under pain of
punishment before the ecclesiastical courts. Specifically, he
continued, all members of the clergy should exclude women
and concubines from their places of residence. Noncom-
pliance would mean the loss of their benefice.[14]

By February 22 the Rat began to despair of action coming quickly enough from Nuremberg. It wrote to Wurmser
and Herlin, bringing them up to date on the proceedings
with the bishop so that they would be able to quell any
rumors, but how much longer, it wanted to know, would
the cities be restrained from taking some sort of common
action? The third estate desired that a free Christian hearing be held. Would this occur, or was every city going to be
left to handle the matter by itself? [15]

The delay that the bishop had granted came to an end;
nothing had been achieved at Nuremberg, and on March
14 the bishop put the married priests under the ban. The
Rat decided to let the matter run its course. The ban was
nailed up on the church doors of all the parishes on April 3.
On April 10 the married priests responded with a call to a
council, in the meantime preaching vigorously against the
"insane action" of the bishop.[16] The Rat made one last at-

14. A.S.T., 47, Proclamation Episc., Feb. 19, 1524.
15. Hans Virck, ed., *Politische Correspondenz der Stadt Strassburg
im Zeitalter der Reformation* (5 vols. Strassburg, 1882–98), 1, 89,
#166.
16. A. Baum, *Magistrat und Reformation*, p. 48 n. 2.

tempt to intercede for them, this time asking the deacon and the cathedral chapter to request the bishop not to press the charges. The bishop, indignant, complained directly to Cardinal Campeggio at Nuremberg. In the end the Diet took no action, the question of a council was pushed off to be discussed at Speyer in November,[17] and the Magistrat was left in an extremely uncomfortable position. The matter had been carried as far as the Cardinal, which was what they had hoped to avoid, and worst of all, the married men were still on their hands. No action was taken to grant them protection, but neither was an attempt made to carry out the provisions of the ban. Firn and Zell remained in their parishes while the Rat awaited the formulation of a general policy at Speyer. During the summer Altbiesser, Hedio, and Capito were married.[18]

Until the spring of 1524 initiative had been in the hands of the clergy. It was they who had begun to preach, and they who had broken from the traditional pattern of celibacy. The populace had been evident only as a mass audience, as parishioners supporting their preachers. Then the pace quickened, and although the burghers did not establish themselves in a position of leadership, they forced the leaders, both clerical and secular, into new positions and new decisions.

The new role was first evident in the petition that requested the Rat to provide parish churches with evangelical preachers.[19] It had been signed by five parishes—St. Aurelie, St. Stephen, St. Martin, St. Laurence, and Young St. Peter. It is impossible to determine with precision who lived in these parishes in the year 1524, but the parish registers for the period from 1540 to 1560 provide a general picture of the occupations and activities of each district.[20]

17. Ibid., p. 49.
18. Altbiesser married his cook, May 23; Hedio married a gardener's daughter; Capito married a daughter of one of the XV, Aug. 1, 1524.
19. See Chapter 7, p. 115.
20. See Appendix B.

Three of the churches were on the outskirts of the town, in areas that were not greatly built up. St. Aurelie was the furthest out, actually at the very gate, known as the White Gate. It was the market-garden area of the city and, possibly most important to its particular development as a parish, it was quite literally surrounded by cloisters and convents. In the thirteenth century, when the city had forbidden further monastic building within the walls, no fewer than four orders had built as close to the city as possible. The new fortifications begun in 1524 brought this area inside the city, and at the time of the Reform, the parish included a cloister and church for Dominican nuns, a cloister and church for Augustine friars, a cloister and church for the proud and noble Teutonic Knights, and a cloister, church, chapel, and hospital for the even more proud and noble Knights of the Order of St. John. As the Reformation wore on, the feelings of the parish toward their monastic neighbors became only too evident. The people of St. Aurelie were simple folk: Roughly a quarter of them worked as gardeners on their own lands or on lands rented from the convents, and the gardeners had long enjoyed a reputation for a certain tough independence. Another quarter of the parish worked as domestic servants and day laborers, usually in one of the convents. The third quarter were in the clothing trades, and the final group were woolworkers or worked in a rope walk, probably located in the quarter.

The parish of St. Stephen stood at the eastern gate of the town, as St. Aurelie at the west. Again there were convents. The parish church was itself a part of the chapter of St. Stephen, a chapter of noble ladies, and the convent of St. Clara was across the canal. Situated where the Ill was diverted around the city in a series of canals, it was the quarter of the rivermen; the register is entirely dominated by boatmen and fishermen. There were also large fields on this side of the town, for the other major profession represented was that of gardener.

Young St. Peter was the other church on the edge of town,

again a chapter church, but the quarter had no convents. The occupational pattern was a bit broader here; there was no one clearly dominant trade, like fishing and boating in St. Stephen's or gardening and domestic service in St. Aurelie. There was still a large group of gardeners, but the dominant occupations seem to have been small trades—the clothing trades, woolworkers, metalworkers (smiths, armorers, locksmiths), masons, and stonemasons. Interestingly enough a few printers and bookbinders show up on the register. In general, it was a group of craftsmen and artisans, not men engaged in broad commerce or trade.

It is possible to infer from these data that in the early period the response to the Reform came from the little people of the city; this is borne out by the consistent reference in the documents to the *gemeinde Volcks*. The Rat is always concerned that the Gemeinde will make an uprising, that the Gemeinde are restless, and that the preachers have aroused the Gemeinde. Further evidence lies in the events of 1524 and 1525, for it was the burghers themselves who now determined the pattern of change. They had heard the Pure Word of God, and it spoke to them of brotherhood, of equality of men in Christ. They translated these words into direct action: action against the privileged, which to them meant the clergy. The latent anticlericalism that existed in all medieval towns now became overt and violent, ending in the closing of the convents and the abolition of the traditional Catholic Mass.

The first move, however, came from the clergy themselves. On November 9, 1523, a deputation of Franciscan friars appeared before the Rat, complaining of the profligate administration of the provincial, which had reduced the monastery to penury.[21] With the permission of the pope, the friars wished to lay aside their habits and to transfer to the city the rights of collection of their benefices. In November the Rat was deeply involved in the marital affairs of Anton Firn and had no desire to become further enmeshed in an internal dispute within an ecclesiastical unit. The Rat re-

21. A. Baum, *Magistrat und Reformation*, p. 99.

plied that the laying off of the habit was not its affair; but if the convent decided to dissolve itself, the Rat would take over the revenues.

The matter was dropped at that point, and it was not until spring that the Magistrat apparently felt that some further legal provisions should be made. With the exception of the knightly orders and the Carthusians, the financial affairs of all the monastic units were supervised by *Klosterpfleger* (convent supervisors) appointed by the Rat. It was the duty of these men to watch over the goods and property of the convents, to keep informed of the sale or exchange of property, and to deduct the city's share from bequests and gifts (the city liberally took half). In 1521 the convents had been forbidden by the Rat to receive alms. Money given for this purpose was taken over directly by the convent supervisors, who put it in the city treasury for direct distribution to the poor.[22] On March 2, 1525, the Magistrat provided, in addition, that the possessions of all convents, chapters, and churches should be inventoried.[23]

The dissatisfied Franciscans interpreted the Rat's action as an authorization and laid off their habits, "some putting on long black robes, others grey student cowls like Luther."[24] The Dominicans were annoyed, and a street fight broke out between them and several burghers, ending with the invasion of the great Dominican cloister (it was the largest in the city) by two hundred burghers. The Ammeister himself had to go in and dispel the crowd.[25]

This was the beginning. A few weeks later a group of gardeners, "moved so full and hard by the Gospel," gathered in front of those convents that they considered most evil and dissolute, creating an angry, threatening crowd.[26] Shortly thereafter six hundred men—handworkers and a "variety of

22. Josef F. Vierling, *Das Ringen um die letzten den Katholizismus treuen Klöster Strassburg zur Zeit der Reformation und Gegenreformation* (Strassburg, 1913), pp. 17–18.
23. Trausch and Wencker, *Chroniques*, p. 152.
24. Ibid., p. 151.
25. Ibid.
26. Büheler, *Chronique*, p. 73.

trash"[27]—gathered at the horse market, again in a violent mood. Although the Ratsherren admonished them to break up and to return to their homes peacefully, they would not, and in the morning they went out to St. Arbogast, the Augustine monastery in the parish of St. Aurelie, and to the Carthusian monastery, which lay beyond, and broke in. The threat was apparently dissipated in a riotous bout of eating and drinking, the provisions having been requisitioned from the cellars and storehouses of the monasteries.[28]

The Chapterherren of Young St. Peter, Old St. Peter, and St. Thomas were dismayed by these outbursts. Convinced that the violence might spread and wishing to protect their property, they left the city "with all their treasures, the ornaments for the Mass, vessels, monstrances, relics, charters, and seals."[29] Their departure had much the same effect as the flight of the nobility in 1420. The burghers saw it as an indication of lack of loyalty and concern for the city. For the Rat it meant a long period of negotiations with the chapters, the bishop, and other members of the ecclesiastical hierarchy—negotiations that demanded the utmost tact and diplomacy.

At the same time the burghers seemed to be satisfied that some changes were being made. They had chased the Chapterherren out of the temple, and the rioting quieted down. On March 16, 1524, the Franciscan and Dominican cloisters were inventoried, including the convent of Franciscan nuns, and for several months new customs and traditional practices were observed side by side. Indulgences were preached during Lent at Young St. Peter, the church where Capito was also preaching. Some of the parishioners objected, took the money from the indulgence coffer, and placed it in the alms boxes instead.[30] On April 19, Diebold Schwartz sang the first German Mass in the crypt of the cathedral under

27. It is well to remember this chronicler was Catholic, but the term gives some indication of social consciousness at the time.
28. Büheler, *Chronique*, p. 73.
29. Specklin, *Collectanées*, p. 503.
30. Ibid., p. 502.

the very choir of the great chapter. The chronicler reports that a great group of people heard it. Considering the size of the area, which dates back to the Romanesque foundation of the church it is hard to believe that more than four hundred persons could possibly come together there. Schwartz climaxed the Mass by distributing communion in both kinds and by offering to baptize children in a German service. These innovations won rapid approval and were quickly established at St. Aurelie and St. Martin as well.[31] Yet at the same time pilgrims continued to flock to St. Aurelie to visit the miraculous tomb. Bucer himself preached strongly against this custom, but the faithful continued to go both there and to the shrine and fountain of St. Odile.[32] An indulgence train carrying St. Anstatt's relics arrived in the city in the early summer. It was exceptionally successful, raising more money than usual—so much so that the authorities[33] took away 2,000 gulden that had been collected in Strasbourg alone and put the money in the alms boxes.[34]

Part of the unwillingness to undertake further innovations may have come from a general uneasiness with regard to imperial policy. On May 15 King Ferdinand had ridden in person into Hapsburg territories lying very close to Strasbourg—Freiburg, Breisach and Ensisheim—to read out a strong mandate against evangelical preaching.[35] This put the imperial authority within fifty miles of the city. On July 15, 1524, the emperor himself, although still in Spain, wrote a sharp letter to the estates of the empire, singling out Strasbourg for censure. He was amazed to find that the decrees of the Diet of Worms had not been carried out, that the clergy of the city had married, and that the bishop had not been permitted to punish them. He reprimanded the estates, noting that their request for a council lay outside their

31. Ibid., p. 501.
32. Ibid.
33. The chronicle does not specify whether this was the Rat or the ecclesiastical authorities.
34. Specklin, *Collectanées,* p. 503.
35. Ibid., p. 505.

jurisdiction—it was a question for the pope and the emperor to determine. He would discuss the matter with the pope, but until the Diet of Speyer the cities were to be bound by the edicts of Worms and Nuremberg.[36]

With this admonition, the summer of 1524 passed by in relative peace. In the fall there was a new flurry of activity on the part of the burghers, again directed at the property and possessions of the church. The Rat in this case placed itself firmly in the position of maintaining order and protecting property rights, a policy which led to a sharp conflict between the burghers and the Magistrat.

Several parishes, notably St. Aurelie and St. Martin, had removed pictures and statues from side altars and from the central altar.[37] From time to time pictures were taken down in other churches; in particular, small shrines in the streets had been subject to vandalism and depradation. To prevent destruction and violence, the Rat provided on September 3, 1524, that all pictures be taken out of the churches and cloisters, that this be done carefully, and that the objects be packed away. No one, under pain of serious punishment, was to destroy or carry off any object from a church. The act was put into immediate effect. Seckler, a fuse maker, and his accomplice, a tailor, and their followers, who had been seen taking pictures out of the churches, were imprisoned and punished.[38]

Further efforts were also made to put the financial arrangements of the churches in order. The Rat's August decision to take over the appointment of preachers to the parishes was followed by an edict on September 3 that provided for regular procedures of appointment and for the payment of the salary of the clergy from public funds. The relationship between the clergy and the civil authority was thus made clear. The Magistrat was determined to observe the provisions of the imperial mandate; the preachers, now

36. Ibid., p. 501.
37. Trausch and Wencker, *Chroniques*, p. 152.
38. Brant, *Annales*, p. 101.

being paid by the city, were to admonish the people to observe the law and to support the city authorities.[39]

On November 5, 1524, the city increased the powers of the convent supervisors. Any sale or loan contracted for without the consent of the supervisor was to be invalid, and a yearly accounting was to be given to him. In addition the act provided that no new monks were to be admitted without the knowledge and assent of the supervisor.[40] Technically this was still a financial decision; the supervisor was to determine whether sufficient revenues existed for the support of new members. In reality the Rat was extending full authority over the convents. At Christmas it ordered all clergy to assume Bürgerrecht, placing them directly under its jurisdiction.[41] So when the new officers of the municipal government stood before the cathedral to take their oath, their powers with regard to the persons and property of the church were more clearly defined than ever before.

It was fortunate, for the unrest that had been sporadic was now consolidating. Furthermore, not only was there turmoil in the city itself, but in the nearby villages the peasants were taking up arms against the convents. On January 15, 1525, the imperial commissioner wrote to the Rat that all Alsace was in ferment, that the *Bundschuh* had reappeared, and that a revolt was being propagated in the name of the Gospel. For this reason he was asking the ten imperial cities in the district to join him at Haguenau to discuss the emergency.[42] The developing radicalism was reflected in a petition to the Rat from the gardeners and wagoners on January 18. They requested the authorities to take over all the possessions of the clergy. These were then either to be divided among the burghers, to be put up for sale, or, perhaps, to be distributed by a lottery. The Rat's decision was that

39. Ibid.
40. Vierling, *Die letzten dem Katholizismus Treuen Klöster*, p. 27.
41. Trausch and Wencker, *Chroniques*, p. 151.
42. Rodolphe Peter, "Le Jardinier Clement Ziegler, L'homme et son oeuvre" (Unpublished thèse de baccalaureate en théologie, l'Université de Strasbourg, 1954), p. 89.

it would be necessary to hire a battalion of soldiers to protect the city, and it called together the Constoffler and the Schöffen to approve such a force.[43]

Evangelical preaching in the villages near the city continued to stir the peasants. The city was involved because one of the preachers was a citizen of Strasbourg, a gardener named Clement Ziegler. Although of humble origin Ziegler was literate and intelligent. In the course of a personal crisis in 1524 he experienced a spiritual conversion and became a self-appointed preacher to his own corporation and to agricultural workers outside the city, teaching that there was nothing in the scriptures with regard to seigneurial privileges or with regard to crushing tithes.[44] The Magistrat of Obernai complained of his activity, requesting the Strasbourg authorities to restrain him. The Rat replied that it would take immediate steps, forcing him to return by virtue of his burgher oath.[45] In the meantime, the farmers of the priory of St. Leonard met to protest payments of dues to their landlords, the great chapter of Strasbourg, while other peasants threatened to invade the convents of Hohenburg, Niedermunster, and Truttenhausen. Despite a strict interdiction against preaching in the area, Ziegler went out to the peasants, and an uprising occurred, led, in part, by a Strasbourg innkeeper.[46]

While unrest mounted outside the city, the gardeners continued to press their demands within. They had consistently charged the Magistrat with conservatism and had urged it to move more decisively against the monastic orders and the Chapterherren. They felt that not only should the clergy take on Bürgerrecht but that they should also have to swear the burgher oath. The Rat was able to avoid this only by pointing out that this would give the clergy full and equal rights, including the right to serve as city officials.[47] By January 1525 the gardeners still felt that the Magistrat was

43. Brant, *Annales*, p. 110.
44. Peter, "Le Jardinier Ziegler," pp. 17–18, 84.
45. Ibid., p. 90.
46. Ibid.
47. Ibid., p. 81.

handling the clergy with kid gloves and making too much of a fuss over the "gentlemen." On their own initiative, the gardeners of St. Aurelie, most of whom cultivated lands belonging to the chapter of St. Thomas, had decided not to remit their rents or to pay any fixed dues or tithes.[48] A small group of them made an attack on the *Pfennigturm,* the tower in the heart of the city which served as a treasury. Some of the most radical hoped that they would get aid from the peasants outside to attack the convents within the city.[49]

Despite the unsettled conditions, five of the convents managed to close without incident. In March 1525 the Franciscans and four of the female convents closed voluntarily. The properties were given over directly to the Rat, which returned to each individual the property he or she had offered on entrance and, in addition, provided a yearly pension to be paid until death.[50] The rest of the property, both real estate and revenues, was to be administered by a new commission of *Klosterherren,* made up of one Constoffler and three representatives of the guilds.[51] The monks and the nuns themselves apparently took up their new lives gladly: "The men took wives, the women husbands, as they wished, and they took off their robes and put on other more respectable [sic] clothing . . . and many clergy learned trades."[52]

At this moment, with open revolt threatening in the countryside and with a hard core of dissidents within the city, the Rat was asked to assume authority over the church service itself. Although innovations had been made in translating the Mass into German and in offering Communion in both kinds, the basic liturgy and order of service had never been changed. Now a group of six burghers came forward, citing a recent mandate of the Rat which requested that if a citizen had a grievance against the church, he should not try to remedy it himself, but should bring the matter before the

48. Ibid., p. 82.
49. Ibid., p. 94.
50. Vierling, *Die letzten dem Katholizismus Treuen Klöster,* p. 30.
51. A. Baum, *Magistrat und Reformation,* p. 106.
52. Specklin, *Collectanées,* p. 508.

Magistrat. This procedure had been joyfully received by the burghers, the petitioners said, because it would create an orderly way of doing things, making it possible to bring about improvement, which all the burghers desired. They therefore presented the following grievances.

Too many godless masses are held every day. The Mass makers, without any authority, indeed despite the Word of God, offer the Body and Blood of Christ for the living and the dead as an atonement for their sins. Christ, however, died once as a redemption for all the faithful. Thus the masses are not necessary and are superfluous, and so they are not true, for there is not one thing in all the Holy Scriptures with regard to such masses. Thus it must truly be that these masses come from the devil, for through them shameless harlots and rogues are granted forgiveness and are exonerated of their sins.

It also troubles us, since no scriptures say it is right, that there is that evil idol [sic] in the choir of the cathedral, which is not only a blasphemous offence to many of our people in the city, but to all people in the whole region. For every day one sees people kneeling before it, and praying to it, while these same people obstinately refuse to pay attention to God's Word as it is preached to them. And the silver idol behind the altar in the choir is also evil, and the idols in the entrance to the cathedral, which were recently made into rubble, and now, more than ever, people light candles in front of them during the day, which is a travesty against God and pious customs. In sum we see all images as evil, for they appeal not to the perfected Christians but to the weak and those whom the Word has not yet possessed. All idols are against the Word of God, and no good fruit can come from them.[53]

53. I have purposely refrained from the temptation of smoothing the translation, rendering "gotz" as statue. "Gotz" means idol, in old German as well as in modern, and it is quite clear that the burghers

Reformation or Revolution?

Further it troubles us because we know what the Word of God is—that one day should be like another. And no one can deny that holidays have brought about great error and evil and you, your honors, are responsible before God to help control them. For on holidays people are stimulated and worked up, so that the opposition is strengthened and the weak become dedicated. In this way the disunity and discord between the burghers is preserved and maintained.[54]

The burghers also urged the Magistrat to regulate the inns, which were centers of gambling, blasphemy, and prostitution, and to close the convents because they practiced and advocated customs against the teaching of the scriptures. Recognizing that these were not simple tasks, the burghers pointed out to the authorities their responsibility for their own salvation and that of all the citizens. The Rat could not expect to serve both God and man, but if it was truly to follow God's Word and His Commandments, there would be peace and unity in the city.[55] The petition was signed by Menschen Jacob der Jung, Andres Siferman, Fultzen Hans, Christman Kenlin, Meinolf Dannenföls, and Peter Sigel. Unfortunately only one of these men appears in the burgher register of the city. Andres Siferman is registered as a carpenter, having acquired Bürgerrecht in 1515 through his wife, the widow of a burgher.[56] Menschen Jacob der Jung was a fisherman and appears as one of the Schöffen of his guild at the synod of 1533.[57] Christman Kenlin, a member of the drapers' guild, was in close touch with the peasants and their revolt; later on in the spring (May 14) he was called

are taking a Mosaic view of the decoration of the church, quoting literally from the Ten Commandments.

54. A.S.T., 87, Une délégation des bourgeois demande l'abolition des plusieurs erreurs papistes, March 1525.

55. Ibid.

56. Charles Wittmer, ed., *Le Livre de bourgeoisie de la ville de Strasbourg, 1440–1530* (3 vols. Strasbourg, 1948–60), 2, 624.

57. A.S.T., 75, Namen daran so von Stifften und Zunfte allhie zu das Synode geordnet, 1533.

before the Rat and asked whether he wanted to stay in the city, respecting the obligations of his burgher oath, or whether he wanted to leave and join the peasants. He elected to stay.[58] There is no record of the other two men, and it is impossible to determine whether this was a group of moderates with one rather radical member or whether they were all of the opinion of Kenlin.

The Rat's response came relatively quickly in an edict issued after Easter, 1525. Since the priests no longer preached and fulfilled their responsibility for instructing the people in the Word of God, the Mass would perforce have to be abolished, and in all the parish churches of the city the preachings of the Word should be substituted for the Mass. The Rat was careful to protect itself vis-à-vis the bishop and the empire by providing that the Latin Mass could still be sung in all four chapter churches.[59]

Although this was the most important decision the Rat had made, its immediate effect was slight in view of the mounting tension. Capito wrote to Blaurer that "the rich are very worried about their fortunes, and even in this city, which is so secure, we are not sheltered from the unexpected. A betrayal was projected, it would seem, but failed." [60] On Easter itself the peasants had risen at Dorlisheim, twelve miles outside the city. A rumor had reached them that the bishop had arrested two reformed priests. A fanatic named Erasmus Guerber organized four hundred men to make a punitive expedition against the convent of Altorf. By the time they reached the convent gates the insurgents numbered two thousand men, among them a group of Strasbourg gardeners who distinguished themselves by their brutality in the ensuing pillage.[61] This incident set off a further wave of violence all

58. Archives de la ville, AA Folio 386. I am indebted to M. Rott for telling me that Kenlin appeared at these hearings.
59. A.S.T., 80, Ratschlag des Gotsdiensthalb, 1525.
60. Quoted by Peter, "Le Jardinier Ziegler," p. 94.
61. Ibid., p. 92. In his *pièces justicatives* Peter gives the document: an eyewitness account of the sack of the convent by one Hans Kunde who was sent as an emissary to Altorf. The original is in Archives de la ville de Strasbourg AA 396, folio 24b.

over the countryside. Armed bands went all over but turned chiefly against the clergy and the convents. Churches were burned and sacked; the favorite targets were the convents, which were totally defenseless against a band of three or four hundred men. The bands would gorge themselves in the larder, drink up the wine in the cellars, take the movable treasures, and depart, sometimes burning the building, sometimes content with their loot. The revolt went on until the end of May; some peasants came to the gates of the city and asked for protection and the Franciscan convent was made into a shelter for the refugees.[62] Finally the princes and lords of Alsace turned to Anthony, Duke of Lorraine, for assistance. With a strong army the peasants were put down in a brutal massacre at Saverne and Scherwiller between May 16 and May 20, 1525.[63]

Within the city itself, on May 6, Capito, Zell, Hedio, and Altbiesser assured the Rat of their support and cooperation. Charges had been made that the revolt without and the unrest within stemmed from the Gospel. The preachers asked the Magistrat to stop this slander against the Bible and suggested that it establish some supervision over the guild rooms so that the common men would not be led into error. The final solution would come by establishing schools in which the young people would be trained to honor God and do their duty. Thus disorder would be averted at its roots. For the present the preachers recommended that the cloisters be closed and the Mass abolished because its continuation provoked incidents and divisions.[64]

On May 15 the Magistrat polled the guilds with regard to the policy the city should follow toward the clergy and their property, in particular toward the clergy who were pouring into the city from the countryside, seeking protection within the walls. The answers revealed a rather wide spread in opinion and attitude, ranging from a feeling of responsibility to the clergy to pure anticlericalism. Six guilds

62. Brant, *Annales*, p. 124.
63. Specklin, *Collectanées*, p. 510.
64. Brant, *Annales*, p. 121.

—boatmen, butchers, drapers, *Friburger, Spiegel,* and *Lucern*—felt that the clerical possessions should not be taxed. The implication is that these guildsmen felt the clergy should be permitted to enter the city freely. The *Steltz,* which consisted mainly of goldsmiths, printers and bookbinders, and bakers, unanimously pledged full support to the Rat, come what may, whatever its policy; two guilds said that they did not want the city to protect clerical property. The gardeners were all "good willed" toward the Rat except for one man who said that the clerical property should be divided up. The attitude of the guilds seems to have been remarkably humane toward the clergy. They were to be protected as fellow human beings, but there was less enthusiasm for protecting their isolated properties. Significantly, the loyalty of the guilds to the Rat was clear and unalloyed. In the end the Committee of XIII recommended that a group of mercenaries be hired to protect the city and that citizens be asked to join the group.[65]

The poll of the guilds and the other evidence indicates that the Peasants' Revolt did not establish a foothold within the city itself. It was an agrarian movement whose objective did not appeal to the urban population. Once the crisis was over in late May, neither the Rat nor the bishop attempted to wreak vengeance on the peasants; indeed, the city urged the Count of Bitsch and Hanau not to press so severely on his people.[66] The city merely ordered the residents of its own market towns and villages to swear a new oath to the Rat.[67] The bishop did not demand individual indemnities from all his peasants, but punished only the leaders. Other lords in the area were much harsher; King Ferdinand demanded a fine of three pounds from all his peasants.[68] At the same time, probably as an attempt to meet the social problems within the city, a new welfare policy began to be formulated. Street

65. Ibid., pp. 123–24. See also Rott, "Artisanat et mouvements sociaux," pp. 147–48, for a discussion of the polling of the guilds.
66. Brant, *Annales,* p. 124.
67. Ibid., p. 125.
68. Specklin, *Collectanées,* p. 510.

begging had been forbidden before, but the act was now strictly enforced, the Rat stating that the poor would be taken care of in their own homes by the city and their support would not be left to the whim of an individual almsgiver.[69]

With the suppression of the Peasants' Revolt the social and economic demands of the early period of the Reform terminated abruptly. There can be no doubt that in these early years members of the lower classes were attracted to the Reform because they read into the new teachings a message of economic salvation. This social revolution was quickly aborted because the change sought by the reformers was neither economic nor political. Their object was order. The church had fallen into disorder and was to be restored to its original force and purity, but the preachers had not envisioned that this would involve changes in the traditional economic and social relationships. They saw the Peasants' Revolt as an unfortunate incident that might weaken their religious movement. Now that the revolutionary attempt had been brought under control, the reformers could turn to what they considered the more critical matter, the process of ecclesiastical reform. It is significant that in the series of developments just reviewed, the Strasbourg reformers—Bucer, Zell, Capito, and Hedio—are conspicuous by their absence. Although they had lent support to a fellow cleric if he married and although they had preached vehemently against the convents and the monks, they had given no support to the gardeners or to the peasants. This had come only from Ziegler who was neither ordained nor, at that time, considered by the others to be anything more than a self-appointed street preacher. While they genuinely believed in a better world, born in a new faith in Christ, they conceived of this in a spiritual rather than a political sense. The modern world has been quick to condemn Luther and the other reformers for their failure to become revolutionists and lead men up out of oppression. It is essential to recog-

69. Büheler, *Chronique,* p. 75.

nize that, to them, the injustice was not man-made but part of the God-created order, and it could be changed not by man-made laws but only by God Himself. Man's task, therefore, was not to concern himself with the immediate economic, political, or social world, which was at most ephemeral. Reality was the other world—the world of God—and man's goal was to prepare himself for citizenship therein. This created the urgency in their doctrine, for failure to act would result not in the mere incidental discomfort and distress of this world, but in eternal damnation.

CHAPTER 10

REFORM: ABOLITION OF THE MASS

ROM 1526 to 1529 the efforts of the reformers were focused on establishing a pure form of worship in the churches of Strasbourg, which would create, in turn, a reform of morals and a return to the way of life prescribed by Christ Himself. Eventually this would involve them in a struggle with the Anabaptists, who differed in their definition of pure worship. In 1526, however, their opponents were the bishop, the canons, and the Roman church, and their target was the Mass. Despite the fact that preaching had been substituted for the Mass in the parish churches, Masses continued to be sung daily in the chapter churches, probably attracting a solid number of citizens who maintained their loyalty to the old faith. The struggle that ensued over the abolition of these Masses provides an example of the intricacy of the process of change. Five groups were involved: the evangelical preachers, convinced that the last vestige of the old way must be eradicated; an articulate group of reformed burghers who saw the Masses as a threat to the prestige and unity of the city; a large group of citizens (perhaps the majority) who remained inarticulate; the bishop and the canons, desperately attempting to preserve the ancient, established, ordained order of things; and the Magistrat, divided within itself on the issue, but confronted with the responsibility of maintaining the peace and burgherlike quiet (a favorite phrase of the documents).

The preachers and then their supporters brought pressure

to bear on the Magistrat through consistent propaganda—
a veritable stream of petitions flowed from their pens. As
late as 1527 the Rat was undecided and appealed to the
bishop to aid it in disciplining the preachers, and in 1528
it still hesitated to take the final step of abolishing all the
Masses. The bishop, for his part, maintained a firm opposition, countering each petition from the preachers with a
letter exhorting the Rat to dispense with preaching and return to the old order of things. Unlike the preachers, however, he had no articulate support from his flock and little
from his clergy. In a rather poignant letter in 1527 he appealed to those Constoffler who had received their land from
the diocese, reminding them of their loyalties as vassals and
asking them to refrain from granting any support to the
city,[1] but there was no response. Beset by these rival claims
to the truth and concerned by the division within the city,
the Rat pursued a policy of cautious neutralism. In the end
the tenacity of the articulate and organized minority forced
the Magistrat into decision and action.

The final campaign against the Mass began in 1526 with
a petition from the preachers whose very title set the tone
of their attack:

> That the Mass is no service but a squalling and a
> slander against God and should be abolished by the
> Christian authorities, and cut down root and branch.
> Thus we wish to show the true service of God, accord-
> ing to the Holy Scriptures, so that we may see the mis-
> takes of the Mass and no longer tolerate them.[2]

The preachers set about to prove that the Roman service
was in direct contravention to the Commandments of Christ
and, thus, in error.

> First, it is well known that to serve God and live ac-
> cording to God's will means that we will love Him with

1. Archives de la ville, VI, 701a, 15, Correspondence concernant
la suppression de la messe. Folio 13, Episc. an den Constoffler, Oct. 11,
1527.
2. A.S.T., 80, Das die Mess kein dienst ist, May 18, 1526.

all our hearts and our neighbors as ourselves, for thereon hangs the Law and the Prophets. This is the whole meaning of all Godly teaching and writings.

The whole duty of the Christian, his real service to God, is to show forth the love of God to his neighbor. Thus, our whole life must be directed toward the service of our neighbors and the care of his needs, following the example given us by Christ in his own life. This love of God and one's neighbor brings it about finally that man follows the commands of God, renouncing of his own volition his sinful lusts to take up, with pain and effort, the Cross which was laid down . . . [by Christ].

This alone is the proper, Christian, true, pious, holy life and the only true way of serving God. What rests on this is good, and commanded by God; what does not is evil and evil to God. . . . Thus we wish to give proof that the Mass not only is a false way of serving God but that it is also wholly opposed to the true way.[3]

The Mass was false because it was not commanded by scripture, and God had explicitly abjured man to do nothing except by His command. The Mass was a work created by man which had entangled the free worship of God in lamentable ceremonies that served to deny and ridicule Christ's sacrifice, his death, and martyrdom. It was thus a blasphemy and abominable, and it did not lead a Christian to love his neighbor and help him as he should.

True Communion did not rest on ceremonies and ritual but was achieved whenever companions in Christ came together to thank the Lord and refresh their Christian ties with each other and all the faithful. It was valid only when he who took of it had received Christ and really believed that He had died for him. Christ had desired and commanded this type of worship, and the Magistrat should rise up, armed with the sword of authority given it by God, and abolish the Mass.[4] Another statement presented by the preachers in the

3. Ibid.
4. Ibid.

same year, 1526, summarized the first petition and repeated the same arguments in the same phrases.[5]

The bishop countered these petitions in two letters addressed to the Rat, one in September, the other in December, warning it not to abolish the Mass because such an action would be a direct contravention of imperial law and because it would repudiate the Christian religion, the church, and long-standing and honorable tradition. The bishop protested against the preachers' interpretation that the Mass was without scriptural foundation; for, indeed, the Sacrament had been founded and originated by Christ Himself, and He had performed it. He urged the Rat not to proceed rashly with the changes advocated by the reformers.[6]

The bishop's words did not fall on entirely barren soil. The following spring the Rat apparently felt that the reformers had gone too far in their demands and, in particular, that their preaching led to a continual undercurrent of unrest. On May 6, 1527, it dispatched a delegation to the bishop bearing four pages of instructions that were really a catalogue of the errors of the preachers. When the Rat had attempted to arrange a friendly discussion between the preachers and the chapters, the reformers had refused to come; furthermore, they had openly criticized and opposed such a conference. The Rat had not hindered the preachers in changing certain ceremonies because the people had been led to believe that this was right and in accordance with the scriptures, but now it was clear that the changes had brought nothing but division and discord. The Rat therefore asked the bishop to take the matter into his own hands and to provide for some supervision of the preachers: they should review their sermons with the bishop. That which dealt with

5. A.S.T., 80, (1) Abschrifft der punkten der durch die predicanten zu Strassburg vermeinen die Mess abzuthan, 1526. (2) Punkten die Messe betreffend vie den Predicanten den Stifftn zur tumult (?) Wartung ubergeben, 1526. These documents are two different copies of the same statement.

6. Archives de la ville, VI, 701a, 15, Correspondence concernant la suppression de la messe. Folio 5, Episc. an den Rat, Sept. 24, 1526. Folio 6, Episcop. an den Rat, Dec. 8, 1526.

scripture should be permitted, but anything else should be forbidden. The Rat asked the bishop to set a date when the preachers could appear before him.[7]

This action on the part of the Rat probably caused consternation in the ranks of the reformers. They were faced with the necessity of justifying their preaching and protecting their gains. On October 5 they addressed a long petition to the Ratsherren, half-submissive, half-assertive, protesting their loyalty, and then they called on the Rat in stronger tones than before to abolish the Mass! Their first concern, however, was to affirm their obedience and that of their followers to the civil authority, and to disclaim any intention of assuming political responsibility, for it was not their task to protect the Word of God—that belonged to the magistrates.

> However insignificant we are, those who give us a hearing and follow us will in no way deny your authority, but they will be honorable and respectable, and will follow and be obedient not to us, poor sinful men, but to the Almighty Eternal God, Who has made you his officials to rule this city and has ordered that you alone must guide and protect it, and you yourselves not we, must rule the city. We also recognize that we are far too insignificant to advise you, or to tell you how to rule the city. Thus we will say nothing here which comes from our own mouths or thoughts, we would prefer in such things to simply bring before you the commandments of God . . . , especially we ask that you, our honored magistrates, who do not hear us preach very often, and who are perhaps not pleased by it, will still listen to our speech . . . for it is our responsibility as your servants in the Lord of God to bring these duties before you. And you, as Christian magistrates, must carry them out.[8]

7. Archives de la ville VI, 701a, 15, Correspondence de la suppression de la messe, Folio 8, May 6, 1527.

8. A.S.T., 80, Der Priester begern die Rat Massen abzustellen, Oct. 5, 1527.

The uncomfortable introduction having been got out of the way, the preachers could launch forth into the familiar list of what was wrong in the city—gambling, drinking, inns open and frequented on Sunday, and noise and disturbance in the churches during the preaching (things had not changed much since Geiler von Kaysersberg). What was new in the petition was the emphasis on the Magistrat's responsibility and authority. The city was a body, and it was the function of the Rat to take care of it, guarding and conserving its health.

It is you that are established by God to abolish evil, and since the people are turned away from God by the Mass, so you must realize [that] you will have no excuse if you permit the masses to continue. You have to punish and abolish obvious evils such as robbery, murder and the like; even more, then, must you punish such shocking robbery of God's honor and the murder of the souls that is committed by the Mass. Therefore, you have the highest authority to abolish it in that you are given greater power to deal with the greater evil. First of all, the recess of the Diet of Speyers, permits it. For each authority, in matters of faith, is to act in such a way that they can answer before God and the emperor. . . . How can those who have mocked God answer before the emperor? After they have been warned to have a fear of God, and want nothing less than to forbid the Commandments of God, consequently you can certainly reasonably hope that the imperial authority will not prevail against you, for you are doing what you should do according to God, the greatest emperor.[9]

The petition reflected the preachers' anxiety. They were by no means sure of their reception; indeed, this document and the preceding instructions to the Rat's delegates indicate that relations between the reformers and the Magistrat

9. Ibid.

were not as harmonious as has sometimes been assumed. It has been thought that after 1524 the two worked together to carry out the reform of the city.[10] In actual fact, relations between the two were often strained and uncomfortable. The reformers' statement that the Ratsherren rarely heard them preach and perhaps regarded their sermons unfavorably is particularly revealing. Mutual trust and respect had not been achieved. The preachers even accused the Rat of indecision and of making excuses for their lack of action: "first there was the *Reichstag*, the *Stett tag*, then the Council, then this, then that, which were in the way." [11] They also charged them with bad faith by going to the bishop and thus "disposing the Mass makers against us." [12] Rather sarcastically the preachers added that at least nothing had come of that latter effort!

Sometime during the year the reformers submitted to the Rat a series of alternative services to be used by the canons instead of the Mass—Bucer and Capito each prepared one. The tone of these recommendations was very different from the petitions for abolition; the intransigence of the latter was missing; these were irenic and moderate. The reformers suggested that the canons could come together in the morning during the winter, at one o'clock in the afternoon during the summer, to sing a psalm—or three or four—to listen to

10. Adolf Baum, for example, believed that the whole question of the Reform was conclusively decided by 1524: "The new teaching was in the ascendancy because not only the authorities but also the majority of the burghers had come over to its side. The *Rat* from now on followed an active policy; it opened the city to all refugees who had been persecuted for their faith, it not only changed the form of the old church rituals, but it attacked church ordinances and church rights at their very roots." *Magistrat und Reformation,* p. 97. Even recent studies such as Wendel, *L'Église de Strasbourg,* p. 26, and H. Strohl, *Le Protestantisme en Alsace,* p. 18, give 1524 as the date the city became Protestant. The assumption has usually been made that there was very close cooperation between the Magistrat and the reformers after that date.

11. A.S.T., 80, Der Priester begern die Rat Massen abzustellen, Oct. 5, 1527.

12. Ibid.

a reading from the Bible, followed by exegesis of a psalm or text. If all the chapter members understood Latin, there was no reason why this could not be performed in Latin, but if there were auditors or singers who did not understand Latin, German should be used. There might even be other ways to organize the service, but it must be focused on the Word of God.[13] The preachers were assuming that the Chapterherren would remain in their traditional positions and that the services would be performed. All that was necessary was to replace the Mass by a simpler liturgical form.

During the fall the Rat continued to discuss the matter and must have come to the conclusion that the solution was to turn the matter over to the Schöffen, for on October 11, 1527, the bishop addressed a stiff letter to the Magistrat stating that he had been informed of their intention to let the Schöffen make the decision on the Mass. It was his duty, he reminded them, to exhort them not to take such an action. Instead, he suggested that they should meet with him on November 25 to discuss the matter so that a solution could be found worthy of the people of Strasbourg.[14] The bishop's letter apparently had little effect; there is no indication that the conference he suggested took place; and on November 30 Daniel Mueg submitted to his fellow Ratsherren a memorandum pleading the desirability of a decision by the Schöffen. It was becoming increasingly evident that there should be a unified religious service in the city, and it was only right that the service should be the one authorized by Holy Scriptures; until a council made a definitive decision for the empire as a whole, the responsibility

13. A.S.T., 80. (1) Bedacht und Fortschlag was an statt der Mass in Münster allhie zu Strassburg und anderen Kirchen mochte furgenommen wurd. (Bucer.) 1527.
(2) Quid errgendum et institutuendum pro vice Missae abrogande.
(3) Ordnung wie taglich, von canoniken der stifft zu Strassburg ein christliche gotsdienst offgericht und geholen möcht (Capitonis manus).
14. Archives de la ville, VI, 701a, 15, Correspondence de la suppression de la messe, Folio 12, Episcop. an den Rat, Oct. 11, 1527.

devolved upon the Schöffen.[15] With that the matter was left. In the following Lent—activity always was intensified in this season—six burghers forwarded a petition to the Magistrat. It is interesting to speculate on the initiative behind this move, although no answers can be provided. Did the preachers request them to make their views known to the authorities, or were they simply moved by the words of the Gospel and the sermons to take action? The petition would seem to be the product of the burghers' own efforts rather than a draft drawn up by the preachers to be signed by a few supporters. The phrasing tends to be awkward, and the almost scriptural flow of language that marks the preachers' style is absent. The arguments presented reflect the teaching of the preachers, yet there are political arguments and concerns that were peculiar to the burghers.

The petitioners began by exposing the error of the Mass. It was a desertion from God's original Commandments and the Christ-like simplicity of the Gospel.

Thus we have considered among ourselves, how we could come to a solution. We have talked earnestly together, and there was little choice but to ask you, entreatingly, Your Honors, to abolish the Mass and thus avoid the Wrath of God. But we are so positively warned and instructed, in all this, by the preachers that we as burghers are subject to your Honors, as God has commanded, that we wish to avoid any evil suspicions and semblance of insubordination. Thus we have not held any assemblies, nor will we, although the Mass is abhorrent to us universally, and we know this from each other very well, and in daily burgher affairs we recognize increasingly that assembly and meeting does not produce a better insight but [rather] a worse example. Do not have any doubt, however, that if Your Honors

15. A.S.T., Varia Ecclesiastica, Ia, I 263–265, Daniel Mueg an den Rat, Nov. 30, 1527.

wished to question the guilds you would find them all in accord, that they would pledge body and goods to your Honors, that truly the Mass, in addition to the fact that it is against God, also discredits your Honors and our beloved city abroad, for they say among themselves that we in Strasbourg have two Gods, and thus we are heretic and divided among ourselves, and if you, our worthy Magistrat, permit preaching, why do you not abolish the Mass, which is in opposition to the preaching and to God? [16]

To the burghers unified religious practice was essential to the peace of the city, for division made conflict within and, more significantly, made it difficult to maintain alliances. No city would want to associate itself with another weakened by internal strife. It was thus incumbent upon the Rat to establish and ordain one service which would be accepted by all, for the honor of God, and action should come quickly:

> Your honors must remember that Josiah the King did not let the law of God be read before the people more than one time, then immediately thereafter he destroyed all the blasphemers in Israel. [Nor] did he ask for the consent of his subjects. And he was praised for this. For the sovereign must always bear the burdens for their subjects, whether the latter understand or desire it.[17]

The petitioners made no claim that all the citizens of Strasbourg wanted the Mass abolished. They were not concerned with the problem of the consent of the governed. The Magistrat had only to order, and the burghers would obey. It was not a question of the will of the majority, in any case; it was a question of the Will of God.

The petition was signed by Bastian Erb, Zeisan Claus,

16. A.S.T., 80, Supplication Etlicher Bürger zumb abstellung der Mass, Mar. 18, 1528.
17. Ibid.

Reform: Abolition of the Mass

Cüntz Heldwÿnsticher, Diebolt Kieffer, Wolff Schmidt, Hans von Ehingen. All the signatures are in the same hand, probably that of the professional scribe who made the final copy. Below the signatures was written, still in the same hand, "who, among the common burghers, have been turned to the Word of God." [18] Bastian Erb is the only member of the group who can be thoroughly recorded. A native Strasburgher, he was first elected to the Rat in 1515 and served as a representative of the drapers throughout the decade of the twenties. In 1532 he was appointed a member of the XXI and, in the same year, became the administrator of the hospital for smallpox and syphilis, a responsibility he fulfilled admirably by expanding and improving the foundation.[19] In 1533 he served as one of the Schöffen from the drapers guild to the synod which formed the Reformed Church of Strasbourg.[20] Cüntz Held gave his profession, winetaster, with his signature—the winetasters were well above the artisan level. Hans von Ehingen and Diebolt Kieffer would also be sent as Schöffen from their respective guilds, the Möhrin and the coopers, to the synod of 1533.[21] Zeisan Claus and Wolff Schmidt appear neither in the *Book of the Burghers* nor on the available lists of the corporations.

A subtle social change is noticeable. In 1524 it was the carpenters who were building portable pulpits, and the gardeners who were opening up the tomb of St. Aurelie. Now it was the drapers and winetasters who were pressing the Reform, perhaps an indication that the movement had penetrated to the more solid elements of burgher society. Certainly the objectives of the early supporters of the Reform—the dissolution of the convents and the destruction of the altars—differed from the complaints of these burghers, who wished to abolish the Mass and replace it with a pure

18. Ibid.
19. Otto Winckelmann, *Das Fürsorgewesen der Stadt Strassburg* (Leipzig, 1922), p. 159.
20. A.S.T., 75, Namen daran so von den Stiffter und Zunfte allhie zu das Sinods geordnet, 1533.
21. Ibid.

liturgy. The nascent social revolution of 1524–25 had been diverted into theological channels, and in the process, the support for the movement had broadened.

Another petition of that same year[22] brought forth similar arguments but reflected in particular the burghers' fear of the imminent threat of the Wrath of God if the Masses were continued. The concept of God the Judge and the fear of damnation moved the burghers in this particular instance. The petitioners were, they stated, responsible first to God and wished to honor Him and obey His Commandments, and they were anxious because the city continued to act against the Will and the Laws of God. Certainly the Rat knew that the true Word of God was scorned and blasphemed by many in the city and that the Masses were perhaps the worst evil, yet they had allowed them to remain.

Therefore, honored gentlemen, awake, watch over our wives and children, do not bring down upon us the terrible Wrath of God—thousands *fear the world, but you must fear God,*[23] for the world can only take away our bodies, but God has power over both our souls and bodies, so we, as people, have much more to fear from God. God has all the power and not men. If, however, some of you have not yet known that the masses are against the true Word of God . . . they should dispose of the mass makers and hear our preachers . . . and come to a good teaching and understanding . . . for one cannot depend on men for these matters for many are called and few are chosen, and whether one is called to high authority or to low, to follow them one must become like the Turks.[24]

22. Archives de la ville, VI, 701a, 15, Supplicatio etlicher dran den burgerschafft die Stadt Strassburg nach abschaffung von papstlichen Mass. Folios 18–23. The document itself is undated, but it appears in the dossier, in an ancient binding, together with other documents of the year 1528. Since the later guild petitions refer to a petition presented on St. John's Day (July 1), this may very well be that document.

23. Underlined in the original text.

24. Archives de la ville VI, 701a, 15, Supplicatio, Folio 19.

Reform: Abolition of the Mass

This paragraph provides further evidence of the particular relationship among the burghers, the Rat, and the preachers. Once again there is the implication that the Ratsherren did not all attend preaching; indeed—and this in 1528—perhaps some of them had not yet heard Zell or Bucer. The confused comment at the end would seem to indicate some division on social lines, that persons of high estate tended to remain adherents of the traditional service. In any case the petition reveals that the city was in no way unanimous in its support of the new faith, for it was the existence of an opposition group that made the burghers plead their cause. The people who continued to go to Mass could not be opened to the Truth, and it was they who placed the whole town in jeopardy.

> Some say it is all beyond their understanding, but nevertheless they stick to the blasphemers of the truth . . . and thus will not hear. Some want to believe like the king, others like their fathers, and all the while *Christ must be a liar* and His Word is slandered.[25]

The existence of two services was particularly confusing for the weak because the Mass was said in the cathedral and the other great churches. Thus they supposed it was the true service, reasoning that if it was evil or wrong the Rat would abolish it.[26] Then, when they heard the Word preached, they no longer knew what to believe. The preaching of two services resulted in internal division—there were two parties in the city—and Strasbourg's external position was weakened because those who had formerly respected the free city now saw that it was irresolute and infirm.

It devolved upon the Ratsherren to end this disunion for they were the fathers of the city, and certainly no father would permit blasphemy in his own house; rather he would serve God reverently. The Ratsherren must do as father Jacob had done and keep all blasphemy from the door. Certainly if some worldly authority ordered a heathen service,

25. Ibid., Folio 20. Underlining in the original text.
26. Ibid.

which led to the raping of wives and daughters and all other sorts of evil, the Rat would intervene and provide something better. Yet the Mass resulted in even greater evil for the wives and daughters of the burghers, because it caused their souls to be lost.[27] Since the abolition of the Mass lay within the authority of the Rat, as provided by the Mandate of Speyer, the petitioners requested it to use its powers in the city, just as a father would use discipline in his own house. The supplication was signed, "your humble, obedient burghers, all of whom wish the ascension of the honor of God and the Kingdom of Christ." [28]

The tone of the document was anxious and apprehensive; the burghers feared that the Rat would not act and that the evangelical cause could not stand alone. It needed official support and assistance. Thus the reforming party continued to press its case and to urge the Magistrat to take action. In the fall of the year a series of petitions bearing the names of the guilds was presented, although there were no official signatures of guild officers, nor did the petitions bear the seals of the corporations.[29] It is open to question whether these supplications demanding the abolition of the Mass were ever voted on by the whole corporation since there were older members in many who were still loyal to the old religion.[30] The documents themselves betray a deliberate organized effort, rather than a spontaneous expression of opinions. Fifteen guilds submitted petitions, written in a similar format, in the hand of a professional scribe. Each

27. Ibid., Folio 21.
28. Ibid., Folio 23.
29. In general a seal was used only on a parchment document, and the petitions were written on paper. Three of the corporations presenting petitions, the boatmen, the masons, and the Möhrin, are known to have possessed seals. Cf. F. J. Fuchs, *Inventaire des archives de la ville de Strasbourg* (Strasbourg, 1960), p. 318.
30. Cf. Röhrich, *Geschichte der Reformation, 1,* 356. Röhrich believed that the five guilds which abstained from the petition did so because the guild master or the Schöffen were opposed to the reform. He also felt that the majority of the guilds probably knew nothing about this petition and that it was handled by a small minority.

petition said exactly the same thing, in the same words, except that some omitted the introductory paragraph of salutation. The only differences are in spelling. It is perfectly clear that each was copied from one original master copy, and they may have been presented to the Magistrat without having been read before their assembled guild companies. The names of the following guilds appear on the petitions: boatmen, butchers, furriers, coopers, winetasters, tailors, smiths, shoemakers, carpenters, gardeners, and masons, as well as those guilds called by the name of the inn in which they met—Spiegel, Friburger, Lucern, and Möhrin. The five guilds not involved were the tanners, the bakers, the goldsmiths, the drapers, and the fishermen. The text read:

Our honored Masters, we have petitioned you on the next Sunday before St. John's[31] and trusted in you as the honored Rat, our gracious lords, that you would bring forward our request with regard to the Mass, directly on the following Monday. [For the Mass] is certainly against God and brings the common *burgerschaft* into animosity one against the other. Since there has been no answer thereon, and since nothing has been done about it, it is our request to the honorable Rat to humbly bring forward this idea once again.

First, a common burgerschaft should be instructed in the truth, and a great dispute exists whether the Mass is a judgment against faith and love, and therefore it is our humble and earnest desire that such blasphemy against God should be abolished by you our gracious lords.

Second, as it was decided by the Schöffen and Ammen that the Gospel should be preached and that we should live and act [according to it], it follows that the mass should be abolished.

Third, thereby God's honor would be furthered, and this is something we should all work on.

31. St. John the Baptist's Day, July 1. Is this a reference to the petition of the humble, obedient burghers?

Fourth, also our neighbors would be better toward us, since now the masses make bitterness and trouble and move them to speak stupidly of us, namely that those of Strasbourg have two Gods, the evangelical God through preaching and the papist God through the Mass.

Fifth, the four masses create a division and schism among the burgerschaft which goes on every day and which will not come to a good end. With the abolition of the mass this would be abolished.

Sixth, that our gracious masters should remember that the citizens have always been obedient and that they have endured much so that no animosity would exist among themselves, and they, the citizens, must now wonder whether our gracious masters pay much attention to them. For they have so often petitioned and have received no answer, while other leaders have acted in accordance with their requests and supplications.

Finally, this we do in humble obedience. We see daily what need there is for it, not only for the honor of God, but for the city in general, and for us all. We wish therefore to entreat you for an answer.[32]

The relationship among the various petitions—those from the preachers, the six burghers, the humble burghers, and the guilds—is of some interest. In addition to certain phrases, such as the "Mass as a blasphemy against God," "Strasbourg has two Gods," there is a common thread of argument in all the evangelical petitions, both lay and ecclesiastical, as far back as the earliest statements in favor of preaching in 1524. The petitioners never claimed to represent the majority. Consistently they stated that they were forced to act by the weak, who still insisted on going to Mass and on following the old customs. It was this obstinate behavior on the part of the other citizens that caused dissension and di-

32. Archives de la ville de Srasbourg, Series VI, 701a, 16, Der Zunft Supplicationes umb Abschaffung der Babstische Mess, 1528.

vision, for instead of accepting the truth, they remained blind. Under these circumstances the only solution was to abolish what was in error so that the truth might flourish. Truth was an absolute that permitted only one solution, and the reformers demanded the same totality of obedience which the Roman Church had required. The force of the evangelical movement lay in this very dogmatism, in its oneness of conviction. Although the bishop was unable to arouse either the faithful or the clergy to unite with him against the enemy, the preachers could count on a dedicated minority, whose beliefs stirred them to action, conscious that they were clad in the armor of righteousness.

In the fall of the year the preachers renewed their offensive. Capito addressed a four-page statement to the Magistrat, urging abolition of the Mass, repeating the arguments he had used before.[33] Bucer also presented a statement whose general tone was clearly revealed by its title, "That the Mass is the worst insult to God and idolatrous and not to be tolerated by any Christian Magistrates."[34] The prolonged attack finally bore results. During the month of December the Rat discussed the question at length. Klaus Kniebis, a member of the XIII and former Ammeister, pressed the case for abolition, citing the unrest, division, and tension in the city, but his major emphasis was theological. Had the Mass been commanded by God? If not, then it should be abolished without waiting further for a council.[35] Martin Betschold, also a member of the XIII, spoke with equal vehemence in opposition to abolition, for it would be a direct contravention of the Edict of Worms and the Recess of Speyers to make any change in the religious practices or customs; and it was his opinion that the preaching of the Pure Word of God instead of bringing the burgher to a new depth of spiritual understanding had only created blas-

33. A.S.T., 80, Capito Entschuldigt seiner red, 1528.
34. A.S.T., 80, Dass die Mess die schwerest gottesschmack und abgottery und von keiner christlichen oberkeit zu dulden sy, Dec. 31, 1528.
35. A. Baum, *Magistrat und Reformation*, pp. 178–79.

phemy, immorality, and profiteering.[36] The bishop addressed yet another letter to the Rat urging it to retain the Masses in the name of God, the Holy Roman Emperor, and peace and unity.[37] The bishop asked the cathedral chapter to add its protest to his own, but the canons, evincing the internal divisions that were so destructive to the Roman church, replied that they were uncertain about the matter and did not want to add to the general agitation.[38] The bishop therefore turned to the pope, the emperor, and the *Reichskammergericht*, but his request for immediate intervention was lost in the procedural maze of the imperial chamber.[39]

On January 10, 1529,[40] the Rat laid the question of the abolition of the Mass before the Schöffen, counseling them not to vote immediately on the matter but to consider the matter carefully, both within their corporations and in solitude at home, in view of the dangers that could befall them from the opposition of the bishop and others. Meanwhile, in mid-January Jacob Sturm wrote from Worms, where he was meeting with Phillip of Hesse, that the city should avoid any defiant or disobedient action as long as the Diet was in session. The question before the Schöffen was then reworded: Should the Mass be abolished, or should the city wait to take action until after the Diet had dissolved? On February 20, when the Schöffen met, 94 voted that no action should be taken and that the Mass should remain until the end of the Diet; 184 voted that the Mass should be abolished *until it could be proved that it was a pious form of worship*. One single vote was recorded that the Mass should never be abolished, now or ever.[41]

The Rat immediately released a nine and one-half–page

36. Ibid., p. 180.
37. Archives de la ville, VI, 701a, 15, Correspondance concernant la suppression de la Messe, Folio 16, Episc. an den Rat, Dec. 8, 1528.
38. A. Baum, *Magistrat und Reformation,* p. 183.
39. Ibid., p. 184.
40. Archives de la ville, VI, 701a, 15, Correspondance concernant la suppression de la Messe, Folio 26, Was der Schoffen der Mass halb furgehaben, Jan. 10, 1529.
41. A. Baum, *Magistrat und Reformation,* p. 188.

justification of the action to the Bürgerschaft. From this it was quite clear that the various petitions had been carefully read and that the arguments put forward both by the preachers and the burghers had had their effect. The threat of the Wrath of God and the lack of scriptural foundation for the Mass were the deciding factors for the Magistrat. The justification reviewed the recent developments. The preachers had preached against the Mass for several years and had described it as a blasphemy against God. As a result, various burghers had petitioned the Rat to abolish the Mass; the Rat had given the matter long and careful consideration as part of its responsibility to guard and protect the Burgerschaft from the future Wrath of God. Its decision to abolish the Mass was based on the terrible consequences that might result if it were continued.

In order to learn the Will of God, we had no other human way than what we could learn through reading or through hearing preaching from the holy Biblical and Apostolic writings. This same Scripture does not leave any doubt but that it is the ancient true Godly writing and it cannot be denied even by God Himself. It is further true that false service to God is specifically called blasphemy and also that God the Lord was often moved by anger both in the Old and New Testament against his people. . . . The Mass for a long time has meant nothing more than a death duty, so it is against the Word of God and the teachings of Jesus Christ . . . and thus a blasphemy before God. Also . . . the Wrath of God should be published and proclaimed thereby. The Mass therefore is unholy, and it is the responsibility of the Magistrat to carry out the Commandment of God.[42]

The Rat had not taken action before because the Will of God had not used its power to make the Pure Word under-

42. A.S.T., 80, Die Herren an die Burgherschafft wegen abschaflung der Mass und annemung Christliche Religion, 1529.

173

standable; the Ratsherren had not been sufficiently instructed.[43] But now God's Word had been made known—His Will and Commandments were clear, and the Rat had no alternative but to act.

These were the theological reasons for abolishing the Mass; justifying this action in terms of the emperor and imperial policy was much more difficult. The Rat had no desire, it emphasized, to put the city in a dangerous position politically or to veto the Edict of Worms. As an indication of its good intent it reviewed the terms of the Edict, outlining the penalties for any imperial citizen who helped Luther by word or deed. Its own actions, it said, clearly did not fall within these provisions. The Rat had never attempted to conceal its desire for further negotiation on the religious question; indeed, representatives of the city had petitioned the Bishop of Hildesheim for a national council to discuss the matter of the abolition of the Mass. The imperial authority, however, had indicated that it had no intention of changing the original mandate and had sent an embassy from the *Reichsregiment* urging the city to take no action against the Mass. The Magistrat, meanwhile, had never ceased to hope that a general council or national assembly would be called to discuss the religious question and that the city would then be able to make a decision in terms of the policy established by such a council. The canons of the Strasbourg chapters for their part had vigorously advised the Rat not to abolish the Mass and had warned it that any move against the old service would arouse the chapters.

Thus, the Rat had been beset from all sides and had found the matter exceedingly difficult to decide. It had therefore determined to turn to the burghers themselves to find out what they wished to do. For this reason it had summoned the Schöffen and Ammen, having agreed to abide by their decision, as was established by ancient custom. And, the Ratsherren piously remarked at this point, it must always be remembered that God Almighty had not sent velvet for man-

43. Ibid.

kind, but a cross. The decision thus had finally been made, and it was to be hoped, the Ratsherren concluded, that it would establish unity and love, for through unity small things could become great, but through division and conflict great things would come to nothing. The last lines were a benediction: "For God will preserve us and keep us, and His peace will be established among us, Amen." [44]

The tone of the mandate was subdued, and every attempt was made to indicate that the Ratsherren had tried every possible alternative. They had waited for a national council, but none had been called. The final decision to call in the Schöffen and Ammen was an evidence of the Rat's political adroitness, for the responsibility for abolishing the Mass fell not on the Rat and XXI, but was divided among the three hundred members of the Schöffen and Ammen. The Ratsherren stressed that they had not initiated the policy but that they had simply carried out the decision made by the other group, as was required by ancient custom. Significantly, at no point in the document was it clearly stated that the Mass was abolished: It was only said that the Rat would abide by the decision of the Schöffen and Ammen; thus the final result was merely that the Mass would be set aside until it was established that it was pleasing to God.

The Rat not only informed the Bürgerschaft in full detail but also wrote the bishop to inform him of the decision. The bishop's reply was prompt and unequivocal. He had attempted all through the affair to give true, fatherly advice, and he was convinced that the matter should not be decided until a council had been held. The action of the Schöffen was against his will and his authority as ordinary of the city. [45]

The petitions viewed as a whole indicate that the process of the magisterial reformation was slower and more tenuous

44. Ibid.
45. Archives de la ville, VI, 701a, 15, Correspondance concernant la suppression de la Messe, Folio 35, Episc. an den Rat, Feb. 22, 1529.

than has sometimes been thought.[46] The abolition of the Mass was perhaps the central element in the program of reform; yet it took five years to achieve it. The petitions of the reformers as late as 1527 indicate that there was little real cooperation between reformers and Rat, nor was the Magistrat eager to enact into law the reforms the preachers felt were essential. The Reform was not the result of a close cooperation between Bucer and Sturm, reformers and Magistrat. It was the result of the zealous efforts of a minority. Leadership came from the reformers, but the burghers themselves developed a group capable of articulating its own ideas and influencing policy. The relentless activity of preachers and burghers together pushed the Magistrat toward decisions that it did not wish to make. It preferred to temporize. It wished to avoid clear-cut statements and definitive policies. Overwhelmingly concerned with the problem of the emperor and still hopeful that it could maintain a tenuous peace with the bishop, the Rat served as a brake on the projects of the reformers. In the end it had not created policy, it had acquiesced in the decision of the militant.

46. See page 161, footnote 10.

CHAPTER 11

THE REJECTION OF RADICALISM: THE ANABAPTISTS

HE Anabaptist movement played a particular and especial role in Strasbourg,[1] providing a strong counterpoint to the themes of the more orthodox Reformation. It developed from many sources, and perhaps nothing could better indicate the proliferative nature of ideological change. Luther and his followers, like Zell and Bucer, had started to preach the Gospel—Anabaptism evolved out of the infinite possibilities of divergent interpretation. It emphasized doctrines that were not central to or were in opposition to Lu-

1. Fundamental work has recently been done on the Anabaptist movement in Strasbourg. This chapter does not attempt a comprehensive review of all the Anabaptist activity but is confined to an analysis of the effect of the Anabaptists on the development of the Reform in the city. The following sources should be consulted for further information:

George M. Williams, *The Radical Reformation* (London, 1962). Detailed biographical material on the individual Anabaptists who came to Strasbourg is available on pp. 241–78. Referred to hereafter as Williams, *Radical Reformation*.

Charles B. Mitchell, "Martin Bucer and Sectarian Dissent" (Unpublished Ph.D. thesis, Yale University, New Haven, Conn., 1960). A careful study of the relations between Bucer and the Anabaptists which had been subject to misinterpretation. Referred to hereafter as Mitchell, *Sectarian Dissent*.

Manfred Krebs and Hans Georg Rott, *Elsass I, Stadt Strassburg 1522–32, Elsass II, Stadt Strassburg 1533–35*, Quellen zur Geschichte der Täufer, 7–8 (Gütersloh, 1959–60). A definitive and comprehensive collection of the documents, carefully annotated. Referred to hereafter as Krebs and Rott, *Elsass, I* or *Elsass, II*. Hans Georg Rott

ther, Zwingli, or Bucer, and most important, it caught up those vague aspirations for social justice and social change that the more orthodox reformers were incapable of assimilating.

Although the data are fragmentary and incomplete, Anabaptism seems to have sprung from and to have drawn its support from the artisan and peasant levels of the social order. A study of Swabian Anabaptism finds that while the rich upper classes and the intellectuals of the imperial cities were not entirely immune, the majority of town dwellers who joined the sectarians were craftsmen and their wives. The overwhelming majority of Anabaptists in Swabia were, however, peasants and village people.[2] In Strasbourg the lists of Anabaptist prisoners record tailors, tinkers, shoemakers, fishermen, weavers, and rummage dealers rather than drapers, goldsmiths, and winetasters.[3] Thus in general the pattern would indicate a particular response to the social emphasis of the doctrines.

Anabaptist teaching was suffused by a sincere and genuine Christian socialism. The sectarians took the words of the New Testament in their most literal sense, seeing in them a blueprint for a new order, patterned on the Christian communities envisioned by the Apostles. The heart of their doctrine lay in their different view of the nature and purpose of the church—essentially they believed that civil society was extraneous, that the true Christian needed only the

---

is the same person as Jean Rott. When publishing in German he uses the German form for his name.

Rodolphe Peter's thesis on Clement Ziegler gives an excellent account of the very early developments. Unfortunately, the thesis is not on deposit in the University of Strasbourg Library. M. Peter kindly lent me his own copy. I have summarized as much of the material as I could in order to make it available.

2. Claus Peter Clasen, "The Sociology of Swabian Anabaptism," *Church History, 32* (1963), 154–55.

3. Krebs and Rott, *Elsass, I,* no. 224, Verhöre in Wiedertäufersachen, October 22–23 (and shortly before), 1530, p. 268 ff. and no. 234, Bericht über einige Strassburger Wiedertäufer, 1530–1546, pp. 288–89.

ILLUSTRATIONS

All of the illustrations are from the
Cabinet des Estampes de Strasbourg

1. Martin Bucer (1491-1551).

2. Wolfgang Capito (1478-1541).

3. Matthäus Zell (1477-1548).

4. Caspar Hedio (1494-1552).

Détail des Bagues de la main gauche.

5. Jacob Sturm von Sturmeck (1489-1553).
(Member of the Rat from 1524-1553)

6. Jean Sturm — Humanist and Teacher.

church, which should be a voluntary association, free of any hierarchy. Rejecting the principle of catholicity, they conceived of a gathered, exclusive society, open only to those who had experienced profound religious transformation or conversion. These persons—both men and women—were the chosen, directly called by Christ to purify the church and the world. It was their responsibility to reestablish the forgotten Christian community of the New Testament, to restore the fallen order.[4] This doctrine of the gathered church led the Anabaptists to reject infant baptism since baptism could be meaningful only after the conversion experience. Adult baptism was a symbol of selection, of entry into the society of saints. Spiritual, otherworldly, critical, and censorious, the doctrines appealed, on the one hand, to the restless and the oppressed, and on the other, to the visionary and the idealistic, and it was men of this nature who became Anabaptists.

They were drawn to Strasbourg for a variety of reasons. One was simply geographic. Anabaptism's major centers were in Switzerland and the Low Countries, and Strasbourg was the crossroads of the main traveled route between the two—since Strasbourg boatmen dominated the Rhine all the way to Mainz, a traveler had to stop to change boats. More important was the particular nature of the Strasbourg Reform and the presence of three men instead of a single, dogmatic leader. Neither Bucer, Capito, nor Zell had a personality like Luther's, which forced other men to accept his beliefs or to leave. The Strasbourg reformers were temperate by comparison, and it was well known that they were neither pure Lutherans nor pure Zwinglians. Men who found themselves in disagreement with the new prophets sought out the Strasburghers as possible confreres. Strasbourg had not developed a definitive doctrine; it had neither a distinctive liturgy nor particular forms of worship. Indeed, Bucer, Capito, and Zell were still open on the important question

4. Franklin Hamlin Littell, *The Anabaptist View of the Church* (Boston, 1952), p. xvi.

of infant baptism. As late as 1524 Bucer wrote that while infant baptism was preferable, providing the parents of the child with the faith and confidence born of the child's acceptance into the Christian community, nevertheless if parents wished to wait on baptism and could do it without destroying love and unity, they should not be condemned for this, but each should act according to his convictions in the matter.[5] Bucer was careful to state that such practice was acceptable only insofar as the parents remained in the bosom of society, but this type of open-mindedness promoted sectarian dissent. Finally, Strasbourg attracted Anabaptists because of its civic reputation for clemency and moderation. While other cities drowned and burned the sectarians, Strasbourg maintained her humanitarian tradition.[6] Her citizens were proud that their penal code had never been as severe as that of other German cities. Sebastian Franck, himself an Anabaptist who sought shelter in the city, wrote that "he who would be hanged elsewhere is simply beaten out of Strasbourg with rods."[7]

When the Anabaptist leaders first arrived, they were welcomed by the Strasbourg reformers, who saw them as fellow preachers, brothers in Christ, or as fellow opponents of Luther. In the early years all were united by their common rejection of the Mass, their opposition to monasticism, and their desire to restore the pure church. In the interminable discussions and colloquies that went on in the ministerial circle, certain doctrinal differences appeared. At first these did not seem too important because there was no single dogmatic formulation, and a man's piety and sincere religiosity were paramount. As the movement developed out of this

5. Text quoted in Peter, "Le Jardinier Ziegler," p. 61.
6. Phillipe Dollinger, "La Tolérance à Strasbourg au XVIᵉ siècle," in *Hommage à Lucien Febvre* (Paris, 1954), p. 245.
7. Quoted by Peter, "'Le Jardinier Ziegler," p. 41. The original statement was made by Franck in his *Chronica*, which he published in Strasbourg in 1531. Having made unfortunate references to the German imperial eagle as a bloodthirsty bird, he was expelled from the city, but not hanged!

early phase, it became necessary to establish new services and liturgies to replace the old and to provide some form of organization and discipline. At this point the differences between Anabaptism and Reform widened and became schismatic. Bucer was the first to recognize the problem, but it was difficult for him to convince Capito and Zell of the inherent dangers of sectarianism. In the end the Strasbourg reformers regarded Anabaptism as an enemy as satanic as Rome itself—the Anabaptists became the opposition against which an orthodoxy could be formulated. To suppress sectarian teaching and practices, a synod was called in 1533, from which proceeded the definitive doctrine and structure of the reformed church of Strasbourg. Thus, Anabaptism at first was an evidence of the vitality and richness of the early Reformation, when new forms and doctrines were explored. Later it became the cathode, in reaction to which the new church was established.

The movement started in Strasbourg with the spontaneous preaching and teaching of Clement Ziegler, a gardener, living in the Krutenau, a suburb to the south of the city, where he rented lands belonging to the convent of St. Nicholas in Undis. His preaching and teaching included all the most confusing elements of sectarianism. In a sense he never was an Anabaptist because he never divorced himself from the traditional church organization, but he was a fundamentalist, a Christian socialist, and an idealist whose doctrines were at once radical, mystical, and unorthodox.

Having experienced a direct revelation of Christ, he undertook to share it with his fellow gardeners—"Why shouldn't I give my life to the whole community, for even if there are dangers in doing so, God helped me out of deep waters in 1524." [8] Having been called, he hoped he could substitute a true Christian brotherhood for the beer, gossip, and card playing of the gardeners' guild hall, and he began to read to his fellow workers, explaining the Bible that was available in German from one of the Strasbourg presses.

8. Quoted in Peter, "Le Jardinier Ziegler," p. 17.

In this way the guilds became an important focal point of the Reformation, not only in Strasbourg but in other cities of Southern Germany and Switzerland.[9]

At the same time Ziegler began to write and to publish. His first treatise, published in 1524, bears witness to an intermingling of the old and the new. Entitled *Von der Vermehelung Marie and Josephs*,[10] it asserted the entirely spiritual nature of Mary's marriage to Joseph, which continued even after the birth of Christ. Ziegler's object, however, was not to encourage the cult of Mary, but to reveal the mystery of the Incarnation, the way in which the Word was made flesh.[11] Two other tracts published in the same year[12] were far more provocative. By 1524 preaching was permitted in Strasbourg's churches, the Mass had been said in German, and communion had been distributed in both kinds, but this did not satisfy Ziegler. In his pamphlets he attacked the monks, the priests, and the reforming preachers in turn: The priests were mere lackeys who did nothing except for money; whereas the preachers preached the Gospel in one breath but still recited the same old prayers for the dead and the exorcisms of the baptismal service, even though they had translated them into German.[13] He deplored the worship of saints and other images in the churches and finished up with a rousing denunciation of the sacraments from baptism to extreme unction.

Ziegler's teaching may have been directly responsible for the vehement action of the parish of Young St. Peter in 1524, which included stripping the church of all its statuary, and for the gardeners' pillage of the tomb of St. Aurelie in November 1524.[14] By the following spring, however, his atten-

9. Ibid., p. 34.
10. On the Marriage of Mary and Joseph.
11. Peter, "Le Jardinier Ziegler," pp. 37–39.
12. *Ein Kurtz Register und Auszzug der Bibel* (A Short Index and Summary of the Bible) and *Von der Waren Nyessung beyd leibs und blut Christi* (Of the Real Reception both of the Body and Blood of Christ).
13. Peter, "Le Jardinier Ziegler," p. 46.
14. Ibid., pp. 54, 56.

tion had shifted to the peasants. A convinced Christian socialist, Ziegler was moved by the condition of the agrarian workers and condemned the heavy financial burden of both rent and tithe. A sense of justice led him into the villages to teach and preach a doctrine of Christian equality. All were brothers before Christ, and the time was ripe for men of good will to unite in a true Christian community, dividing the goods of the world evenly among all.[15] Yet he found only too quickly that his message was misinterpreted and twisted by the fanatics among the peasants, and he was appalled by the brutality, tyranny, and excesses of the leadership. Disillusioned, he returned to Strasbourg, convinced that the Kingdom of God could not be built by the hands of men, only to find that his supporters in Strasbourg had abandoned him for the more zealous Anabaptism of Balthazar Hubmaier.[16]

A former professor of theology who had led the reform of Waldshut in the Black Forest, Hubmaier had arrived in the city in 1525, advocating the restoration of the economic and social customs of the primitive church, including community of goods.[17] Under his influence the first Anabaptist congregation was organized and began to hold meetings. Five Anabaptists brought before a police tribunal in 1526 testified that, led by Jacob Gross, a disciple of Hubmaier, they had met in a house in the suburb of Ruprechtsau. Gross taught from the scripture, and adult baptism had been practiced. They described the form of worship, which began with a common prayer in which they asked God to give them strength to bear the Cross; then each member interpreted passages from the scripture according to his own understanding. In his own testimony Gross explained that although he was loyal to the Magistrat and would perform customary civic duties of the watch and protection, he would not kill another man. As another unorthodox element, the group

15. Ibid., p. 85.
16. Ibid., p. 65.
17. Williams, *Radical Reformation*, p. 252.

practiced division of goods, sharing the fruits of their individual labor. The record lists as participants a potter, a tailor, a tanner, a cooper, and several women.[18] Although the group was thus known by the police at a fairly early date, the record reveals that it remained active until the Synod of 1533.[19] It is difficult to trace the relations between this group and the refugees coming in from other cities who seem to have maintained their own groupings.

Ziegler never joined this Ruprechtsau congregation, partially because he was unwilling to contribute to disunity among the burghers, having seen the result of excess and violence among the peasants.[20] On December 18, 1525, he purchased Bürgerrecht, and even served as a tithe collector.[21] From then on he withdrew from his more provocative activities and wrote tracts that became increasingly visionary and mystical. Never ordained, and thus never given an official church appointment, he served the people of Ruprechtsau during the plague, when their ordained priest fled. He cared for the sick and the dying, oblivious of the danger to himself, and assumed the duties of the pastor in the emergency but was never given the post. Although the Anabaptists exhorted him to join their society of saints and although the reforming preachers refused to accept him as a colleague, he maintained the integrity of his own beliefs, but within the collective body of the Christian church. The only native Anabaptist leader, he never had an Anabaptist congregation.

In March 1526 Anabaptists from all over Southern Germany began to arrive in Strasbourg—Hans Wolff (a weaver from Benfeld), Martin Borrhaus (known as Cellarius),

18. Krebs and Rott, *Elsass, I,* no. 67, Verhör der Wiedertäufer Jörg Tucher, Jacob Gross, Wilhelm Echsel, Matthis Hiller und Jörg Ziegler, 1526 (end), pp. 62–67.
19. Ibid., passim.
20. Mitchell, "Sectarian Dissent," p. 184.
21. Krebs and Rott, *Elsass, I,* no. 40, Clemens Ziegler wird Voller Bürger der Stadt Strassburg und Wirkt als Zehntrechner im Vorort Ruprechtsau, December 18, 1525 and 1526, pp. 49–50.

The Rejection of Theological Radicalism

Michael Sattler, Ludwig Hetzer, Hans Denck—all but Wolff major leaders of the movement. Hetzer and Cellarius settled down to live with Capito, who saw them as fellow Hebraists; they worked with him on a translation of the Old Testament. They did not press their views on either the reformers or the burghers, but Hetzer moved on after a year's stay.[22] Denck was more active. He made immediate contact with the Ruprechtsau group and preached openly to all who would listen. Two of the Ratsherren found him preaching in the old Dominican cloister to some four hundred burghers.[23] The reformers met him in an open disputation on December 25, 1526, and he was expelled from the city.[24]

The reformers' correspondence from this period shows them struggling with the intolerance and dogmatism of the Anabaptists. The sectarians, they discovered, were firmly convinced of the absolute right of their own beliefs, but they were entirely unwilling to grant the reformers the same prerogative; indeed, they did not hesitate to castigate the preachers for their errors and lay bare their falseness to the world. Capito, in a letter to Prugner, the reformer in Mülhausen, descibed a typical incident. Wolff had publicly attacked Zell in the cathedral while the latter was preaching. Capito deplored the self-pride and vanity which the Anabaptist had displayed.[25] In December Bucer wrote to Farel, admiring the piety and character of Cellarius, contrasting it with Denck, who had thrown the Strasbourg church into confusion. The implication was clear that Bucer would be delighted to see Denck leave.[26]

The Magistrat kept a weather eye on the whole develop-

22. Williams, *Radical Reformation*, p. 251.
23. Krebs and Rott, *Elsass*, I, no. 65, Ratsverhandlung über die Disputation der Strassburger Prediger mit (Denck), December 24, 1526, p. 61.
24. Williams, *Radical Reformation*, p. 251.
25. Krebs and Rott, *Elsass*, I, no. 50, Capito an Prugner, Bericht über ungebührliches Benehmen des (Hans Wolff) im Strassburger Münster., June 10, 1526, pp. 54–55.
26. Krebs and Rott, *Elsass*, I, no. 62, Bucer and Farel, Über Cellarius und Denck, Dec. 13 (1526), p. 59.

ment. On February 21, 1526, when Bucer, Engelbrecht, and Zell informed it that children were not being brought in to be baptized, the Rat ordered that on an assigned day all unbaptized children were to be brought in and that no further changes were to be made from traditional procedures.[27] It acted quickly and with dispatch to expel Wolff and Denck, and at the end of the year brought the Ruprechtsau group before the tribunal for hearing. At the very end of the year, December 31, the Rat issued a statement that the Anabaptists were to be sent away.[28]

February and March of 1527 saw an increase in sectarian activity in the Rhineland. The Rat of Nuremberg wrote to its counterpart in Strasbourg on March 21, warning it against Anabaptists and their disruptive influence.[29] In July, Bucer wrote Zwingli that the Anabaptists wearied the reformers by refuting the scriptures openly and denying the satisfaction of Christ,[30] but he followed this with a letter saying that the Rat was considering some action and that three men had already been taken into custody.[31] On July 27, 1527, the Rat issued its "first" [sic] mandate against the Anabaptists. Since the Anabaptists were unwilling to recognize the authority of the magistrates, in defiance of all the commandments of scriptures, and since they had actively stirred up unrest and dissension, they must all leave the city, and all the citizens were warned that they were not to give them shelter, food, or drink but were to turn them away, under pain of punishment.[32]

27. Krebs and Rott, *Elsass, I*, no. 44, Ratsbeschluss betr. die Kindertaufe, Feb. 21, 1526, p. 51.
28. Krebs and Rott, *Elsass, I*, no. 68, Ratsverchandlung betr. die Wiedertäufer, Dec. 31, 1526, p. 67.
29. Krebs and Rott, *Elsass, I*, no. 79, Der Rat von Nuremburg an den von Strassburg, March 21, 1527, p. 79.
30. Krebs and Rott, *Elsass, I*, no. 88, Bucer an Zwingli, Über die Strassburger Wiedertäufer, July 8, 1527, p. 115.
31. Krebs and Rott, *Elsass, I*, no. 89, Capito an Zwingli, Bericht über die Strassburger Wiedertäufer, July 9, 1527, p. 116.
32. Krebs and Rott, *Elsass, I*, no. 92, Erste Strassburger Ratsverordnung gegen die Wiedertäufer, July 27, 1527, pp. 122–23.

The Rejection of Theological Radicalism

The edict apparently had little effect. By the spring of 1528 the unity and peace of the reformers themselves was in peril; the preachers were rent by the fear that Capito himself had defected from orthodoxy. Martin Cellarius had lived in Capito's house from the time of his arrival in 1526. No longer associating with his Anabaptist friends, he had lived the life of a quiet, religious man.[33] Even Bucer had extolled his virtues to Zwingli, and while he admitted that Cellarius retained his original opposition to infant baptism, in view of the orthodoxy of the rest of his views, Bucer felt that this one defection could be forgiven.[34]

Then in April 1528, Capito published his *Commentary on Moses,* and his discussion of infant baptism was open to the charge of Anabaptist influence. When Bucer admonished him, Capito replied that he could see no other interpretation of the scriptural source.

Bucer was deeply concerned. He saw Capito's book as a threat to the unity of the Strasbourg movement and wrote to Zwingli and Oecolampadius urging them to use their influence on Capito. The latter responded to the plea of the unity of the church; by June the crisis had passed, and the responsibility for Capito's flirtation with unorthodoxy was placed squarely on Cellarius. The incident marked a turning point for the reformers. Until that moment none of them had fully realized that the differences in opinions were so serious; the Anabaptists had been a burden rather than a threat. Now the ministers became increasingly sensitive and alert to the dangers of the sectarian movement. But curiously, their attitude still did not harden against the Anabaptists as individuals. Capito and Zell, in particular, believed that they could deflect these men from radicalism by pastoral counsel; they continued to harbor Anabaptists as guests and to discuss doctrinal matters with them. Even Bucer was irenical. His *Commentary on John,* published in the aftermath of the

33. Camill Gerbert, *Geschichte der Strassburger Sectenbewegung zur Zeit der Reformation, 1524–1534* (Strassburg, 1889), p. 65.
34. Mitchell, "Sectarian Dissent," p. 112.

emotional strain of the Capito incident, stated that the Anabaptists were his brothers and not to be considered as heretics. They were pious and sincere, and their one error with regard to baptism was small; nevertheless he felt that it could lead to greater errors.[35]

The Magistrat was fighting the battle on another line and was increasingly perturbed by the Anabaptist disavowal of the civil authority. The men refused to swear obedience to the Rat or to accept responsibility for shouldering arms. In May, while the reformers were worrying about Capito and Cellarius, the Rat discovered that the Anabaptists were still holding meetings within the city. On May 28 it issued a mandate underscoring its first edict: everyone was to refrain from participating in such meetings; anyone who did join such a group would be exiled forthwith.[36] In August, Capito and Bucer, at the direction of the Rat, examined a group of Anabaptists from Augsburg who had been arrested and imprisoned; they were exiled after the hearing.[37] Despite this action refugees, particularly from Augsburg, continued to enter the city. In October a group of fourteen Anabaptists were arrested while holding services in a private house; the group included Jacob Kautz and Reublin, who were prominent leaders. They were imprisoned. Bucer and Zell, visiting them as a Christian duty, were met by the stinging reproof that the preaching of the Gospel in Strasbourg had borne no fruit and that the city was as sinful as ever.[38] A hearing was held before the Magistrat, and the two men were expelled. Both of them, however, were sick; Kautz was permitted to go to Capito's house, in the hope that he might be converted.[39] Thus the reformers still clung to the belief that these men could be brought to the truth and the light, and

35. Ibid., p. 122.
36. Krebs and Rott, *Elsass, I*, no. 135, Ratsbeschluss über das Verfahren gegen die Wiedertäufer, May 28, 1528, p. 162.
37. Krebs and Rott, *Elsass, I*, no. 148, Wiedertäuferverhöre, August 13, 15 and 17, 1528, pp. 180–82.
38. Mitchell, "Sectarian Dissent," p. 127.
39. Ibid., p. 130.

even after the Cellarius incident, Capito was entrusted with the task.

Despite the policy of exile and imprisonment, the hearings, and the Rat's mandate, in 1529 another large influx occurred. Court records for the first months of 1529 show a series of hearings of men charged with Anabaptism, most of them artisans from all over Germany. Prison records show forty-four imprisonments.[40] The Swabian League had taken official action against the Anabaptists by this time; the Palatinate, all Hapsburg territories, and Switzerland were closed to them, so that even with the mandate of exile, Strasbourg seemed a sanctuary. One record noted one hundred Anabaptists in the city, men who had been expelled from Augsburg.[41] Along with the émigrés came a new group of leaders —Caspar Schwenkfeld, Melchior Hofmann, and Pilgram Marbeck—who now confronted the reformers.

Caspar Schwenkfeld, a nobleman and an early supporter of Luther, had rejected Luther's doctrine of Communion and baptism. He was warmly received in Strasbourg by the reformers, who considered him a victim of religious oppression and regarded him as an ally and a friend. He lived quietly at Capito's house for two years, assisting the cathedral clergy and doing some preaching before private groups (he was still a layman). He continued his opposition to Luther's concept of Communion, but as time went on, Bucer and Zwingli were attempting a rapprochement with Luther, and Bucer became increasingly cool toward Schwenkfeld. Finally when Capito became convinced that the death of his young wife was a Divine judgment caused by his support of the sectarians, he too, broke with Schwenkfeld (1531).[42] Schwenkfeld, rejected by the orthodox reformers, refused to join either the reformed church in Strasbourg or to associate with the Anabaptist groups, which he felt were no better than Bucer and the rest.

40. Gerbert, *Strassburger Sectenbewegung*, p. 91.
41. Mitchell, "Sectarian Dissent," p. 136.
42. Williams, *Radical Reformation*, p. 257.

It were well if they [the Anabaptists] would put more stress on catechetical instruction in the Christian faith, rather than taking everyone into their congregation and appointing him to be a pastor. . . . It appears that they consider all who are not of their group as Godless and will have nothing to do with them, refusing to take in all who are weak in faith.[43]

Hofmann was easier to deal with. He was a mystic whose preaching had become increasingly prophetic; by the time he reached Strasbourg, he felt that he was a chosen prophet of God.[44] He openly opposed the reformers and had the temerity to ask the Rat to provide the Anabaptists with their own church so that they might worship in their own way. When he published two books without submitting them to the city censor, the Rat expelled him forthwith.[45]

Pilgram Marbeck's presence had far more impact on the community itself than either Schwenkfeld or Hofmann. Arriving in Strasbourg first in September 1528, Marbeck was an accomplished engineer whose Anabaptist activities had resulted in exile from his native Tyrol. He immediately joined the local Anabaptist circle but then left town to direct lumbering operations in the Black Forest.[46] In 1529 he was back in the city, gathering about him friends and followers to become a major spokesman of evangelical Anabaptism, as against the spiritualistic interpretation of Schwenkfeld,[47] for the Anabaptist movement itself was splitting into factions based on differences in emphasis and interpretation.

The Strasbourg reformers were beset by large groups of Anabaptists and a vigorous leadership. By now all the preachers recognized that even as individuals the sectarians were dangerous and serious opponents, but they disagreed on methods of procedure. Bucer was convinced that the matter

43. Quoted in Ibid., p. 259.
44. Gerbert, *Strassburger Sectenbewegung*, pp. 142–43.
45. Ibid., pp. 146–48.
46. Williams, *Radical Reformation*, p. 253.
47. Ibid., p. 273.

should be handled firmly by the civil authorities; Capito still felt that private admonition had not been given a sufficient trial, that the preachers had not tried to understand the consciences of the dissenters;[48] Zell hesitated before a forceful policy of suppression. His wife Katherine was an openhearted and generous woman who gave the protection of her house to all whom she felt were persecuted and misunderstood. Zell did not deter her and hung back from official action. He did join Bucer in requesting an open disputation with the Anabaptists in March 1529,[49] and he continued to interrogate prisoners with him, but the major effort of the reformers at these encounters was an attempt to answer each Anabaptist, point by point, either in writing or in open discussion. The records for the year contain a series of written defenses by both sides. It was an appeal to reason which would fail.

The Magistrat had a firmer policy—to administer the edict as effectively as possible by imprisoning those who came in, bringing them up for hearing, and expelling them from the city. The success of its efforts is perhaps reflected in a series of polemical tracts which appeared in March 1529, attacking the city for its shameful treatment of the Anabaptists. The Magistrat was aroused by this, and depositions in their own handwriting were collected from some thirty Anabaptists as a means of having a record of handwritings so that further libelous manuscripts could be traced.[50]

With the great group of refugees who had poured in from Augsburg, the Magistrat was increasingly apprehensive and fearful of an uprising,[51] and during the early months of 1530 it did everything in its power to hew to the letter of the law

48. Mitchell, "Sectarian Dissent," p. 152.
49. Krebs and Rott, *Elsass, I*, no. 178, Die Prediger bitten den Rat um ein öffentliches Gespräch mit den Wiedertäufern, sowie um Abstellung der Laster und des Wuchers. Das Gespräch wird verweigert, March 20, 1529, p. 233.
50. Krebs and Rott, *Elsass, I*, no. 175, Schriftproben und Namen der eingekerkerten Wiedertäufer, March 11–18, 1529, pp. 227–31.
51. Mitchell, "Sectarian Dissent," p. 136.

and carry out the mandate of exile. On April 23, 1530, Melchior Hofmann, seemingly insensitive to the Rat's attitudes, petitioned that a church be set aside for the use of the Anabaptists. The Ratsherren were far more interested in a book he had published on the Apocalypse than they were in providing a church for the sectarians. Eventually they called everyone involved in the publication into a hearing.[52] They continued to carry out the policy of exile—in May they expelled Carlstadt—and on September 24 renewed the mandate against the Anabaptists, urging all the burghers, their friends, and relatives to remain strictly by its provisions.[53] In October a series of hearings were held as part of their general effort to enforce the mandate, and the testimony at these hearings provides a clear view of Anabaptist activity at the time. The witnesses called in were not necessarily Anabaptists, or suspected of Anabaptism, but were men and women who had some knowledge of conditions in different parishes. The reports give a picture of clandestine activity and point to the existence of at least four or five Anabaptist cells operating within the city. The membership, however, seems to have been largely drawn from the refugees from Augsburg, Rotweil, or other southern cities.

The first man to testify, Assmus Hirt, a fisherman, admitted that he had harbored an Anabaptist but said that it had been done unwittingly. The man was a trapmaker from Rotweil, and a great many of his friends went in and out, but he, Assmus, had not known what they were doing.[54] Huck Clog, the wine measurer at the Green Man tavern, said on oath that there were many Anabaptists present but that he could not point out particular individuals. At the Pflug (another

52. Krebs and Rott, *Elsass*, I, no. 211, Ratsbeschluss gegen Melchior Hofmann, April 23, 1530, p. 261.
53. Krebs and Rott, *Elsass*, I, no. 222, Erneuerung des Wiedertäufermandats vom July 27, 1527, Sept. 24, 1530, p. 268.
54. This and the following testimony are all found in Krebs and Rott, *Elsass*, I, no. 224 Verhöre in Wiedertäufersachen, Oct. 22–23 (and shortly before), 1530, pp. 270–78.

inn) there were a great number who did not want to have anything to do with the Strasbourg preachers, and these people were all from Esslingen, Rotweil, and Stuttgart, and they rushed in an out of the furriers' tavern as well. A young girl named Ursula, a maid at the Pflug, testified that, yes, she knew a lot of Anabaptists, and she had been castrated by them because they sought brotherhood with her.[55]

Heinrich Jacob's wife admitted to attending Anabaptist meetings. They had sat and read from the Testament, and then one day they gave a reading which made her jump out of her chair, and she had asked, "Is that what you teach? Then God protect me from it." Jacob Schoner's wife had had much the same reaction. She had gone to a few meetings at a locksmith's and there had seen good teachings from the scriptures, but then they had started baptizing and criticizing the preachers, and she had not gone any more. Johann Latomus, the priest at St. Nicholas, testified that he and his colleague had had a great deal of trouble with Anabaptists in the parish. They came together at Hansen Von Than's house and also at the clockmaker's and talked a lot of rubbish and called the preachers baying dogs. Then when he preached, they came in the church and made a lot of mischief. He knew meetings were also held at the stonemasons', at the Rucker tavern, that the furriers had let them use a tailor's house for their meetings, and that the armorer Horb at the butchers' gate had a great crowd of Anabaptists coming in and out. Finally he charged that Lucas Hackfurt, the welfare officer, was a member of the group and gave out

55. The text here is difficult. The German reads "Sie waiss inn usszuschneiden, dann sie suchen bruderschafft zu ir." In a footnote the editor speculates as to whether "sie verschneiden" means castrate, and then raises the question whether this was meant figuratively; or whether it might mean "aufschneiden" (to cut open), or in the figurative sense, to rape or despoil. In any case it would seem as though sexual intercourse of some sort was involved. Several of the Anabaptists sects did attach spiritual significance to the sexual act. See Claus Peter Clasen, "Medieval Heresies in the Reformation," *Church History*, 32 (1963).

alms only to other Anabaptists. With the exception of Hackfurt, he said, all the men were from Augsburg, Horb, or Rotweil.

Diebolt Schwartz, the preacher at Old St. Peter, was also asked to testify. He said he did not like the procedure, but he did think some of the parishioners were attending neither his preaching nor anyone else's. Anndres Paner said flatly that they were a peculiar people and that there was nothing good about them. Jörge Meffert and his wife gave an account of their troubles with an Anabaptist neighbor, a man from Freiburg, who had moved in next door, had shown a great deal of animosity, and now never spoke to them at all.

A general picture emerges from the separate accounts. There were obviously three or four centers: the inn named the Pflug, the clockmaker's behind the Dominican convent, and the house out by the butchers' gate, as well as outdoor meetings, and other private homes and dwellings. The implication is that the meetings were relatively small and made up of refugees. The individuals, themselves, seem to have been troublesome and quarrelsome, a constant thorn in the flesh; they made difficulty in their parishes and in the parish churches; they were constantly criticizing the Strasbourg clergy; they did not behave in a neighborly way; and they were clannish and exclusive.

The Rat renewed its efforts to round them up and get them out of the city. More hearings were held in late October and November.[56] On November 28, 1530, the Rat announced that it had come to its attention that many were not having their children baptized; from that date civil action would be taken against any who let their children be baptized at home.[57]

Yet despite these valiant efforts on the part of the Magis-

---

56. Krebs and Rott, Elsass, I, no. 225, Ratsbeschluss gegen die Wiedertäufer, Oct. 31, 1530, no. 226, Abermaliges Zeugenverhör wegen der Wiedertäufer, no. 228, Verhör mehrer Wiedertäufer, Nov. 17, 1530, pp. 279–81.

57. Krebs and Rott, Elsass, I, no. 230, Ratsverhandlung über die Haustaufen, Nov. 28, 1530, p. 283.

trat, as soon as it got rid of one group, another seems to have come in. In 1531 the situation was exacerbated by the arrival of two radical nonconformist dissenters and by renewed attempts by Marbeck to actually establish an organized Anabaptist church. He confronted the reformers directly, criticizing them for trying to evangelize the whole population when they were unprepared. The common people, the masses, he said, should live under the commandments of the Old Testament; only the chosen few, the Anabaptists, were capable of living under the new law, the law of the Gospel. The debate went on between the two sides all through 1531. In the end it was significant because it was in defending themselves against Marbeck, in answering him point by point, that Bucer and Capito began to formulate the doctrines for the new church.

The final dénouement, however, arose from the activities of Sebastian Franck and Servetus. Franck had his *Chronicle* published by a Strasbourg press in 1531, stating before the censor that it was simply a history book. In fact, it contained passages that could be construed as an attack on the House of Hapsburg (it was here that he called the imperial eagle a bloodthirsty bird), and delegates from the city were immediately called before the Archbishop of Mainz to defend their laxity. Servetus, meanwhile, published his book *On the Errors of the Trinity* through a Haguenau press, while living in hiding at Strasbourg. It was a shocking book to the sixteenth-century mind, placing in doubt the triune nature of God. It was criticized from all sides—Catholic, Lutheran, Zwinglian, let alone the imperial authorities. These incidents forced a change in policy. The Magistrat had seen clearly that for the last two years the Anabaptists created only unrest and difficulty within the city. The reformers had doubled their efforts to refute the Anabaptist doctrines point by point, but now it was clear that refutation and exile were not enough. The city's religious doctrines would have to be clearly and publicly proclaimed, and a system of supervision and discipline established, so that only those doctrines were taught in the Strasbourg churches. The answer to radicalism was orthodoxy. The reformers were well prepared for the task, for the endless written debates with men like Kautz, Reublin, and Marbeck had forced them to come to common agreement within the ministerial circle. In late November 1532 the preachers and the supervisors of the churches asked the Rat to convene a synod for the city as a means of eradicating sectarian activity. Only if there was a common understanding as to what constituted true Christian teaching, they argued, could the sects be controlled and suppressed.[58] On November 30 the Ratsherren accepted the suggestion and appointed a committee composed of Jacob Sturm, Martin Herlin, Andreas Mueg, and Sebastian Erb to organize the meeting.[59]

A final evaluation of the significance of Anabaptism to the Strasbourg movement as a whole is difficult. How many Strasburghers were even really involved? And for how long? Having been members, did they remain in the group? The testimony of at least two women would indicate that after a few meetings some people withdrew. There is the particularly curious incident of Lucas Hackfurt. Apparently there was some truth in the allegations made by Johann Latomus, for on July 30, 1531, Hackfurt formally and publicly recanted his "unchristian beliefs" before Bucer, Capito, Hedio, and Latomus at Zell's house and was received again into the fellowship of the church. He had strayed but had returned.[60]

58. Krebs and Rott, *Elsass, I,* no. 348, Vorschläge der Prädikanten und Kirchenpfleger an den Rat zur Bekämpfung verschiedener Missstände und Sekten und zur Abhaltung einer Synode, shortly before Nov. 30, 1532, p. 575.

59. Krebs and Rott, *Elsass, I,* no. 349, Ratsbeschluss betr. obige Eingabe der Prädikanten, Nov. 30, 1532, p. 578.

60. Krebs and Rott, *Elsass, I,* no. 252, Der Almosenpfleger Lukas Hachfurt widerruft seine Ansicht vom unchristlichen Charakter jeglicher Obrigkeit und wird im Pfarrhaus des Matthäus Zell von Bucer, Capito, Hedio, Latomus und Altbiesser Wieder in de Kirchengemeinschaft aufgenommen, July 20, 1531, p. 334.

The Rejection of Theological Radicalism

As for the actual numbers involved, the records go from the relative handful—twenty or twenty-five persons—in the Ruprechtsau group, to the four hundred in the Dominican cloister, to the one hundred from Augsburg. But how many were there as a permanent group? This we cannot establish; we do know that there were some five or six groups, meeting clandestinely and furtively, first in one house, then in another, and that perhaps the majority of the members were émigrés, refugees from outside. The reformers wished to curb these gatherings chiefly because they were afraid they would attract the weak and wavering, but even more because the Anabaptist preachers revelled in attacking the preaching of the reformed clergy. Their favorite charge was that the work of the reformers bore no fruit. Strasbourg was as evil and immoral as ever, they taunted, because the true Word had not been revealed.

The Magistrat was even more seriously concerned by the Anabaptist cells, for they taught and practiced overt civil disobedience. All Anabaptists refused to take oaths, and the city constitution was centered on the solemn act of the *Schwörbrief*, the mutual oath taking between magistrates and citizens. Furthermore, a sixteenth-century city could not afford the luxury of a group of pacifist residents who would not bear arms to protect it. Thus the Rat took the major initiative in the actual suppression of the congregations and from 1528 on tried to keep the group under control through imprisonment and exile.

The reformers dealt with the leaders, apparently never making an attempt to go out to one of the Anabaptist congregations and refute its errors. Their only contact with the ordinary membership was in the courts, where Bucer, Capito, or Zell often handled the questioning. The reformers' attention focused on the preachers and writers, and it was here that their actions seem contradictory. Although they urged the Rat to proceed strongly against the sects, their relations with individual men were marked by a fundamental humanitarianism. Some of these men annoyed them, attacked them, or were openly defiant; yet even Bucer seems to have felt that this was a proof of error, not of an evil nature. Thus Kautz, weak and ill after a long imprisonment, was taken to Capito's house to recover and to be converted. Schwenkfeld was never really expelled, even after the reformers had broken with him. This quality of mercy is particularly evident in a memorandum addressed by the ministers to the Magistrat in June 1535. While the Christian magistrate should protect the church against false doctrine and schism, which rub and chafe like a piece of breast armor, they should also be sure that no one was ever denied the Christian instruction that might restore him to righteousness. Furthermore, no person should ever be more heavily punished than his offense warranted or be imprisoned in idleness without need. A wise, true magistrate, the preachers concluded, would find a way to make unthoughtful persons like the sectarians useful to the community and would not permit them to be tortured or put to death.[61]

The most remarkable incident involved Servetus. The man was an obvious heretic, and yet he was hidden and protected. Capito first gave him refuge in 1530, when he was making arrangements with the Haguenau printer. It may have been that Capito had not seen the manuscript, but once the book was published, there was no doubt in anyone's mind that it was openly heretical. Bucer's action was extraordinary. He immediately wrote to Servetus that it was unfortunate that the book had been published without consulting him. However, what was done, was done, and Servetus must realize that he had put himself in a very dangerous position; certainly the civil authorities would proceed against him. Yet Bucer pledged that he himself would not turn Servetus over to the authorities (in direct contravention of the

61. Krebs and Rott, *Elsass, II*, no. 673, Durch der Strassburger Rat von den Predigern der Stadt eingefordertes Gutachten, wie eine Christliche Obrigkeit sich gegen die Wiedertäufer verhalten solle. Shortly before June 3, 1535, pp. 463–64.

Rat's mandate and his responsibility, as a sworn burgher, to obey the Magistrat).

> You may expect from me not the least danger. But as to your intention of staying . . . I have warned you before not to do so. In my opinion the Magistrat will scarcely suffer you, if discovered, to remain. But as for me, you will not be molested, while you are here, so long as you disturb and seduce no one, and I should like to see you given permission [to stay] long enough for me to examine your work.[62]

Furthermore, Bucer kept his word and did not divulge to the Rat where Servetus was, for it is not until five months later that the Magistrat learned the heretic was living in the city and ordered him to leave.[63] There is no plausible explanation for such defiance of authority. Clearly Bucer did not feel that Servetus was a threat to the Strasbourg church itself; his ideas were far too extreme. But it was a dangerous risk to take, both for himself and for the evangelical church, which he represented. It was perhaps an emotional rather than a rational act. Bucer was unwilling to force Servetus to leave, knowing that torture or death were the inevitable end.

In the last analysis this may be the best explanation of Strasbourg's particular treatment of the Anabaptists. A genuine and effective humanitarianism—in part a heritage from Brant, Geiler, and Wimpfeling—made them unwilling to torture, drown, or burn their fellow men.[64] The calling of the

62. Mitchell, "Sectarian Dissent," p. 155.
63. Ibid., p. 157.
64. The only exception to this was the drowning of Claus Frey on May 22, 1534. Frey was a political radical, involved in the Peasants' Rebellion and had marked spiritualist tendencies. He abandoned his legal wife and was united with another woman through a "Spiritual marriage." He came to Strasbourg with the latter woman in 1532 and was imprisoned for adultery. After months of imprisonment, he was drowned, having stubbornly refused to terminate the adulterous relationship. See Clasen, "Medieval Heresies," p. 401; and Krebs and Rott, *Elsass, II*, no. 573 and footnote 1.

synod was yet one more example of this attitude. The final solution to the problem of the sectarians lay in discussion, in a rational procedure, in which all those in dissent would be heard and the Pure Word of God defined. The truth would manifest itself.

CHAPTER 12

THE NEW CHURCH

Y 1530 there were increasing pressures to create a new church—pressures not only from within the ecclesiastical circle, but also from without. Anabaptist activity had created confusion and dissension in the city; discord had threatened to divide the reformers themselves. Malcontents among the teachers contributed further to the invective and criticism hurled against the reformers. External political pressures were also mounting, for Strasbourg had maneuvered herself into a particularly vulnerable and sensitive position.

In 1530 the Imperial Diet convened at Augsburg. The German Protestant princes and the delegates from the major Protestant cities were in attendance and were prepared to make a major effort toward conciliation. To this end Melanchthon had drawn up a statement of the Protestant doctrine, the *Augustana*. Part of his purpose in preparing these articles was to make clear the differences between Luther, on the one hand, and Zwingli and the sectarians, on the other.[1] The imperial party, strengthened by the fact that Charles V had just been crowned emperor by the pope in Bologna, rejected the efforts at conciliation and demanded instead that the Protestants return to the Catholic church by the following year. The Protestants demonstrated their unity by signing the Augustana, which came to be known as the

1. Hajo Holborn, *A History of Modern Germany* (2 vols. New York, 1959), *1*, 212.

Confession of Augsburg, and created the Schmalkaldic League for their common defense.

Unfortunately, because of its Lutheran emphasis, Strasbourg had been unable to accept the Augustana and instead, joining with three Swiss cities, had submitted an alternative confession of faith known as the *Tetrapolitan*.[2] This declaration attempted to heal the breach between Luther and Zwingli and took a middle position between the Lutheran doctrine of transubstantiation and Zwingli's concept of the sacrament as a memorial service. Neither Luther nor Zwingli could accept the compromise, and the result was that Strasbourg had isolated herself from the German Protestant states and was in an extremely vulnerable position vis-à-vis the emperor. Unsupported and open to attack, with only the smaller Swiss cities as allies, she was finally forced to shift her policy. Jacob Sturm opened negotiations with the Schmalkaldic League. The League insisted that Strasbourg accept the Augustana, and the Magistrat was willing to do this on the condition that the Tetrapolitan would still remain in effect.[3]

Strasbourg was still in a precarious position when admitted to the Schmalkaldic League in April 1531. In a period when doctrinal lines were sharply drawn, her dual acceptance of the Augustana and the Tetrapolitan seemed to represent either wily indifference or flagrant persiflage. The Swiss cities scathingly charged that Strasbourg had abandoned the truth for political ends. The Lutheran cities, for their part, regarded their new ally with suspicion, convinced that she was unreliable and unstable and still too close to the Swiss. These were the external pressures that made it essential for Strasbourg to clarify her doctrinal position. Internally the relentless pressure of the Anabaptists made it equally urgent to establish an ordered church.

By 1530 Bucer had developed a relatively clear idea of the function and responsibilities of the church, its position in

2. The Swiss cities were Lindau, Constance, and Memmingen.
3. Wendel, *L'Eglise de Strasbourg*, p. 31.

the body politic, and its relationship to the civil authority. However, while the Magistrat was willing to accept his leadership on doctrinal matters, it was less willing to adopt his plans for a church based on close cooperation between the clergy and the civil authority. The city fathers were reluctant to share power with the reformed ministers, power that had only just fallen from the hands of the Roman Catholic clergy, and the cooperation Bucer sought was one-sided at best. In Strasbourg he was able to create only a state church. The broader church he envisioned would take shape only in other cities, at a later time.

In his earliest tract, printed in 1523, Bucer had broached his idea of a church of the whole community. The clergy, he said, were the representatives of Christ and the successors of the Apostles.[4] The secular authority stood only just below the clergy, for their responsibility was to maintain good order and to protect the pious community (*gantz gemeyn*) by upholding the common peace and justice.[5] Part of their responsibility, indeed the most important part, was to rule according to God's Commandments and make them known to the people,[6] for the laws of God should provide a model for the laws of men.[7]

Bucer's ideal was a Christian community in which the clergy and the secular authority would join together to serve the common good. Because he was brought up within the city walls, his thought reflected certain elements of late medieval urban political theory. A city was God-ordained— founded by God or at least by a bishop or a saint through divine intervention. The laws of the city were established by God, and the function of the city officials was to carry out these laws, to honor God, and to support God's own institution, the church. The city embodied the *corpus Christi-*

4. Martin Bucer, *Das ym selbs niemant, sonder anderen leben soll, und wie der mensch dahyn Kummen Mög,* in Stupperich, *Bucers Deutsche Schriften 1,* 52.
5. Ibid., p. 55.
6. Ibid., p. 56.
7. Ibid., p. 57.

anum in microcosm[8]—within its walls the magistrates were responsible for the general well-being of the populace.

In the early years of the Reformation, Bucer reiterated this idea in various forms.[9] The church and the magistrate had the same goal: to lead men to Christ. It was the magistrate's duty to protect the church, to prosecute heretics, and to punish any clergy who failed to live a Godly life. The clergy for their part were to teach the Word so that the civil authorities would know the truth.[10] From 1525 on, petitions and proposals addressed to the Magistrat flowed from his pen—in all of them he urged the Rat to assume its responsibilities for the spiritual and moral well-being of the citizens of Strasbourg. He exhorted its members to follow the example of the patriarchs of the Old Testament, to gird up their loins and take action. He dwelt at length on their obligation to abolish the Mass because it was a blasphemy against God. Not only did he urge the Ratsherren to expel the Anabaptists but worked closely with them in the endless examination of suspects, in hearings, and in public confrontations. Consistently he cited those scriptural passages which spoke of a close association between church and state such as the stories of the kings of Israel and the New Testament passages concerning God's bestowal of His sword on the magistrate.[11]

8. Moeller, *Reichstadt und Reformation*, pp. 13–15.

9. Zwingli's view was very similar. He emphasized that the church and the populace of the city were the same body. Ibid., pp. 40–41.

10. Ibid., pp. 43–44.

11. These references are recurrent in the materials on the abolition of the Mass and in the materials urging action against the Anabaptists. See especially:

A.S.T., 80. Der Priester begern dei Rat Massen abzustellen, Oct. 5, 1527.

A.S.T., 80. Supplication etlicher Bürger zumb abstellung der Mass, Mar. 18, 1528.

Archives de la ville, VI, 701a, 15, Supplicatio etlicher dran den burgerschafft die Stadt Strassburg nach Abscheffung von papstlichen Mass (probably 1528). Folio 12.

For the Anabaptist materials, see Krebs and Rott, *Elsass*, I, no. 178 (1529); no. 244 (1531).

In the early years of the Reform in Strasbourg a close association between the Magistrat and the reformers did seem to exist. The clergy preached the Word to their congregation and counseled, exhorted, and advised the Magistrat on matters of ecclesiastical policy. The Rat took on the burden of financial management of church properties, of administration, appointments, and salaries. This particular division of functions, which seemed natural and rather effortless at the time, worked partially because it was a period of crisis and partially because in these very early years there was little attempt to define or formalize procedures and thus little opportunity for conflict. The "church" or Strasbourg at that time was based on a series of informal and ad hoc arrangements. The evangelical preachers met once a week, probably from 1524 on, in a group known as the *Konvent*. Here they discussed doctrine and general problems of the church, but they made no attempt to issue directives to individual churches or to regulate services or practices.[12] When it was necessary to provide for the appointment of preachers, they turned to the Magistrat.

The Rat in the period from 1524 to 1530 was notably unwilling to commit anything to writing and left any new ecclesiastical arrangements as informal as possible. It took over the appointment of the parish priests in a vaguely worded decree, but established no regular procedure for appointment, nor did it provide for any system of supervision. In actual practice, an individual parish would propose a particular candidate to the Rat, and the latter made the official appointment.[13] With such a loose arrangement the Magistrat could claim that no change had been made that violated the terms of the Nuremberg mandate. Even the financial support of the evangelical preachers was carefully provided for within the traditional ecclesiastical framework. After the chapter exodus in 1524, negotiations between the Rat and the chapters simply transferred the salaries of the former parish

12. Wendel, *L'Eglise de Strasbourg*, p. 46 and note.
13. Röhrich, *Geschichte der Reformation, 1,* 190.

priests to the reforming preachers;[14] thus the reformers were paid out of regular revenues of the Roman church. Again the Nuremberg mandate was observed

The pressure for a more precise system arose not only from the makeshift quality of these arrangements but from mounting disapproval on all sides. The German Protestant cities and the Swiss cities disparaged the Magistrat; Lutheran adherents in the town took exception both to the Magistrat and to the reformers; and the Anabaptists criticized everyone—Lutherans, Magistrat, and reformers. The Anabaptists, however, were the most harassing, and it was in answer to their charges that the reformers arrived at a more explicit definition of the church. There were three major elements at issue: the nature of the church itself, the definition of the true doctrine, and the maintenance of the doctrine, once defined. Consistently, in arriving at their own definition, the reformers were governed by the need to refute the Anabaptists; this provided a negative emphasis, a defensive rather than an affirmative approach to the problem.

In January 1529 the preachers wrote to the Rat, censuring the teachings of the Anabaptists Kautz and Reublin. Reublin had been preaching the doctrine of a gathered church, inward and invisible, open only to the elect. The reformers vigorously rejected this concept on the grounds that the scriptures, particularly the Epistle of Paul, described an external, outward, perceptible, visible church, open to all men, the whole community of people, who formed Christ's flock.[15] They rejected the concept of election, believing that God chose all for salvation who followed Christ, who had faith in eternal life—all these He gathered into His Church.[16]

14. This arrangement provides an insight into the aims and attitudes of the chapters. Although the Chapterherren offered some resistance to this particular proposal, they accepted it in the end. They felt no commitment to oppose the Reform conclusively—indeed, they were even willing to let the chapter funds be used in its support, as long as their own benefices were not disturbed.

15. Krebs and Rott, *Elsass, I*, no. 171, Die Strassburger Prädikanten an den Rat, Jan. 23, 1529, p. 202.

16. Ibid., p. 203.

Thus the Word of God must be preached to all, so they might know the truth and turn to God.

Kautz had preached that the office of the pastor was open only to those secretly called by God and further stated that a man thus called was subject to no earthly authority. The preachers denied this narrow concept of the ministry— rather, they believed, any man who preached the true Word of God was sent by God, and it was not necessary that he receive a secret call. It was only the Apostles who had been specifically called to go from place to place and preach the Gospel. St. Paul himself had precisely differentiated their task from that of the prophets, the preachers, and the teachers.[17] While the reformers did not develop this point with regard to the special nature of calling any further, significantly, at this very early stage, they did add another function, that of the elders, whom they compared to the bishops.[18]

Bucer then conceived of the church as identical with the whole community—the *Bürgerschaft* was the church, and the civil authorities were responsible for carrying out God's Commandments, both in His church and in His city. Pushing it one step further, this meant that the people themselves should be responsible for providing the necessary discipline within the church, with the help of God's particular servants—the preachers, teachers, and elders.[19] This polity reflected the pragmatic conditions of urban society; similar plans were suggested in other cities as well. On December 14, 1530, the Magistrat of Basel, under the guidance of Oecolampadius, instituted Articles of Faith, which each citizen was obliged to accept, as he accepted his basic obligations of citizenship. Oecolampadius proposed that supervision and enforcement should be given to the ministers, with a clear jurisdiction, independent of the civil authority. The Basel Magistrat, however, placed supervision and discipline in the hands of laymen—three pious, upright, and coura-

17. Ibid., p. 205.
18. Ibid.
19. Bornkamm, *Martin Bucers Bedeutung*, 58, Heft 2, p. 14.

geous men chosen from each parish to maintain a serious and faithful watch over their fellow parishioners. The power of excommunication was also given to them. In practice, of the three men from each parish, two were always members of the Magistrat, and only one was chosen from the parish at large.[20]

Bucer followed this development with interest. In February 1531 he wrote to his friend Ambrosius Blaurer in Constance recommending the Basel plan.[21] In May he had the opportunity to work more closely on the problem. He, Oecolampadius, and Blaurer were called to Ulm to assist in organizing the new church there. They provided close ties between the clergy and the civil authority: a synod, composed of ministers and laymen, was to meet twice a year to discuss policy and doctrine; the responsibility for discipline within the church, including the power of excommunication, Bucer wished to place in a board of eight—three magistrates, three citizens, and two ministers.[22] The civil authorities in Ulm balked at the idea of discipline. Excommunication was still associated in their minds with papal tyranny, and they had little enthusiasm for continuing the practice. They were particularly unwilling to place such authority in the hands of a combined board of clergy and laymen. After several months of hesitation the Council of Ulm provided that a citizen guilty of religious error should come before the Council itself. The Council would then decide whether to banish him or whether to command the ministers to excommunicate him "by order of the Council." [23]

In spite of the fact that in Basel and in Ulm the civil authorities had been unwilling to place the power of discipline in the hands of the clergy and in spite of the rejection of a similar proposal made by Capito in Berne,[24] there was no diminishing of Bucer's confidence in the eventual estab-

20. Wendel, *L'Eglise de Strasbourg*, p. 180.
21. Ibid., p. 181.
22. Eells, *Martin Bucer*, pp. 120–21.
23. Wendel, *L'Eglise de Strasbourg*, pp. 46, 181–82.
24. Ibid., p. 182.

lishment of a truly Christian order in Strasbourg, with a group of *Pfleger* to watch over the church, just as various other Pfleger watched over hospitals, orphans, widows, the poor, and the schools.[25] Such a system would protect the city from Anabaptist preaching and teaching since it would provide for careful supervision of the clergy.

In the summer after his return from Ulm, Bucer and the other reformers worked with the Rat to prepare the first formal ecclesiastical ordinance for the city. Following the traditional pattern, it provided for a lay committee, to be known as *Kirchenpfleger*,[26] to be established for each parish, composed of three members: one drawn from the Schöffen, one from the Magistrat, and one from the burghers at large.[27] Essentially it created seven parish committees, drawn from the magistral class, with wide powers of supervision and control. The members were to concern themselves, in particular, with the pastors and their curates, admonishing or punishing them if they learned of anything "reprehensible in their lives, their doctrines, or their preachings."[28] If the doctrine of a particular minister was seriously questioned, he was to appear before all the Kirchenpfleger, but the ordinance did not go so far as to provide a specific penalty such as excommunication. Wendel believes that Bucer conceived of this ordinance as a means of providing closer control over the parish clergy, that he was not thinking of the broader problems of ecclesiastical discipline at this time and had no idea of vesting the power of excommunication in a lay group.[29] The Kirchenpfleger were rather to serve as model Christian magistrates and, in this spirit, were given the broad

25. Bornkamm, *Martin Bucers Bedeutung*, 58, Heft 2, p. 14.
26. In some documents, and in some of the secondary sources, a differentiation is sometimes made between the members of these committees at the parish level, where they were called *Kirchenspielpfleger*, and the same men as members of a united group of 21 members where they were called *Kirchenpfleger*. Here the term *Kirchenpfleger* is used for both—the practice of many modern secondary sources.
27. Wendel, *L'Eglise de Strasbourg*, p. 46.
28. Ibid.
29. Ibid., p. 182.

responsibility of improving the religious life and moral standards of the citizens. To this end they were to meet every three months with the Konvent of ministers to discuss the state of religion and the church within the city.

Both the reformers and the Kirchenpfleger took this last provision seriously, and their concern for improvement of the religious life of the city moved them to positive action. During one of their meetings in 1532, both clergy and laymen agreed that the citizens scorned the Word of God as it was preached to them and continued to lead frivolous, unchristian, profligate lives. A petition was drawn up to present to the Rat, suggesting a series of remedies. All citizens should be required to attend at least one Sunday service, with their children and their servants; something should be done to stop people walking about and gossiping during the sermon; there should be more religious education in the schools; the pupils should be exposed not only to the liberal arts but to the fear of God; capable young men should be sought out and given financial assistance to undertake theological studies, or the city would soon find itself without trained preachers. Several of these were familiar problems with familiar solutions.

The end of the petition, however, suggested a new approach. It proposed that a synod be called for all the rural churches dependent on Strasbourg, to provide some supervision and oversight. Further, it recommended that all the former decrees and ordinances with regard to church services and public morality should be revised, codified, and then read publicly once a year. It was also suggested that, following the example of the primitive church, deacons and deaconesses should be elected to care for the sick and the needy.[30] The concept of the Christian community is manifest in this petition—the city would look after not only the churches within the walls, but also those in the rural dependencies; ecclesiastical regulations, like civil law, would be codified. The mention of deacons is significant as an example of

30. Ibid., pp. 53–56.

The New Church

Bucer's use of the Apostolic church as a guide and standard. The Rat responded to the petition in its usual way—by appointing a committee to examine the proposals. The men appointed—Jacob Sturm, Martin Herlin, Andreas Mueg, and Sebastian Erb—were all confirmed followers of the Reform and distinguished members of the Rat. Their appointment indicated the importance the Magistrat, as a whole, attached to ecclesiastical problems.[31] Nevertheless, four full months went by before the committee made its report. They accepted all the educational recommendations, but suggested that the synod be expanded to include the urban parishes as well as the rural churches. The participants were to include the twenty-one Kirchenpfleger and two laymen from every locality (urban parish or rural village) as well as everyone who wished to complain about the conduct of any preacher. In addition a pre-synod, consisting of the Kirchenpfleger and the urban ministers, would be held.

These arrangements provide an interesting insight into the process of decision making in the sixteenth century. The pre-synod would approve the major draft of the Articles of Faith, and thus it would be impossible for an outsider or a small rural group to dominate the larger assembly. Policy was formulated before the meeting was held, and there was no idea of permitting free debate or discussion on such an important matter as Articles of Faith. The general synod would provide an opportunity for public confrontation with the opposition. The sectarians could state their disagreement publicly and thus could be censured. No one expected that their arguments would change the final form of the Articles. The meeting was conceived more in the spirit of a disputation than as a modern constitutive assembly. One final point should be noted: the introduction of lay delegates placed the clergy in the minority. The reins of authority and decision were to be kept firmly in the hands of the Magistrat.[32]

The report of Sturm et al. was accepted by the Rat on

31. Ibid., p. 57.
32. Ibid., pp. 58–59.

211

April 12, 1533, and preparations for the synod were soon underway.[33] By mid-April, Bucer, working at that moment in Basel, had sent back to Capito, Hedio, and Zell a rough draft of XXII Articles of Faith.[34] This preliminary formulation started by confirming "our confession which we delivered up at Augsburg" because it "set forth the doctrines which should be maintained and taught in purity."[35] While the majority of the articles dealt with the creed, communion, and baptism, four were concerned with the church and the functions of the clergy and the magistrates. The highest fellowship, it stated, existed among the faithful, namely, a true church, which was a Christian community where no one sought his own ends but rather desired to serve the needs of others, each member attempting to build the faith of his fellows through prayer, teaching, and good example. The ministers of this church were established by God as servants of His Holy Gospel and were responsible for expounding His Word daily and with zeal. The magistrates, for their part, should regulate everything with regard to the citizens, insofar as possible, by God's commandments, and should admonish the clergy to preach the truth. Finally the articles stated that whoever scorned the church and did not take the Sacrament would not achieve oneness with Christ, for forgiveness of sins could come only through the church.[36] Clearly the reformers were thinking in terms of an associative relationship, with a sharing of responsibility between the clergy and the civil authority. Equally clearly they were willing to give administrative and supervisory authority, even over themselves, to the magistrates and had reserved for themselves only purely ecclesiastical functions.

On May 31 the Kirchenpfleger and the Konvent of ministers, meeting in their prescribed joint session and joined

33. Krebs and Rott, *Elsass, II*, no. 357, Ratsbeschluss betr. Abhaltung einer städtischen Synode vor der allgemeinen Stadt-und Landsynode, Apr. 12, 1533, p. 3.
34. Ibid., no. 358, Bucer an Capito, Hedio und Zell, p. 4.
35. Ibid., p. 6.
36. Ibid., pp. 7–8.

by the committee of four from the Rat, drew up a memorandum covering the purposes of the synod and its agenda. Once again the establishment of a Christian order within the city emerged as paramount in the minds of the planners. The synod would bring together the Kirchenpfleger, the clergy, and others who could give them aid and counsel so that the Holy Gospel would be preached more boldly and with more purity and uniformity—thus it would bear more fruit. The group would also concern itself with uniformity in the administration of the Sacrament and all other ceremonies and would remedy, insofar as God willed it, the misunderstanding and errors of the sects.[37] The agenda covered three points: first, the accepted doctrines would be combined in articles and debated orally or, if necessary, in writing, at the discretion of the participants; second, church ceremonies would be discussed; and third, there would be an opportunity for censure and criticism of the moral life and teachings of every preacher, rural and urban.[38] Attached to this memorandum was a revised set of articles prepared by Bucer.[39]

In this second draft Bucer cut the twenty-two original articles to sixteen, and thoroughly reworded and revised them. The tone was now sharper and more defensive; in article after article Anabaptist teaching on a specific doctrine was pointedly refuted. Most significantly, the article with regard to the church was fundamentally changed. It no longer spoke of the "True Church" as the Christian community; emphasis was now placed on individual Christians who, united in the Body and Blood of Christ, would live in greater love and unity, having Christian concern for one an-

37. Ibid., no. 370, Bedacht der Kirchenpfleger, Prädicanten und Helfer über die abhaltung der angeordneten Synode, shortly before May 31, 1533, p. 21.

38. Ibid., p. 22. Note, in terms of procedure, that the articles would be drawn up before the Synod started and that debate would be in writing "if the participants felt it was wise."

39. Krebs an Rott, *Elsass, II*, no. 371, Die der Synode Vorgelegten Glaubens artikel, shortly before May 31, June 5–10, 1533, p. 25. See especially Editor's Note on authorship, p. 32.

other and thus, gently, discretely, would instruct, admonish, exhort, and encourage one another. Discipline was justified by an article which cautioned that it was wrong to state that a Christian could not instruct and warn his fellow Christians in a brotherly way.[40] A succeeding article attempted to allay fears of a new papism by providing that no one need be excluded from the common brotherhood except those who committed the great blasphemies specifically described by St. Paul.[41] The description of the duties of the ministers was deleted from this draft of the articles, in its place was a paraphrase of the Gospel that those who were bound on earth would also be bound in Heaven, that those unbound in the church of Christ would be unbound in Heaven, and that the power to bind and to loose lay not in any man—even a pope or a bishop—but lay only in the Word of God.[42]

While the church and its ministers were not mentioned, the duties of the magistrates were described at length in two of the final three articles and were then further explained in a supplement running to several pages. The magistrates, holding the sword and the highest secular power, were servants of God and must obey the commandments of God in their laws and the spirit of Christ in all that they directed, taught, or promulgated. All their efforts should be directed to the sanctification of God's name, the furthering of His kingdom, and the achievement of His will. It was their duty to provide that God's teaching be zealously and purely explained and made known to everyone. They must always protect and defend the good and destroy the evil. The articles closed on a negative note—it should not be said that the magistrates could not punish the perversion of Christian teaching and the subversion of the people to false and blasphemous worship.[43]

40. Ibid., p. 28.
41. These gross sins would include immorality, the works of the flesh such as impurity, licentiousness, idolatry, sorcery, enmity, strife, drunkenness, and idleness.
42. Krebs and Rott, *Elsass, II,* no. 371, p. 28.
43. Ibid., p. 29.

Important changes were made between mid-April and early June, changes which were profoundly significant because the June draft was to be accepted almost without revision by the synod. Since Bucer wrote both versions, it can only be assumed that the omissions with regard to the church and the clergy were deliberate and conscious. In view of the proceedings at the synod it would seem that increasingly, as the time for the meeting approached, the emphasis in Bucer's mind was on the need to destroy the Anabaptists and to purge the town of them. Since they were capable, in open disputation, of attacking his concept of the church *and* the Christian community as one, he may have deleted it to avoid argument and the inevitable criticism that certainly this ideal had not been achieved in Strasbourg. This would also explain the stress on the power of the magistrates. Bucer wanted it to be clear beyond any shadow of doubt that the Rat had the right, indeed the obligation, to maintain the purity of the Strasbourg church. The fact that he spelled out these particular articles even more explicitly is a further indication of the importance he attached to them.

The final article revealed most lucidly the true purpose of the synod—it was a warning to the intractable. God the Father, it stated, who made us all from nothing, would use the Word and the magistrates to destroy all evil through our Lord Jesus Christ, but weapons of wrath would still remain for those who would accept neither the Word nor the magistrates, for they would be thrown finally into the everlasting flames. To say there was no everlasting damnation was to contradict God in all His Scriptures.[44]

To attain the immediate goal of controlling the Anabaptists, Bucer was willing to postpone the establishment of the true church, the church of the Christian community. It was not that his ecclesiastical ideas were not clear at the time—he had a firm idea of the nature of the church and an equally clear idea of its substance and organization. In the course of the preparation of materials on the synod he

44. Ibid.

designated the three major offices of the later congregational church: the ministers, the deacons, and the elders. Drawing on the experience of the early church, he justified the calling of the synod on the grounds that similar gatherings of the clergy and the elders had been held in early times to subdue the sects.[45] He was careful in his draft to explain his use of the term "elders," stating that they were to be differentiated from the preachers, whose function was to proclaim and interpret the Gospel, while the elders' task was pastoral, to protect and lead God's people so they would be piously taught and live blessed lives.[46] From the two drafts a clearly established church organization could have been created. Perhaps these ideas were opposed by the Kirchenpfleger or by the committee of four Ratsherren. Perhaps Bucer himself felt that the Anabaptist problem took precedence over details of church organization, that unless the sectarians were silenced, there would be no church. In any case he abandoned the proposals, and they were not reintroduced.

The urban synod convened at six o'clock in the morning, June 3, 1533. The four Ratsherren who had formed the original organizing committee were now the presiding officers. The twenty-one Kirchenpfleger, the pastors, vicars, and the teachers from the Latin schools constituted the working members, and they proceeded without delay to the draft of the sixteen articles. There were several stormy sessions in which Engelbrecht, the pastor of St. Stephen, and Sapidus, from the Latin school, who had always been rather independent, attacked the proposals unmercifully. The presiding officers were perturbed by the delay, Sturm in particular because he was due to leave for Schmalkald and was afraid the general synod would have to be postponed.[47] By the end of the week, however, the articles, having sustained no

45. Krebs and Rott, *Elsass, II,* no. 370, p. 21.
46. Wendel, *L'Eglise de Strasbourg,* p. 91 n. 5. Wendel believes that this is the first recognition of the special function of the elders, as differentiated from the preachers.
47. Ibid., p. 75.

substantive changes, were ready for presentation to the general synod, and the pre-synod ended with the mutual examination characteristic of the Reformation. The vicars made their complaints with regard to the ministers; the ministers, in turn, criticized the work of the vicars. The comments were personal rather than doctrinal—Capito had become involved in the business affairs of a printing press; Bucer was proud and stubborn, given to rash judgments, and his sermons were too long. The ministers found the vicars proud, unwilling to submit to authority, and not always clear on important doctrinal points.[48] This scrutiny was routine. The main purpose of the meeting had been to inform the urban ministers with regard to the provisions of the articles.

The general synod convened on June 10, 1533, in the Church of St. Madeline, one of the former convent churches. A good deal of excitement and tension surrounded the meeting, and the Rat feared civil unrest. The door of the church was strictly controlled, the guards were given elaborate instructions as to who might enter, and an ordinance of June 7 stated that "everyone else should stay home and remain quiet." [49] The synod devoted very little time to the XVI Articles. The first twelve were accepted without discussion or debate at the end of the first day's meeting. Articles XIV to XVI were only briefly discussed and then approved. The object of the synod was not to debate them exhaustively but to make them known to all the clergy, urban and rural, and to assure the support of the rural parishes.

The articles adopted, the synod could proceed with the urgent business of rooting out unorthodoxy and impure doctrine.[50] Thus, the major drama hinged on a four-day debate

48. Ibid., p. 81.
49. A.S.T., 45, 1, Folio 87.
50. In resumé the XVI Articles provided for early baptism, as a sign of Christian initiation by which the individual was consecrated to God and adopted by Him. The doctrine of Communion was particular to Strasbourg, for it taught that in Communion Christ himself was offered, and thus the communicant received His body and blood but in such a manner that the bread was not necessarily His body or

between Bucer and the principal sectarians—Clement Ziegler, Melchior Hofmann, Caspar Schwenkfeld, Claus Frey, and Martin Stör. These men criticized the XVI Articles severely, and although Bucer argued point for point, the Anabaptists remained unshaken. Finally the presiding Ratsherren announced that anyone with further objections to the articles should present them without fear of censure, but no one rose to speak. The Ratsherren then withdrew, sending Martin Herlin back to say that if anyone had failed to speak because he was afraid, he should present himself to the Kirchenpfleger of his parish, but that in the future no maledictive attacks would be tolerated. Capito then closed the session.[51]

The synod had only partially achieved its aim. An orthodox doctrine had been agreed upon, but no provisions had been made to preserve and protect it beyond the very general statement with regard to the powers of the magistrates. Furthermore the articles had to be promulgated into law before they became operative. Two days after adjournment the four presiding officers suggested to their fellow Ratsherren that the Kirchenpfleger should call before them those who had refused to come before the synod.[52] Yet even this did not silence the opposition. The record of the following months shows constant hearings, statements of doctrine by the sectarians, rebuttals by the reformers, with Hofmann, Schwenkfeld, and Frey particularly articulate in defense of their own doctrines.

---

the wine His blood and that the elements were not transformed, because the body and blood would then become perishable. But with the bread and the wine and the Word, the communicant was offered the true body and blood that is the community of Christ. This view refused to localize the presence in the wine and the wafer and, typically, stressed the effect of the Word as one of the major factors in the change in the elements.

Articles XI–XIII covered the matter of discipline substantially as recommended in Bucer's second draft, and Articles XIV–XVI, on the powers of the magistrates, were virtually unchanged from the draft.

51. Wendel, L'Eglise de Strasbourg, p. 91.

52. Krebs and Rott, Elsass, II, no. 387, Die Synodalpräsidenten berichten über den Schluss der Synode, June 16, 1533, p. 91.

While the Rat made no move to promulgate the decisions of the synod into a formal ordinance, the need for controls became more pressing. A committee appointed by the synod presented a memorandum in mid-October, providing for standardization of church practices and supervision of doctrine and preaching. Uniform procedures were established for the celebration and use of the sacraments, for the religious education and training of children, and for weddings and church attendance. Most important were the provisions for the selection of the clergy and for their supervision and discipline, including excommunication. Purity of doctrine would be maintained by an Examining Committee of seven —two Ratsherren, two preachers, and three Kirchenpfleger —who would hear all those whose doctrines were questioned and examine them in a Christian way; doubtful doctrines would be referred to the Rat itself.[53] Provisions were made for a weekly meeting within each parish of the ministers, their helpers, and the two parish members of the Kirchenpfleger.[54]

Responding to this memorandum, the Rat convoked a fall meeting of the urban synod.[55] Only the provisions for the maintenance of true doctrine were accepted. The Examining Committee was given the responsibility for appointment and examination of the clergy, which would provide a basis for surveillance over doctrine.[56] The provision for supervision and discipline within the parishes, however, met with concerted opposition. Criticizing it as a radical departure, the synod referred it to the Rat for further action.[57]

At the end of the year no action had been taken on the proposals made by either session of the synod. The Magistrat had, as usual, appointed a committee to consider the recom-

53. Krebs and Rott, *Elsass, II,* no. 433, Vorschlag der Synodal-Kommission für die geplante Kirchenordnung, Oct. 13, 1533, p. 136.
54. Ibid., p. 136.
55. Krebs and Rott, *Elsass, II,* no. 435, Ratsbeschluss betr. Abhaltung der Herbstsynode, Oct. 13, 1533, p. 44.
56. Krebs and Rott, *Elsass, II,* no. 441, Protokoll der Herbstsitzung der Synode, Oct. 23 and 29, 1533, p. 179.
57. Ibid., p. 181.

mendations and draw up an ordinance, but no report was forthcoming.[58] Anabaptist activity had in no way diminished, and Bucer wrote angrily to a Swiss friend that the Anabaptists created nothing but misery.[59] In the meantime both the Rat and the ministers were much embarrassed by the fact that Melchior Hofmann, imprisoned for printing heretical books, had become ill and was refusing food. Letters were received from as far away as Holland bewailing his plight. The Ratsherren having no desire to make a martyr out of him, carefully reviewed in writing their solicitous treatment of his illness. Whether this incident made them less willing to take action on the recommendations of the synod is difficult to know, but it drew them into the limelight at an unfortunate time.[60]

By January 1534 the ministers were impatient, and when the new Ratsherren, having taken their oath, foregathered as a body in the cathedral, Hedio preached a forceful sermon with regard to their duties and responsibilities. His words indicated that the reformers had not forgotten their vision of a Christian community with clergy and magistrates working together to create an environment within which Christian love and neighborliness could flourish. "The welfare of a state," Hedio asserted, "is based on the clergy, the school teacher, and the magistrates." [61] The clergy for their part, had left no stone unturned to achieve the necessary reforms of the church, church customs, schools, and charitable institutions, but the threat to the city lay in the sects, in false doctrine, and in schism and dissent—it behooved the Magistrat to protect the true ministers of the Word and to take action against those who disturbed the peace of the church.[62]

58. Wendel, *L'Eglise de Strasbourg*, p. 108.
59. Krebs and Rott, *Elsass, II*, no. 443, Bucer an Marg, Blaurer, Oct. 23, 1533, p. 182.
60. The record of the incident is voluminous. See Krebs and Rott, *Elsass, II*, nos. 395, 396, 400, 417, 428, 451, 452, 461, 467, 468.
61. Krebs and Rott, *Elsass, II*, no. 492, Hedio's Ratspredigt über die Pflichten der Obrigkeit, Jan. 14, 1534, p. 262.
62. Ibid., p. 263.

The sermon drew no response from its auditors, and two weeks later Bucer, accompanied by Capito, Hedio, and Zell, went before the Rat to press the matter of a final formulation of the decrees of the synod. They were asked to present their case in writing, and four days later they submitted a sharply worded warning. The ministers had put their faith in the synod and had worked hard to make it a success, but nothing had come of it. Under the circumstances they would be obliged to denounce the situation from their pulpits. It was the responsibility of the Magistrat to enact legislation which would carry out the recommendations of the synod, for the Magistrat was the instrument and the servant of the arm of God, which meant that it was responsible for organizing the life of the community according to the will of God. The power to organize the church was not only the right of the civil authority, but its most sacred right. The Rat should therefore proceed first to define the true Christian doctrine of the city, then to name the preachers responsible for teaching this doctrine, and then to establish a method of discipline to maintain the purity of teaching and preaching. Furthermore the preachers should be protected from slander and calumnious attacks. Action must be forthcoming if the Magistrat wished to protect the city from the wrath of God and eternal ruin.[63]

Within two weeks the Magistrat took action. It addressed itself first to the problems of doctrine by reviewing the Tetrapolitan, the confession of Augsburg, and the XVI Articles. These were seriously studied and discussed—the Tetrapolitan was specially printed and distributed among the Ratsherren so that each member could study it at leisure, "because it is very long so that one can hardly understand it in a single day's meeting of the Rat, where no one remains seated to the very end and [thus] when the end is reached, one has forgotten the beginning." [64] On March 4, 1534, the

63. Wendel, *L'Eglise de Strasbourg*, pp. 109–11.
64. Quoted from Brant's *Annales* in Wendel's *L'Eglise de Strasbourg*, p. 112.

Magistrat accepted the recommendations of the synod, voting that the Tetrapolitan and XVI Articles should serve as the Articles of Faith for the city.[65] On April 13 its resolution was further affirmed in an act which provided that anyone who still opposed the articles must leave the city in eight days.[66]

Even before the latter action the new policy had begun to take its effect. From March 8 on, one sectarian after another departed. On April 5 Bucer or one of his colleagues defended the Magistrat from an anonymous critic by asserting that such vigorous prosecution lay entirely within the right of the civil authority.[67] It was not until late June, however, that the Rat completed the new ecclesiastical ordinance.[68] The Rat, albeit hesistantly, since it smacked of a new papacy, required that all the city officials should attend one sermon every Sunday, and the Ammeister was to visit the guilds and exhort them to more zealous church attendance; this they were willing to do partially to ensure the preachers of an audience.[69] On matters of organization the Rat remained conservative and cautious. It was unwilling to give the clergy the authority to maintain pure doctrine and was even less willing to give them the right to discipline the lay congregation.

The ordinance reaffirmed the XVI Articles and the Tetrapolitan as the accepted doctrine of the city; no one was permitted to teach or preach any other doctrine or to contradict the tenets of the articles. An Examining Board was estab-

65. Krebs and Rott, *Elsass, II,* no. 518, Der Rat beschliesst, bei der Tetrapolitana und der 16 Artikel der Synode zu bleibem, Mar. 4, 1534, pp. 285–86.
66. Krebs and Rott, *Elsass, II,* no. 535, Ratsbeschluss wonach hartnäckige Wiedertäufer innerhalb 8 Tagen mit weib und kind räumen Soll, Apr. 13, 1534, p. 301.
67. Krebs and Rott, *Elsass, II,* no. 527, [Bucer (?)] Setzt sich mit einem ungenannten Geger über das Recht der Obrigkeit in Glaubenssachen einzugreifen, Apr. 5, 1534, p. 295.
68. Krebs and Rott, *Elsass, II,* no. 577, Ratzverhandlung und Beschluss, June 19, 24, 26, and 27, 1534, p. 353.
69. Ibid., p. 354.

lished, composed of three Kirchenpfleger and two Ratsherren, to hear any person accused of preaching against
the established doctrine.[70] In case of need these five men
might call in two members of the clergy. The synod's provision for vesting parish discipline in the Kirchenpfleger and
minister together was rejected; indeed the item of parish
discipline was ignored altogether, and the oversight of the
parish clergy was put in the hands of the Kirchenpfleger
alone. They were responsible for seeking out those who
preached falsely, whether openly or not. The accused would
be referred to the Examining Board or the Rat for final
disciplinary action.[71] Association between the clergy and the
civil authorities was confined to the meetings of the clerical
Konvent. Three members of the Kirchenpfleger would sit
with the ministers and serve as elders. Again the Magistrat
maintained the upper hand, for these three lay members had
the right to remove any matter they deemed of sufficient
importance from the hands of the Konvent and refer it to
the whole body of Kirchenpfleger or even directly to the
Magistrat. Appointment of the clergy was placed in lay
hands. Candidates were to appear in the empty parish
church, before the parish Kirchenpfleger and the Examining
Board. Having been passed on by this group, the candidate
would preach before the congregation. The Kirchenpfleger
would then select twelve men from the congregation and,
with them, conclude the choice. The appointment was confirmed by the Magistrat—only formal installation was given
to the ministry.[72]

The ecclesiastical ordinance as finally promulgated, then,
created a state church, organized in seven parishes. The
Kirchenpfleger, a magistral committee selected on a principle of parish representation, carried the major responsibility for the church. They controlled its financial affairs,

70. Ibid., p. 358.
71. Wendel, *L'Eglise de Strasbourg*, p. 173.
72. Gustav Anrich, *Strassburg und die Calvinische Kirchenverfassung*, Rede bei der Rektorats-Übergabe, Tübingen, May 3, 1928, p. 20.

made decisions with regard to property and allocation of funds, and were responsible for appointing the clergy and their helpers and for providing their salaries. They had the broader responsibility of supervision and oversight of the church and of maintaining its vigor and its moral fiber. The Examining Board, a lay group consisting of three members of the Kirchenpfleger and two members of the Magistrat, had specific responsibility for the maintenance of true doctrine, now plainly defined by the XVI Articles. Thus, the church and its doctrine were in the hands of the civil authorities. The one clerical body, the Konvent, was limited to a loose advisory function and was closely supervised by the three members of the Kirchenpfleger who could translate any matter from the Konvent to their own group or directly to the Rat.

Surely Bucer and his colleagues must have been disappointed by the final form of the ordinance of 1534. Many of their original proposals and many made by the synod had been ignored, and their own function had been decisively and determinedly limited. Bucer had taught that the church should be all-encompassing, giving meaning to the lives of all the people, creating a community of love and service, watching over the citizens and ministering to them through teaching, discipline, and admonition.[73] The ordinance of 1534 came nowhere near this ideal, for it provided neither cooperation between the magistrates and the clergy nor supervision and discipline for the individual Christian. In effect the Rat had created an organization not too far removed from the model of the imperial church of the fourth and fifth centuries, and had provided discipline only for the group which needed it least—the clergy. Yet in 1534 Bucer did not challenge the investment of so much ecclesiastical authority in lay hands. The goal of the reformers was to create within the city walls a Christian commonwealth, the City of God. They had no illusions that they could achieve this by themselves; they saw themselves as part of a cor-

73. Ibid., p. 19.

224

porate whole and continued, both in Strasbourg itself and in other cities, to develop the concept of cooperation. They still wrote of the four officers ordained by God: the minister, the magistrate, the teacher, and the elder—each with his own work to perform to fulfill God's purpose.[74] In the fall following the promulgation of the ordinance, Bucer assigned to Musculus the task of translating Augustine's *Ad Bonifacium* into German to provide a strong historical justification for civil assumption of authority in religious matters. Bucer, himself, wrote in the foreword that the translation had been undertaken "to confute the new error that the magistrate should assume only worldly responsibilities."[75]

Consistently the reformers urged the magistrates to take more action. Taking their role as *ministerium verbi* literally, they exhorted the Rat to bestir itself in God's Name. In August 1535 a delegation of ministers appeared before the Rat to assert that all the troubles and difficulties, beginning with the Peasant's War, had been caused by the Wrath of God. Only if decisive changes were made would conditions be ameliorated. The Ratsherren should remember that they were baptized Christians and should go to church regularly, but above all, that they were the shepherds for the citizens and should sustain and guide them. To this end they should direct both adults and children to attend catechism four times a year; they should instruct the school teachers to send their pupils to church, and most important, they should appoint three or more zealous men to supervise the enforcement of the ecclesiastical ordinance, for never had there been more divorce, drunkenness, and gambling than in the last sixteen years.[76] The Rat's response to this was to issue an edict forbidding the citizens to walk around in the church during service (shades of Geiler von Kaysersberg!), ad-

74. Ibid., p. 13.
75. Krebs and Rott, *Elsass, II*, no. 646, Bucer äussert sich Kurz zur stellung der Obrigkeit in Religionssachen, Mar. 10, 1535.
76. Krebs and Rott, *Elsass, II*, no. 691, Mündliche Beschwerde der Prediger, Aug. 7, 1535, p. 473 and no. 692, Schriftliche Eingabe der Prediger an den Rat, Aug. 7, 1535, pp. 474–75.

monishing parents to send their children to church, and (at great length) forbidding any citizen from giving aid or shelter to an Anabaptist, on pain of serious punishment.[77] The request for a disciplinary board was again ignored.

Although they were unable to establish a system of discipline or surveillance over lay morality in Strasbourg, the reformers were able to come closer to the model of the primitive church in other cities. In 1535 Capito drew up an ecclesiastical constitution for the Frankfurt Magistrat. In substance it was close to the Strasbourg ordinance, except that the Kirchenpfleger were called "elders" and a specific provision was made for deacons. The Frankfurt Konvent was given authority to discipline, although the final authority still rested in the Rat.[78] Bucer's plan for the church of Hesse, embodied in the Ziegenhagen Ordinance (1539), was the most complete expression of his idea. Reviving the design of the church created by the Holy Ghost, every parish, in addition to preachers, would have presbyters or elders, some chosen from the Rat, some from the populace. As elders they would supervise the ministers and wield disciplinary authority over them.[79] It would also be their responsibility to see that all children born in the parish were baptized and attended catechism[80] and that the adults took communion.[81] The strongest disciplinary action, excommunication, was vested in the elders and ministers acting together, but it was to be resorted to only in cases of obstinate refusal to undertake Christian duties.[82]

Eventually Strasbourg's ideal of an associative church was broadly disseminated by Jean Calvin. Arriving in the city

77. Krebs and Rott, *Elsass, II*, no. 698, Mandat wegen besuchung der prediger und meidung aller sectirischer lehr, After Aug. 7, before Sept. 19, 1535, p. 478.
78. G. Anrich, *Calvinische Kirchenverfassung*, p. 22.
79. Ibid., p. 23.
80. Martin Bucer, *Ordenung der Christlichen Kirchenzucht. Für die Kirchen in Fürstenthumb Hessen*, 1539, in Stupperich, *Bucers Deutsche Schriften, 7*, 263.
81. Ibid., p. 267.
82. Ibid.

at a crucial moment in his own life and in that of the Strasbourg church, Calvin synthesized his own experience with that of Bucer and developed a congregational church, which effectively adapted the essential elements of the Apostolic church to the realities of sixteenth-century urban politics. In 1537 Calvin and his associate Guillaume Farel had attempted to establish their own system of church discipline in Geneva. The Magistrat there was to name "honorable men" in all the quarters of the city who would be responsible for supervising the moral and religious life of their fellow citizens. Unseemly behavior would be reported to the clergy, who would admonish the individual, and if the person did not improve, he would be excommunicated.[83] The Geneva magistrates refused to establish such a system, and Calvin and Farel refused to proceed with the reformation of the church without the authority to discipline, and the result was the exile of the reformers. They arrived in Strasbourg in 1538, and Calvin served as a teacher in the Gymnasium and as minister to the French congregation.[84] Unable to establish a system of discipline for this church under the stipulation of the ordinance of 1534, he carried out with literal precision the order for the celebration of communion and turned away from the table all those who had not previously presented themselves to him or to his vicars.[85]

During Calvin's years in Strasbourg, he was able to observe the relationship between the clergy and the Rat, and this served to strengthen his original conviction that discipline was indispensable for a well-ordered church. Bucer's emphasis on the Apostolic church gave Calvin a new source of scriptural support for his own doctrine. Significantly, in

83. G. Anrich, *Calvinische Kirchenverfassung*, p. 17.

84. An account of the details of Calvin's residence in Strasbourg may be found in Jacques Pannier, *Calvin à Strasbourg*, Cahiers de la Revue d'histoire et de philosophie religieuses publiés par la Faculté de Théologie protestante de l'Université Strasbourg (Strasbourg, 1925), *1*, 12.

85. François Wendel, *Calvin, sources et evolution de sa pensée religieuse* (Paris, 1950), p. 38.

the first edition of the *Institutes,* published in Basel in 1536, and the Strasbourg edition of 1539, he made no mention of elders, deacons, or doctors; there was no provision for a Konvent of pastors or for a consistory, nor was there any mention of these in the early Genevan catechism.[86] Not until he had returned to Geneva did Calvin incorporate these elements of the Strasbourg formulation with his own thoughts, creating from this synthesis the church of Geneva. While the Geneva Council deliberated on this proposal, Calvin wrote to Bucer for reassurance, describing his anxiety and his hope for the acceptance of his plan.[87]

It is difficult to assess, with finality, the source of any man's ideas. Establishing a system of church discipline was a common problem in the period when Calvin was formulating his *église bien ordonné,* and the solutions tended to have certain common elements. Nevertheless there were marked similarities between Bucer's *Kirchenordnung* and the Geneva system. Both Bucer and Calvin believed that the church was founded on *Jus Divinum:* God had ordered Christ, His deputy, to establish it.[88] In Geneva, Calvin carried out the division of functions between the four officers—ministers, teachers, elders, and deacons—which Bucer had proposed.[89] A consistory of the ministers and their helpers was established; it was similar to the Strasbourg Konvent and held the same weekly sessions.[90] The significant difference was that in Strasbourg Bucer was never able to achieve all the elements of the Apostolic church. On his return to Geneva Calvin was in a far stronger position than the reformers ever occupied in Strasbourg. He had been recalled by the Magistrat which had found that it could not keep the peace with-

86. G. Anrich, *Calvinische Kirchenverfassung,* pp. 17–18.
87. C. A. Cornelius, *Die Rückkehr Calvins nach Genf* (München, 1888), p. 23.
88. Anrich, *Calvinische Kirchenverfassung,* p. 13.
89. Ibid., p. 26.
90. Ibid., p. 25; and also, Wendel, *Calvin, sources et evolution de sa pensée religieuse,* p. 47.

out him,[91] and he could therefore force through innovations that otherwise would have been unacceptable.

While Calvin was resident in Strasbourg, the reformers, frustrated by the stubborn opposition of the Rat to any system of church discipline, resorted to a new means of accomplishing their aim, namely, subterfuge.[92] This tactic had been effective in other areas, and the reformers now felt that they could achieve their aim of discipline without the formal structure of law. In 1544, as a part of this plan, they called an executive committee meeting for the preaching ministers at exactly the same time as the biweekly meeting of the Konvent with the Kirchenpfleger, perhaps to discuss the matter of discipline. Unfortunately, there is no report of the outcome, but it can only be interpreted as a move to outflank the Kirchenpfleger and the Magistrat.[93]

In 1546 Bucer made his last attempt to establish a system of discipline at the parish level. In a memorandum to the Magistrat he suggested a voluntary system in which the church members would submit themselves freely to discipline. The movement would start with zealous preaching from every pulpit with regard to the defects of the church and the failure of lay morality. These sermons would be followed by a series of house visits to the pious, where the ministers would have the opportunity to teach the ways of a truly Christian life. Citizens thus prepared would then be called together, and the ideal of Christian community would be set before them. This group would then choose two or three of their best men as elders, who with the Kirchenpfleger would supervise the ministers, the community, and the congregation. As a beginning of this new order, the ministers would pledge themselves to obedience and sub-

---

91. G. Anrich, *Calvinische Kirchenverfassung*, p. 27.

92. Ibid., p. 24; also Werner Bellardi, *Die Geschichte der "Christlichen Gemeinschaft" in Strassburg* (1546–1550), Quellen und Forschungen zur Reformationsgeschichte, *18* (Leipzig, 1934), p. 21.

93. Bellardi, *Die Geschichte der "Christlichen Gemeinschaft,"* p. 22.

mission to this brotherly discipline and the elders would make a public avowal of their faith.[94]

The Rat's reply to the memorandum was a sharp rejection. There was no need for any provision for discipline beyond the Kirchenpfleger; indeed Bucer's proposal was an attempt to usurp authority from the civil officers.[95] Relations between the two groups were increasingly tense. In April 1547 the Rat called the ministers before it because there had been civil unrest after a series of sermons which criticized the Rat.[96] The ministers were prepared with a memorandum that made the usual complaints with regard to the state of the church and moral life. The Rat recognized that it was on the verge of a serious conflict with the ministers and that the latter had no intention of backing down. Characteristically, the Rat fought for time by appointing a committee to answer the petition of the ministers; the affair dragged on all summer, the Rat constantly being prodded by the reformers. By January 29, 1548, the Rat had completed the task: A new ordinance had been formulated, and one hundred copies were printed to be read out in the guild halls.

Unfortunately it was too late, for the parishioners had already, as in the case of the married clergy, taken matters into their own hands and acted independently. As the summer progressed with no action forthcoming on the part of the Magistrat, several of the ministers had assumed the initiative. Young Johann Marbach, pastor of the church of St. Nicholas, had organized a disciplinary system in his own church and parish. Other churches followed, and the Rat struggled in vain, issuing orders to wait for the new ordinance. On November 8 the issue was drawn at Young St. Peter. The congregation had called a meeting for this day long before the outbreak of difficulty over discipline. The minister, Paul Fagius decided to permit the meeting to take place, despite a Rat's mandate forbidding all congregational

94. Ibid., p. 25.
95. Ibid., p. 28.
96. Ibid., p. 31.

meetings, justifying his action on the grounds that it was his duty to educate and lead his parish. By so doing, he placed God's Commandment above the secular authority.[97] On November 9 Bucer, Fagius, Marbach, and Lenglin were again called before the Rat to answer for their actions. The ministers stated bluntly that they had come before the Magistrat in the spring, petitioning it to take action in purifying the church, but that the Ratsherren had refused to accept their due responsibilities. They had been left with no solution but to go directly to the parish, to call the pious Christians together and practice brotherly supervision and discipline among each other.[98] The Rat refused to accept this excuse and ordered the ministers to undertake no further action within their parishes until the ordinance was promulgated.

The ministers were able to maintain their common front only briefly. Shortly after the November session with the Rat, the clergy divided on the issue of reserving the reception of communion to members of the Christian community. The older members, Zell, Theobold Nigri, and Johannes Latomus, argued that the Rat's prohibition against further innovation should be observed. Fagius, Marbach, Conrad Schnell, and Johannes Lenglin, following Bucer's leadership, justified the withholding of communion as a means of educating the parish and strengthening its moral fiber.[99] The group was too small to be split, and the division ensured the victory of the Rat. It came quickly. The congregation of Young St. Peter again attempted to call a meeting in double defiance of the Rat's ban. Since Fagius had not called the meeting, he did not attend, but three parishioners were sent to get him and he went, although on the following day he wrote to the Rat, asking them to excuse his conduct. The Rat then ordered the Kirchenpfleger to bar any person attending congregational meetings from regular church serv-

97. Ibid., p. 40.
98. Ibid., p. 41.
99. Ibid., p. 48.

ices on Sunday.[100] Faced by this injunction, the congregational movement in Strasbourg crumbled.

In the end the result was bitterness—a bitterness that was perhaps particularly deep because the ministers had for so long believed that the Rat would work with them toward a common purpose. Hedio tried to heal the gap, serving as a mediator between the Ratsherren and his colleagues. On December 11, however, Zell was moved to criticize the presence of the Kirchenpfleger at the meetings of the Konvent and went on to say that a Christian owed more obedience to God than to the magistrates.[101] To justify his position, Bucer prepared one last treatise, entitled "On the Community of the Church." [102] Callously, the Rat refused him permission to print the book. The definition of pure doctrine was now fully in control of the state, and the leader of the movement was forced to conform by order of the civil authority.

100. Ibid., p. 52.
101. Ibid., p. 59.
102. Ibid., p. 61.

PART III

The Impact of the Reform

1534–1548

CHAPTER 13

THE OLD CHURCH: 1524–1548

T was the old church, patently, which received the full impact of the Reformation. Its central service was abolished; the monastic orders disappeared; the parish churches were absorbed; and the effective authority of the remaining units dwindled to the vanishing point—but the Roman Catholic church in Strasbourg survived.

The weakest units in the ecclesiastical structure were the monasteries, and these broke under the stress of change. It is important to note that they were not destroyed or overthrown. They collapsed. It began with the delegation from the Franciscan cloister that appeared before the Magistrat in 1523 asking permission to lay aside their habits and relinquish to the Rat the right to collect their revenues and prebends. The Rat did not encourage the brothers but six months later provided for the inventory of monastic property if the monks renounced their vows. The Franciscans thereupon laid off their cowls, and in 1524 and 1525 other monks and nuns followed.[1]

It would appear that this exodus was largely voluntary. Many of the men and women in orders felt that they had been forced into conventual life, and dissatisfaction with monasticism had mounted throughout the fifteenth century. The voluntary nature of the change is reflected in the very small number of men and women who remained behind. By 1530 there were only four monks left in the Augustinian mon-

1. See Chapter 9.

astery of St. Arbogast,[2] and by 1534 only one solitary monk in the Carmelite cloister.[3] The nuns were as eager to leave the cloister as the men. All ten nuns inhabiting the convent of St. Marx left in 1525, and all the sisters of St. Catherine, except for three elderly women.[4] By 1529 there remained only three nunneries, and these were to survive the Reformation.

> The nuns of St. Margaret, St. Claus in Undis, and Zu den Rawern were allowed to stay, as they had always conducted themselves well in all ways, but the Mass was abolished, and every Sunday there was preaching at midday in all these cloisters, and it was also allowed that they could go out on Sunday morning for church, but they went out very little and stayed cloistered as before.[5]

The closing of the monastic houses was not instituted by the Magistrat but by the monks and nuns themselves. Furthermore, the Rat did not adopt a radical program to extirpate all traces of monasticism. They required an inventory of goods and property and assumed the direction of financial affairs. This was not an entirely new assertion of authority, since the Rat had already acquired some supervisory powers over the sale or exchange of monastic property in the preceding century. The moderate temper of the Rat was apparent in the flexibility of the arrangements. When a monastery closed, individual monks or nuns were not forced to leave; they could remain in their old quarters. The Augustinians continued to observe their regular services.[6] Women who wished to remain in orders moved to one of the three functioning cloisters. If an individual chose to renounce his

2. Adeodatus Vermeulen, *Der Augustiner Konrad Treger* (Rome, 1962), p. 111.
3. A. Baum, *Magistrat und Reformation*, p. 116.
4. Ibid., pp. 120–21.
5. Specklin, *Collectanées*, p. 523.
6. Vermeulen, *Der Augustiner*, p. 112.

vows, the Rat gave him a pension and returned the money he had deposited at his entrance.[7] The younger men were taught a craft so they might become self-supporting.[8]

The major result of the monastic dispersion was that the Magistrat came to control the property and revenues of the various orders. This was not, in all cases, advantageous. The notorious mismanagement of the Franciscan provincial meant that the city assumed more creditors than revenues, and in most cases administrative and financial changes were essential if the properties were to become productive. On April 13, 1524, the Magistrat appointed a committee of eight to handle these affairs and to make inventories of all the cloisters. On December 30, 1527, a more permanent administrative arrangement was instituted. The original group was replaced by one of the usual standing committees of the Rat. Four Ratsherren—one a Constoffler and one from each of the three major committees—would serve as Klosterherren for life with full responsibility for the remaining monastic clergy and for the administration of the property and revenues of the orders.[9]

The committee proceeded slowly with its task. It was assumed that no disposition would be made of monastic buildings as long as elderly clergy remained in residence, and no major changes were made until 1530, when the Augustin's church of St. Arbogast was pulled down, as was the gate of the cloister of St. Marx, and the stones were used for the walls and the bulwark at the Weissenthurn, at the western gate of the city. The Franciscan cloister was converted into a hostel for the poor and unfortunate. In the year 1529–30 alone, more than sixteen hundred persons were given shelter there. The Dominican cloister was the largest in the city; the church itself had a magnificent double nave, and there were numerous other buildings and wings. Revenues from

7. The best account of the actual administration of the pension system is in ibid., pp. 111–13.
8. A. Baum, *Magistrat und Reformation*, pp. 101–02.
9. Ibid., p. 106.

the order were assigned to the city hospital, the hospital for contagious diseases, the orphan asylum, and the leper house; the buildings later housed several schools and a library.[10] The monastic properties were thus adapted to a variety of public purposes, and the Klosterherren seem to have tried conscientiously to designate them for educational or charitable functions in keeping with the pious intentions of the original donations.

By 1530 only the three female convents remained. The knightly orders were, however, untouched by the Reform. The two houses, the Teutonic Knights and the Knights of St. John, had always maintained a position of independence and autonomy. Drawn from the highest nobility, arrogant, rich, and powerful, they had never permitted the Magistrat to assume any supervisory control over their financial affairs, and the Knights of St. John were by far the wealthiest order in the city—even the Rat borrowed money from them.[11] In the confusion of the Reformation their wealth did not decrease, but increased, and in the years after 1529 the Knights of St. John and the three cloisters of nuns were the nucleus of Catholicism. They, alone, defied the orders of the Rat with regard to the abolition of the Mass and the establishment of a new order of service. The Magistrat assigned a minister to preach to the knights from the scriptures. The knights forced him to say Mass and eventually obliged the Rat to modify the ordinance with regard to the Mass, permitting the three cloisters and the knightly orders to celebrate the traditional service. The knights, however, chafed under the restrictions laid upon them by the new religion and finally left the city. Only the Grand Commander and a custodian remained behind to protect the property.[12]

The four chapters were deeply affected by the Reform. They were more closely involved in the ecclesiastical life

10. Büheler, *Chronique,* p. 80.
11. Karl Hahn, *Die Katholische Kirche in Strasbourg unter dem Bischof Erasmus von Limburg, 1541–1568* (Frankfurt am Main, 1940), cf. p. 89 n.
12. Ibid., p. 89.

of the city than the monastic orders because they controlled half of the parish churches, appointing the priests and providing their financial support, their houses, and any other emoluments. They also collected the revenues, distributed alms, and controlled the financial affairs of these churches. Any change in the parishes would inevitably affect them.

Despite these parish responsibilities, however, the chapters regarded themselves as independent entities. Throughout the fifteenth century they had endeavored to assert their autonomy vis-à-vis the bishop, while claiming their ancient clerical freedom from the temporal authority. They had formed temporary alliances with the Rat against the bishop but had always avoided any agreement that would give the Magistrat supervisory power over their financial affairs or judicial authority over their members. They had agreed only to the payment of *Schirmgeld* in recognition of the protection afforded them by the city—except for this, they held themselves apart, insisting on their separation.

There is little doubt that the Rat saw in the Reform a means of settling this ancient division. The clerical state-within-a-state created insolvable administrative and judicial problems; the insularity of the clergy was aggravating in the close society of a medieval town. Thus, while the Ratsherren were still unwilling in 1524 to take overt action in support of preaching, they were willing to move decisively to abolish clerical privilege. In November of that year they sent a delegation to the chapters requesting that the chapter members assume Bürgerrecht and accept the duties of citizens, including the obligation of swearing loyalty to the Rat.[13]

The formal edict was promulgated on January 22, 1525. The canons had no desire to give up their ancient rights and privileges or their hard-won independence, and even before this final enactment, the Chapterherren of Young St. Peter, Old St. Peter, and St. Thomas left town, taking with them all the treasures and movable property they could carry.[14]

13. A. Baum, *Magistrat und Reformation*, p. 67.
14. See Chapter 9.

No one knew where they had gone, and the Magistrat was incensed, feeling that the treasures belonged to the city and could not be considered the private property of the chapters. Determined to force the canons to return with their goods, the Rat resorted to a ruse to find them:

For one canon of the St. Thomas had a beautiful "madonna" in Strasbourg, and it was known he could not stay away from her long. They [the officers of the Rat] caught him at her home, made him divulge the secret of where the clergy were, and then let him go free.[15]

But even when the Magistrat knew the canons were at Haguenau and Offenburg, the affair was not quickly settled. A long legal battle ensued; the chapters appealed to all the courts of the church and finally carried the matter to the *Reichsregiment*. The issue was not the acceptance of the reform. The canons showed little interest in doctrinal matters. Their aim was to protect their benefices and prerogatives. They registered few complaints when the altars in their churches were taken down or when changes in the service were made, but they refused to assume Bürgerrecht. They were unwilling to be placed in a position of legal equality and feared the loss of their financial independence.

In 1528, after three years of negotiation, the city and the canons arrived at an accord, leaving the management of chapter property in the hands of the canons. Thus, in the same year the Mass was abolished, the canons were assured that their lands and revenues would remain intact, and they were restricted only in that they could make no sale of land without the consent of the Magistrat. In return, it was provided that the chapters would continue to support the clergy of their own parish churches, despite the fact that these posts were now filled by reformed preachers. They were to give the Rat 150 gulden a year to cover these salaries and to provide a dwelling or 8 gulden a year for rent, and

15. Specklin, *Collectanées*, p. 506.

they abrogated to the Magistrat the right of appointment to these churches.[16] The goods and treasures that had been taken away were to be returned and inventoried; nothing was to be removed henceforth without the knowledge of the city. Each chapter was to reimburse the Rat for the salaries paid by the city during the exodus, as well as to pay a flat indemnity of 1500 florins.[17] Finally the canons were to accept Bürgerrecht and take the burgher oath.

For their part the Rat agreed to guarantee the chapters protection and to permit them to sing and read their own services. The chapters were authorized to retain their ancient autonomy over their internal affairs. Canonical benefices were not to be disturbed by the city, and the canons would continue to make all appointments to the chapters. The cathedral chapter retained its privilege of electing the bishop.

The accord was a victory for the city—they had finally brought the Chapterherren under their jurisdiction. On the other hand, it is essential to recognize that at the very moment when the city had abolished the Mass, careful provisions were being made to protect the wealth and property of one of the most important groups of the Roman church. The prestige of the chapters had been a decisive factor: they had powerful friends and connections in the imperial court as well as in the church, and the Rat did not wish to press the issue further. The agreement also reflected the Rat's reluctance to force issues of conscience. If an individual was willing to fulfill his civic obligations as a loyal, obedient citizen, he could believe as he pleased.

Unfortunately, on their return to the city, the canons did not attempt to set an example of pious religious life. Even a Catholic historian remarks that they lived more profligate lives than before. With no real function and no public services to conduct, their lives were spent in idleness and vacuity.[18] Their only concern was to preserve their wealth and

16. Adam, *Evangelische Kirchengeschichte,* p. 87.
17. Trausch and Wencker, *Chroniques,* p. 157.
18. Hahn, *Katholische Kirche,* p. 69.

position, and one chronicler reported that they were eminently successful:

All the foundations were permitted to remain, with their canons and vicars; the Great Chapter in the cathedral, those of St. Thomas, Old St. Peter and All Saints. This made the clergy fat with all their rents, dues and income, so they had their managers and administrators as always.[19]

The exception to the pattern was the chapter of St. Thomas, which had always occupied a different position and had been more closely associated with the city. Drawing most of its membership from Strasbourg's patrician families, it was a local institution, and when the Reformation came, a majority of the canons of St. Thomas accepted the new doctrines and supported their provost, Capito. It was only a small minority of the canons who, remaining loyal to the old faith, fled from the city in 1524. This minority returned in 1529 and took up residence again, but the chapter remained Protestant throughout the years of the Reform. The wealth of St. Thomas—its benefices and revenues—was a major source of support for the new church. Capito, however, did not remain provost. Apparently to avoid the criticism that he himself held an important and lucrative benefice, he resigned his post in 1525 and became a preacher, receiving three gulden weekly to cover his own salary and those of his curate and sexton.[20]

The Strasbourg chapters were materially unaffected by the Reform. They lost control of their parish churches, but this meant no economic loss. The canons had not taken their parish responsibilities seriously for decades and were perhaps relieved to let someone else shoulder that particular burden. For the rest, the canons of the cathedral and Young and Old St. Peter continued to function as elite elective bodies, providing life incomes for the scions of noble or

19. Specklin, *Collectanées*, p. 523.
20. Röhrich, *Geschichte der Reformation*, 1, 195.

patrician families. They remained narrow and self-centered, withdrawn from the life of the community, separate in spirit if not by law, and an example of the tenacity of the established institution in the face of change.

Wilhelm von Hohnstein, Bishop of Strasbourg, has been represented as pacific and ineffective by nature and unwilling to offer any forceful resistance to the reform. In fact, issue by issue, incident by incident, he offered a firm and determined resistance to the Magistrat and the reformers, creating for himself the role of spokesman for the minority. By the mere fact of his existence he created a continuing obstruction to change and made it impossible for the reformers to move quickly or with certainty. The old ideology and the old institutions were neither quickly nor totally extinguished—they endured, and their survival was in large part due to the stubborn resistance of the bishop.

From the very beginnings of the Reform the bishop's attitude was neither permissive nor tolerant; as early as 1520 he urged the Magistrat to take definitive action against the first evangelical preachers. As he was faced with the further development of preaching and with the marriage of the reformed clergy, the bishop opposed the preachers—he admonished them; he cited them to come before him; he attempted to expel them; and he carried the case of the clerical marriages to Cardinal Campeggio.[21] In all these efforts he failed but not because of his own weakness. The Magistrat wavered; the Chapterherren refused assistance; imperial and papal policy was immobilized by delay; and he was deserted.

Yet he remained firm in his resolution to resist the Reform, as was evident in the struggle between the chapters and the Rat. The chapters were ancient enemies of the bishop; for over a hundred years they had done everything they could to undermine his authority. Yet when the canons fled the city, it was the bishop who assumed the role of protector and friend. In the first days after the flight several chapter

21. See Chapters 7 and 9 for the detailed account of the bishop's actions against the reformers.

members, who had been left in the city, were captured and imprisoned by the soldiers of the watch while attempting to escape. The bishop immediately interceded, claiming that this civil action restricted the rights and freedoms of the chapter and interfered with his own due authority. The imprisoned clergy were to be released to him.[22] The bishop then complained to the Reichsregiment in Esslingen[23] and tried to obtain support and assistance for the chapters from the Archduke Ferdinand and from the *Landvogt* of Lower Alsace.[24] When the Rat stated that it would undertake negotiations only if the chapter members and their goods were once again within the city, the canons appealed to the bishop, who advised them to remain outside the city and to press the matter at the Reichsregiment, then meeting at Ensisheim.[25] In 1526 the bishop took the case to the Diet of Speyer, asking for imperial assistance for the canons;[26] the following year he carried the matter to the Archduke Ferdinand, in residence at Kentzingen.[27] He had used every weapon at his disposal, and he had given the chapters aid and support which they would never return.

During the long negotiations between the city and the canons the bishop fought to maintain the ancient privileges of the clergy. They could not take the burgher oath, he said, because the assumption of these civil responsibilities would interfere with their spiritual duties;[28] he objected to the inventory of chapter property and warned the Chapterherren not to bring back their treasures. Although he did not gain these points, the settlement was by no means a defeat for the chapter and reflected the bishop's effectiveness as a negotiator.

22. A.S.T., 47, II, Folio 25, Episc. an den Rat, Sept. 8, 1524.
23. Ibid., Folio 26, Episc. an den Rat, Sept. 11, 1524.
24. A. Baum, *Magistrat und Reformation,* p. 138.
25. Ibid., p. 141.
26. A.S.T., 47, II, Folio 24, Appelat. Episc. Wilhelm contra der Stadt Strassburg, Aug. 17, 1524.
27. A. Baum, *Magistrat und Reformation,* p. 144.
28. A.S.T., 47, II, Folio 24, Appelat. Episc. Wilhelm, Aug. 17, 1524.

As far as reform was concerned, the bishop was ready to recognize that the clergy needed constant discipline, and he issued one mandate against concubinage and the immoral behavior of his clergy.[29] He was willing to permit changes on a few minor points of usage, but for the rest he intended to maintain unchanged the doctrines, dogma, and forms of worship of the Roman church. His position was carefully developed in a document prepared during the struggle over the Mass.

I. With regard to the Christian faith and the accepted ceremonies of the church there is nothing to alter; also the seven Sacraments should remain. Only with regard to baptism is there one thing that needs to be changed, that the question to the godfather should be asked in German. Furthermore, every Sunday after Ember days, the Gospel and invocation should be read in German, and the meaning should be explained to the people in a sermon.

II. Abolition of Abuses.

1. Masses. Masses should not be said for money but for God's sake, so that the priest should not be overburdened, for the priests should not be compelled to say the Mass. On Mondays and Fridays, the Epistle, Gospel, and Collect should be explained in the sermon, and once or twice yearly the whole Mass [should be explained]; furthermore, the lesser and the great canon should be translated into German. The traditional fees for funerals and soul Masses should remain. However, the authorities should have consideration for the poor, [and] they should compel no one to have a funeral.

2. Baptism. No more than two persons should be asked to stand as Godfathers.

3. Confirmation. The suffragan should travel at least twice yearly through the diocese for this undertaking and should explain the meaning of it.

29. Ibid., Folio 16, Feb. 19, 1524.

4. Priestly ordination. No unlearned man should be ordained priest.

5. Marriage. Unmarried cohabitation is forbidden; the married partner is otherwise free, even when the other partner is living.

6. Confession. No confessionals shall be placed in dark corners; no secret but only open penance shall be enjoined. The confessor shall be able to absolve all known sins with the exception of open heresy, murder, and ban. They shall refrain from all awkward, vexing questions, which could serve to anger the penitent, but attempt to induce true penitence, faith, and works.

7. Supreme Unction. The oil should not be spilled or soiled.

III. So that all the Sacraments can be offered gratuitously, the priests must receive an adequate salary.

Further, the preachers should preach the Gospel according to the right and true interpretation laid down by the teachers of the Christian Church, without tumult but in peace and unity, according to the recess of the Diet of Augsburg. The number of holy days should be reduced since they divert people from work. . . . Maintenance of fasts should not be proclaimed under the threat of the ban and deadly sin but should be proclaimed for the blessedness of the soul. The seven daily readings should be read with understanding and without thoughtlessness, and every chapter should establish a post for a learned man who will explain the psalms to the unlearned priests so that they will know what they are reading. The parishes should be visited at least once a year, and nothing should be printed without the knowledge of the bishop and the authorities.[30]

The recommendations reflected the loyalty and constancy of the bishop to the doctrines and traditions of the Catholic church; more significantly, they indicated the direction the

30. A. Baum, *Magistrat und Reformation,* pp. 163–65. Baum renders the document in modern German.

Roman church would take in its own reformation. Administrative and financial reforms would be made, but there would be no change in doctrine, in the form of worship, or in the sacramental observances of the church. The meeting for which the document was prepared never took place, and the bishop's proposals were never made public.

Consistently encountering the defeat of his efforts, Wilhelm von Hohnstein continued to assert himself in the spiritual and temporal affairs of his diocese. He had become a shepherd without a flock, but he ignored this and continued to play the role of the active administrator. In October 1529 he addressed two petitions to the Rat reminding it of King Ferdinand's request for help against the Turks, and the necessity of a new crusade.[31] He continued to serve as a friend in court, addressing requests to the Rat in favor of individuals whose cases were before the municipal courts. He intervened in a case between the wife of Benedict Steinmetz and the widow of the late Conrad Wölfflin, who were involved in a dispute over the inheritance of the latter;[32] he requested the city to urge Bernhard Straub, a burgher of Strasbourg, to pay the money he owed to Hans Quinckner of Sarburg;[33] he intervened in the case of a burgher named Valtin Lutz, a grain merchant who owed money to the villagers of Bahlenheim, pressing the city to force him to pay;[34] he requested the Magistrat to grant Steffan Scheudenbogen, a burgher of Saverne, a safe conduct for the Strasbourg fair so that he might buy and sell in peace;[35] and he petitioned the Rat to permit Diebold Karcher and his wife to return to the city after having been banished for a year.[36]

These petitions indicate that the bishop was still regarded as a court of appeals by burghers who felt they had not re-

31. M. Virck, ed., *Politische Correspondenz, 1,* nos. 662, 668.
32. Archives de la ville, Série AA, no. 1554, Folio 326, Aug. 21, 1524.
33. Ibid., Folio 328, July 21, 1525.
34. Ibid., Folio 328, Aug. 29, 1525 and Sept. 26, 1525.
35. Ibid., Folio 331, June 29, 1526.
36. Ibid., no. 1559, Folio 480, July 25, 1534.

ceived justice in the civil courts or who wished to hasten or press a decision. He looked after private petitions, and cases involving wills and inheritances—his traditional area of jurisdiction—continued to be referred to him.

During the 1520s and 1530s the bishop and the Magistrat corresponded on financial matters—usually involving money owed by the bishop to the city—and the episcopal councillor and delegation from the Rat met to confer on joint financial problems at fairly regular intervals.[37] Since it was the bishop who owed the money, this is hardly notable. More significant was the bishop's activity in the economic affairs of the diocese. Sometime around 1530 he undertook to improve some of the dikes along the Rhine and asked the Rat to assign the engineer Diebold to him in order to complete the plans.[38] The city apparently cooperated since in a later document, between 1534 and 1537, the bishop asked that two more men, skilled in their art, be sent to work on the project.[39] He was also involved in a dispute between the furriers and one of their guild masters. Apparently it was an affair of long-standing; several letters had been written indicating that the furriers had not carried out their responsibilities to the master. The bishop intervened in favor of the master, asking the Rat to instruct the furriers to abide by their obligations as guildsmen.[40]

In 1533 Wilhelm was particularly concerned by the high

37. The summary listings of the bishop's correspondence give an idea of the relative frequency of these meetings. See J. Brucker, ed., *Inventaire sommaire des archives communales de la ville de Strasbourg antérieures à 1790* (4 vols. Strasbourg, 1878–1886), 3, 93–94.
38. Ibid., 3, 94. Although this document is listed in the inventory, it has unfortunately been lost or misplaced, for in a thorough search of the portfolio it could not be found.
39. Ibid., 3, 96. This document, too, has been lost.
40. Archives de la ville, Série AA, no. 1559, Folio 446, Apr. 17, 1534. The master furrier involved was one Diebold Pfaffenlapp. The city had already been involved in litigation on his behalf concerning their right to grant him, coming from Balbrunn, Bürgerrecht. Balbrunn was an episcopal town, and that is perhaps why the bishop became involved later on. See *Inventaire des archives de la ville,* Série V, p. 129, V, 73, no. 2.

price of grain and its possible impact on the economy of the region. It was a period of poor harvests. Prices had risen, and speculators were buying up grain and selling it outside the region. On September 5, 1533, he wrote to the Rat, proposing a conference on September 23 to revise the existing ordinances[41] and thus protect the burghers of Strasbourg and its surroundings from high prices and want. The Rat replied that the date was inconvenient, so the meeting was rescheduled for October 15.[42] The importance of this exchange was that the Rat made no attempt to refuse the invitation but recognized the bishop's right to assume leadership in such a matter. The meeting was held, and an ordinance formulated and apparently circulated for comment. The city objected to the wording of certain proposals, submitting their revisions in writing, but the bishop replied that he disagreed, that nothing should be changed, and that the ordinance should be promulgated as it stood.[43] On December 24, 1533, the bishop wrote the Rat urging it to carry out the ordinance strictly and with severity; it should not permit outsiders to preempt grain or to make large purchases; the object of all the citizens in the region should be to keep the supplies available for the local population.[44] Thus, in a moment when it was extremely important, the bishop took the initiative to regulate the grain trade, called a conference involving the participation of the various cities of the diocese, proposed the ordinance, and administered it. It should be noted that this occurred just after the synod had been held.

The bishop's correspondence indicates that he never abdicated his authority over his diocese. During the height of the Reform he performed his judicial functions and continued to carry out his responsibilities as a temporal lord. His relationship with the Rat did not change dramatically; there was a good deal of correspondence on chapter affairs,

41. Archives de la ville, Série AA, no. 1557, Folio 437, Sept. 5, 1533.
42. Ibid., Folio 442a, Oct. 2, 1533.
43. Ibid., Folio 442b, Oct. 28, 1533.
44. Ibid., Folio 436, Dec. 24, 1533.

especially during the exile of the Chapterherren, but the actual number of pieces on this matter does not seem to be greater than the usual correspondence with regard to conflicts between lay and ecclesiastical jurisdiction. The actual numerical count of letters sent by the bishop to the Rat, while it fell at the height of the crisis over the Reform, maintained a remarkable degree of consistency: 69 pieces from 1509 to 1514, 67 from 1522 to 1526, 48 from 1527 to 1530, and 58 from 1534 to 1537.[45] Even during the crisis itself relations were not entirely inimical. A traditional respect for the authority of the other remained. In 1527, which was not a very happy year for the Rat and the bishop, the latter nevertheless apprehended two burghers who, in the dead of night, had escaped from Strasbourg and were attempting to flee the city. He placed them in custody and wrote to the city for further instructions.[46] This is not the act of a sworn enemy, and the evidence as a whole indicates that the conflict between the two was limited to the ecclesiastical issue; each continued to recognize the legitimate authority of the other within its customary jurisdiction.

The attitude of the bishop toward the reformers, however, was in sharp contrast. They were the enemy, and there was no attempt at mediation or reconciliation from his side. In the very first years of the Reform he cited them to come before him, and when they failed to obey his prohibitions of preaching and marrying, he excommunicated them. They were then dead, as far as he was concerned—unregenerate, unrepentant, they were for him damned forever. Curiously enough, after a silence of fourteen years it was the reformers who resumed correspondence with the bishop.

It is impossible to know their precise motivation. By 1538 the reformers certainly realized that they had lost effective power over the church and were beginning to be disillusioned by their experiences as copartners of the Rat. Perhaps they

45. Brucker, *Inventaire sommaire, 3,* 89, 90, 93, 95.
46. Archives de la ville, Série AA, no. 1555, Folio 341, Jan. 17, 1527.

felt that the bishop would provide the weight and authority that they themselves did not possess. They may also have wished to extend their efforts to reestablish the unity of the church. They had worked constantly from 1535 to 1537 to achieve an understanding between the Lutheran and Zwinglian churches, and by 1537 a large number of South German cities and states had accepted a concordat written by Bucer.[47] Their success here may have given them genuine hope that they could negotiate with the bishop as well, for they proceeded to address a sixteen-page letter to him, asking him to resume his position as the bishop of Strasbourg. The document is of sufficient interest to present the major arguments in their original form.

> In the beginning we resolved to use the greater knowledge of Christian teaching and the reformation of the Church that Our Lord straightly communicated to us, as a means of improving the Mass and other ceremonies. . . . So Capito presented a proposal for the improvement of ceremonies and proper ordering of church services to the Chapters, and our Lords and *Magistrat* have several times presented this to you. As Your Grace and several of the beneficed priests in the city have never wished to consider such a proposal, we have now let it go for over eight years, and during that time our calling has waited in the hope that it would not be given of the Lord that we must bring about the whole reformation of the church in the city. Our consciences, however, will not excuse us from inaction. For while so many are called to this service, we cannot forsake the hope that we will be able to bring about the true worship.
>
> As we cannot then excuse ourselves for the time that has already elapsed, so we do not wish to proceed any further in the same thing. Thus we have in the name of

47. These included Frankfurt, Worms, Landau, Wissembourg, Esslingen, Augsburg, Memmingen, Kempten, and Reutlingen. The Swiss cities failed to respond. See Adam, *Evangelische Kirchengeschichte,* pp. 235–37.

the Lord, written to Your Grace that through the Redemption of Christ and for the salvation of so many souls, this disunity of church services in the city and territories of this diocese should be ended, by Christian desires and purposes. Your Grace will subsequently call together many pious men, as many as Your Grace wishes and desires, to come together graciously . . . [and] we would make manifest to this group the Christian moderation of our belief and proceedings so that Your Grace will have evidence and see that in this matter we seek nothing but the salvation and improvement of the church.

It is known to you . . . that we now for so many years have performed all the pastoral and episcopal services in the city . . . and that this is an intolerable defection from the order of the church, and Your Grace will know well how we wish to return these functions to Your Grace, and so we request that Your Grace will lift those same duties from us. . . . They are oppressive and unbearable to us.

On the other hand Your Grace is not to handle us as heretics . . . for if we were really false, we would not try to restore you to your bishop's authority and we request that you hear us and negotiate with us.

Thus we state by this writing that we believe firmly and with the help of God will never weaken therefrom . . . that which is in the Holy Scriptures, and also in the holy fathers and the canons . . . and this we teach and practice in our worship. . . . And it is not only the Holy Scriptures that are decreed by God but He also gave the canon of the church, which we have as set down by the holy councils and other holy fathers . . . and should others find that the customs and usages which we have discontinued, which others still hold to, are against the ways of the Christian religion . . . we would willingly discuss those matters with pious, learned men and give and receive Christian advice.

We believe and teach the one Godhead and the three-fold quality of the person of the divinity, the humanity of Christ, in whom the two qualities are mixed in one person. Also we believe in Original Sin, in the Resurrection, in the Truth of the Gospel, in Holy Baptism, in the Sacrament of the Body and Blood of our Lord Jesus Christ, and in the oneness of the Church.

We believe that the Church Fathers and Canons gave to each church the freedom to create the best ordinance. Thus we feel that the Latin Mass should be replaced by the Mass in the common language so it can be the teacher and instructor of the people, and should be celebrated as the Last Supper of Our Lord Christ, and we have changed the old custom only in this way.

We use in the common prayer and songs of the church the common speech so that all can understand and then know better the spirit of God as revealed in I Corinthians, 14, and this the Holy Fathers and Canons would recognize as necessary, for that we should sing in Latin . . . is not ordered in any conventicle or required by any one of the Holy Fathers.

The matter of marriage is more troublesome, for the ancient holy fathers always have held that the service of the church lay outside of marriage. . . . But this was established a long time ago and has resulted in sinfulness on the part of the clergy, and thus we feel that it is better for the clergy to marry than to live in open sin. All that we think on the matter is too long to be included in one short writing, but we wish to make it clear to Your Grace that we have not wished to turn away from the true ordinance of the church as written down by the Canons and the Church Fathers, but what we have altered is in the customs of the church where these things were subject to great misuse or were left within the freedom of every church.

And we want Your Grace to know that no malice remains on our side and that Your Grace should still therefore remain as the bishop and highest pastor of this church with us, and [Your Grace] will once again solely direct the churches in Strasbourg. And we hope, by the will of Christ, that you will forgive us that we have taken over the church, which we have been guilty of . . .

And we wish once again to become priests under you and to submit to your visitations and to examination by you. According to the canons and the imperial law in every province a Synod should be held and every bishop should examine the priests and servants of the church and reform them. So we call Your Grace no further than to such an episcopal visitation, examination, and reformation of us and others who would serve the church of the diocese.

We have, on behalf of the church of Strasbourg . . . many shocking misuses to complain about in terms of the teaching, ceremonies, and life of the church and use of church property . . . and all these supposed servants of the church, according to the Holy Canons, should be banned, not only from the church but also from the Christian community. . . . As bishop you have let these unworthy men stay, so that there are few God-fearing men among the priesthood. . . .

Many of these things we know bring great sorrow to Your Grace, and you would like to see them reformed. And we really seek for nothing more than a truly Christian reformation and improvement of the church . . . and we hope to serve Your Grace in Christ.[48]

It was a sincere attempt on the part of the reformers to restore the bishop to his position of authority if he were willing to accept the German Mass and the marriage of the clergy. They proposed a return to the episcopal form of church organization, in which the bishop would work with

48. A.S.T., 47, III, Folio 1, Versuche den Bischoff zur Reformation zu bewegen, Die Drei schrifften der prediger an den Bischoff, Dec. 12, 1537.

a synod. The final administrative authority would rest with the bishop, who would examine the diocesan clergy and conduct yearly visitations. The pastors reiterated their acceptance of the authority of the church fathers and the canons as equal to the scriptures and asserted their willingness to discuss contested points.

The bishop had no desire to enter into any negotiations whatsoever. He did not acknowledge the letter, and the reformers sent a second, this one abrupt and stiff in tone. They had written in December asking him to hear them and discuss with them the Christian management of the diocese. They had received no answer. By failing to reply, the bishop had disregarded his responsibility to God for the welfare of his people. While bearing the title of bishop, he had refused to hear those who requested a hearing. This he could not deny even to the blackest heretics. If they did not receive an answer from him, the preachers would be forced to continue to carry out the orderly reformation of the church by themselves.[49]

Again the bishop failed to answer, and a month later a third letter was sent, appealing to him in the name of Jesus Christ, as bishop of all the people of Strasbourg, not to scorn the words addressed to him but to grant a hearing to the reformers. If no reply should come to this third attempt, the ministers would be led to conclude that no answer was the answer, and they would mourn not only his failure to accept his episcopal responsibilities but also his unchristian character, for they had not demanded anything new but only what was ordered twelve hundred years ago in Council and maintained by all right and pious bishops and churches. They prayed that God would open his heart to the Word and grant him salvation while there was yet time, for they wished to serve the bishop in honor and service.[50]

49. Ibid., Versuche den Bischoff zur Reformation zu bewegen, Das andere schreiben an den Bischoff, undated but probably Feb. 1538, according to the following document.

50. Ibid., Versuch den Bischoff zur Reformation zu bewegen, Das dritte schreyben, Mar. 18, 1538.

The bishop finally replied to the third letter, curtly and somewhat sardonically. The conference proposed by the reformers would be unfruitful, for even if it led to a better understanding in Strasbourg, religious conflicts would remain in the rest of the empire, and the confusion would only be worse. Furthermore, the recess of the Diet of Augsburg forbade any changes whatsoever. As far as the diocese was concerned, he would gladly take action, but he was hindered in any attempt at correction by the Magistrat.[51] The bishop's attitude never changed: He recognized neither the Reform nor the reformers.

In 1541 Wilhelm von Hohnstein died. The Magistrat and the reformers were persuaded that his successor might be willing to discuss reconciliation. They wrote jointly to the cathedral chapter reviewing Wilhelm's failures, citing his unwillingness to cooperate in any movement toward pacification, and urged the chapter to elect a reforming bishop. The city wished to maintain the reforms already achieved or at least not to retreat from them. Therefore it was essential that the canons consider a man who was favorable to the Reformation of the diocese, cleansing it of simony and abuses.[52]

A fair number of the canons were friendly to the Reform, although not actual supporters,[53] and the chapter as a whole considered that it would be wise to avoid an extremist who might attempt drastic revision or solution. There were four possible candidates, two of whom were fanatical Catholics. The canons chose Erasmus von Limburg, the archdeacon of the chapter, a humanist who had manifested an interest in the Reformation. By nature he was a mild and tractable man with a conciliatory disposition.[54]

51. M. Virck, ed., *Politische Correspondenz*, 3, 719.
52. A.S.T., 47, III, Folio 2, Schreiben der Prediger und Rath nach Hohnstein's Tod, 1541.
53. Hahn, *Katholische Kirche*, p. 6. It is well to remember that Hahn is a Catholic historian.
54. Ficker and Winckelmann, *Handschriftproben*, 1, 41.

The ceremony of the election brought the two sides together for a brief moment. It was a Catholic occasion with a Protestant service:

> In the year 1541 Erasmus von Limburg was elected Bishop of Strasbourg by the high worthy Chapter of the Cathedral. At the time no Mass was sung, but Dr. Caspar Hedio preached a sermon in the morning and admonished the people to prayer, and after [the Bishop] was chosen, he was led to his palace and with him Duke Georg von Brunswick and Count Bernard von Eberstein, both canons. And then they went to the collation. After this the Bishop rode away to Kochersperg [sic], and the duke and the count rode next to him, and the Bishop did not ride into Strasbourg as the other Bishops had but also he did not come back to Strasbourg until the 19th of September, 1552.[55]

At the time of Erasmus' election there was some possibility that a concordat might be achieved between the reformers and the Catholics. Imperial policy, at that moment, stressed "Union and Reform." A meeting had been held between the two parties in November 1540 at Haguenau under the sponsorship of King Ferdinand, followed by a religious conference at Worms and the meeting at Regensburg in the spring of 1541. The Strasbourg reformers had been important members of the Protestant delegation to the latter and were far more convinced than the Lutherans of the desirability of an agreement. If they could establish a concord with the Catholics in the city, it would do much to strengthen the course of religious unity in the empire. Immediately after the election the reformers wrote to Saverne, asking Bishop Erasmus for a hearing. The bishop did not follow the precedent of his predecessor; he replied, but requested time to organize his affairs. In mid-July the Magistrat, appealing to the decisions at Regensburg, asked him to assign a group

55. Büheler, *Chroniques,* p. 85.

from the cathedral chapter to meet with the ministers for the discussion of steps for reestablishing the unity of the church.[56] The bishop ignored the request, but the Rat repeated it on September 4. Finally the bishop called a conference to meet at Mölsheim on October 18, 1541.

The delegation from the city included three of the leading Ratsherren—Peter Sturm, Mathis Pfarrer, and Martin Herlin. Bucer and Hedio represented the ministers. The Catholic group included the deacon of the cathedral chapter; Johann Christoph von Simmern; Count Bernard von Eberstein; the advocate Tüschelin; and the chancellor of the chapter, Welsinger. Bishop Erasmus himself took part in the proceedings. The municipal delegates were genuinely convinced of the desirability of achieving unity, but unity on their own terms. They felt that the only obstruction before had been Bishop Wilhelm, and they were quite sure that Bishop Erasmus would be willing to accept the major tenets of the reformed doctrine.[57]

Bucer opened the conference by calling for the reform of Christian teaching, in the use of the sacraments, and in the ordering of the church. Chancellor Welsinger answered him, stating that the chapter would consider abolishing abuses and taking steps toward a unified theology. The city delegation was unprepared for such a move; they had not thought of a negotiated theology but had assumed that the bishop would accept their doctrines without any resistance. They themselves had no desire to compromise or negotiate. The gap between the two groups was still there. "Religious unity" meant the acceptance of one's own point of view. The conference failed, and Bishop Erasmus returned to Saverne, from whence he stolidly resisted the encroachments of the city on his episcopal authority. He quarreled with the Magistrat over the form of the oath he had to take in order to make his traditional entry for his consecration, unwilling to accept the ancient formulation that he would "further and

56. Hahn, *Katholische Kirche*, p. 109.
57. A.S.T., 47, IV, Reformations gesprach in Mölsheim, 1542.

increase the freedoms of the city." [58] The city had enough freedom already. He renewed his predecessor's objections to the ordinances with regard to the clerical assumption of Bürgerrecht, and attempted to regain possession of the church property the Magistrat had appropriated.[59] He mounted a solid opposition to the changes the Reform had brought.

The Reform did not break down the Catholic church in Strasbourg. The old church maintained its basic structure. It lost the parishes, the monasteries and the convents, but it held the units that were important from a financial and economic point of view. The upper echelons of the Catholic hierarchy—the chapters, the ecclesiastical courts, the episcopal administration, and the bishop—survived. The old church did not absorb or assimilate the new doctrinal ideas but rejected them, and out of this rejection the Counter-Reformation was born.

58. Hahn, *Katholische Kirche*, p. 112.
59. *Ibid.*, p. 126.

CHAPTER 14

THE NEW INSTITUTIONS:
EDUCATION AND WELFARE

HE impact of the Reform on the church was not what the reformers had expected: The old church was unchanged and, in the end, was driven to reassert more strongly than ever its traditional dogmas and doctrines; the new church was not the Apostolic church restored, but a state church, controlled by the lay authorities. Only in the fields of education and social welfare did the reformers create changes close to their original conceptions, present new ideas, and establish institutions to make them effective.

Their greatest success lay in the establishment of a system of city schools. The old schools, attached either to the chapters or the convents, did not survive the early years of the Reform—they broke up. The teachers either joined the new movement and resigned their school appointment or rejected it and left the city. The reformers were prepared to fill the vacuum—education was an important element in their program, vital to an ideology based on the Word and its interpretation—and the preachers considered themselves educators as well as ministers. To them education and spiritual renewal were interdependent; through the first, the latter would be achieved, for learning and knowledge opened men to the all-creative Word of God. The teacher was one of the four God-ordained officers of the Christian commonwealth.

They began with adult education. By the fall of 1523 Zell was preaching in the cathedral, and Capito had begun to preach at St. Thomas. Bucer had no ecclesiastical post but "undertook the exposition of the Epistles to the Colossians in Latin and in German, and peasants, gardeners, craftsmen and people of all sorts streamed in [to hear him]."[1] It was probably December when several burghers[2] petitioned the Rat to open these lectures to the public, stating that the lessons were not in conflict with Christian belief and should be made available to all the citizens, for thus their knowledge would be extended, and they would hear the Gospel which was essential to their salvation.[3] The Rat's reply was to prohibit the meetings. A few months later it permitted Bucer to resume teaching, but this time he was to lecture only in Latin. This restriction meant that only the educated could attend, but it was assumed that they could be trusted to listen soberly, without resorting to extravagant action. The assumption itself provides an insight into the class concepts of the period. By 1524, however, the Rat no longer regarded the lectures as dangerous or as a threat to the peace of the city. They were given official recognition, and during the following year a bell was rung to inform the citizens when a lecture was about to start.[4]

Adult classes were a beginning, but the reformers were troubled by the inadequacy of primary education and took the initiative in recommending improvement of the schools. In January or February 1524 Luther had appealed to the magistrates of all German cities to organize schools for children.[5] In their very first petition, addressed to the Magistrat

1. Letter of Nicolaus Gerbel to Johann Schwebel, Christmas, 1523. Quoted in J. Baum, *Capito und Butzer*, p. 240.
2. Johann Baum believed that the "burghers" in this case were really the reformers themselves, who by their assumption of Bürgerrecht could so sign themselves at this time.
3. A.S.T., 84, Folio 2, Declaration de plusieurs bourgeois au Magistrat qu'ils se font expliquer l'Evangile de St.-Jean par Bucer, 1523.
4. Charles Engel, *L'École latine et l'ancienne académie de Strasbourg, 1536–1621* (Strasbourg, 1900), p. 14.
5. Martin Luther, "Letter to the Magistrates of all German Cities," in *Luther's Works*, Jaroslav Pelikan and Helmut T. Lehmann, eds.: *The Christian in Society II*, Walther Brandt, ed., (55 vols. Philadelphia, 1962), 45, 354–57.

on August 31, 1524—only eight days after the decision of the Schöffen to permit the teaching of the Gospel—the reformers brought up the question of education. The major focus of the request was on the establishment of a committee of Ratsherren to carry out the provisions of the mandate on preaching of December 1, 1523, but appended to this was a final paragraph in which the reformers noted that it was their duty as Christians and as citizens to strive for the piety of the whole city and to protect it from harm. Thus they wished to note that the youth of the city should be provided with pious, learned schoolmasters and brought to a Christian knowledge of God and of the useful things of the world, for, they continued, the hope of the common good (*gemeynen nûtz*) rested on the youth.[6] This concept of the common good was a new and original contribution of the Strasbourg reformers and probably originated with Bucer himself.[7] It broke the bonds of the medieval ecclesiastical educational ideal and, in a sense, went further than the concept of the humanists, whose approach was individualistic rather than collective. Here was a statement of educational goals in the broadest social terms—to educate the individual for the benefit of the whole community. Furthermore, the Rat should assume the supervision over a function that had hitherto belonged to the church alone, and from henceforth, Christian and burgher education should go hand in hand.[8]

Four days later, on September 3, a second petition from the reformers, again written by Bucer,[9] asked that a new committee of Ratsherren be established to handle the schools. The reasons offered were the same as before: Good schools would benefit the burghers and lead to the proper service

6. Ernst-Wilhelm Kohls, *Die Schule bei Martin Bucer in ihrem Verhältnis zu Kirche und Obrigkeit* (Heidelberg, 1963), p. 50.

7. Kohls is responsible for the research on and publication of the documents which reveal Bucer's concept of "gemeynen nûtz." He bases his conclusion that it was Bucer's conception on his knowledge of the Bucer manuscripts. Cf. ibid., pp. 51–52.

8. Ibid., p. 50.

9. See Kohls' note in Stupperich, *Bucers Deutsche Schriften*, p. 396.

of God, for through education, young people would be correctly instructed and thus molded toward a Christian life. And now was the time; the Rat had an exceptionally favorable opportunity to reform the schools, to lift them out of their mediocrity.[10] The remainder of the petition was vague and general, directed against gambling, dice, and the wine Stuben, but the Rat was attracted by the section on schools, appointed a committee to consider the matter, and asked the reformers to develop their recommendations further.

On February 8, 1525, the reformers presented an amplified memorandum. They reiterated that schools were a means of achieving a better moral and spiritual life in the city, for the people would be instructed and would be more friendly toward each other when they were freed from ignorance and from the coarse and rough demands of raw nature. Furthermore, among a truly educated people, there would be none of the error that had kept the world from the light and turned men away from God.[11] To achieve a proper ordering of the schools, they suggested that the Rat should appoint three or four of its members to serve as a permanent school committee, assisted by two of the ministers. The committee would be responsible for hiring the teachers, providing their salaries, and consulting with them in regard to teaching and books; they would visit the schools every month to see that all were learning diligently. They should provide six schoolhouses for boys, and six for girls, so that both sexes would become pious, God-fearing citizens. In these schools the children would be taught to read and write in German. Four secondary schools could then be formed from the old chapter schools of Old and Young St. Peter, St. Thomas, and St. Stephen; each should be provided with pious, learned teachers—a preceptor and an assistant—to teach Latin, Greek, and Hebrew.[12] To prevent the students from learning evil habits, each should spend only half the day in school;

10. Stupperich, *Bucers Deutsche Schriften,* p. 397.
11. Ibid., p. 400.
12. Ibid., p. 401.

the other half should be spent at home with his parents, learning to work with his hands under his father's direction.[13] The schoolrooms of the four chapters could be used, and the monies the chapters had used for school purposes could now be assigned to the new public institutions since in this way church property would be assigned to the "common good." [14] Further revenues would be available from the Franciscans, the Wilhelmites, the Augustinians, and the Knights of St. John since they had also supported schools. If this were not enough, revenues from the Carthusians and the nuns' cloisters might be assigned "since they are particularly rich and powerful and yet do very little for the community." [15] The petition concluded with the hope that action might be taken quickly and not postponed endlessly.

The novelty of the reformers' recommendations lay in placing all the schools under a centralized direction and providing unified administration of both elementary and Latin schools. Medieval custom had tended to leave elementary instruction to chance, usually in the hands of private instructors who operated in complete independence. Now these schools were to be carefully organized and supervised as the first unit of a larger system. The plan also envisioned selection and supervision of all teachers by a public authority, again an innovation, since this control had been the prerogative of the particular convent or chapter directing a school. Finally, there would be a unified curriculum in all the schools, developed by the school committee and the teachers, working in concert. This comprehensive plan would have delighted Wimpfeling and Brant but was not drawn from their earlier recommendations. It was based, rather, on the pragmatic situation of the moment, and on Zwingli's experiences in Zurich, for on January 29, 1525, Bucer had written to his colleague, asking him to send details on the form and administration of the Zurich schools. Zwingli had

13. Ibid., p. 402.
14. Kohls, *Die Schule bei Martin Bucer*, p. 55.
15. Stupperich, *Bucers Deutsche Schriften*, p. 403.

emphasized the importance of freeing the teachers from their dependence on the students by providing for salaries and also suggested some outside supervision of the schools.[16]

Immediate action in Strasbourg on the reformers' proposals was impossible. The crisis of the Peasants' War intervened and neither Rat nor reformers had time for schools. In the interim two former clerics, Lucas Hackfurt and Otto Brunfels, opened private Latin schools so that some instruction was available. When peace was restored, however, the reformers returned to the problem and on August 10, 1525, petitioned the Magistrat to take action on the educational program. Five days later the Magistrat appointed Hedio and three members of the Rat to visit the convents and chapters and open negotiations for the use of some of their revenues for public schools. The delegation was not enthusiastically received and reported that it feared nothing could be done without violence.[17] Only the chapter of St. Thomas said that it would be willing to contribute forty gulden.[18]

On February 9, 1526, a year and a day after the original petition, the Magistrat took a decisive step; it established a permanent school committee drawn from the very highest ranks of the Ratsherren. Three men, to be called *Scholarchen,* were to be selected from the XIII, XV, and XXI; the group would always include one former Stettmeister, one former Ammeister, and an active member of the Council of XIII. They were to be assisted by two inspectors or visitors drawn from the preachers and teachers. In this one instance the reformers' recommendations had been accepted, and the reformers themselves were to have an effective role in developing and controlling the schools. The first Scholarchen appointed were Jacob Sturm, Nicolaus Kniebis, and Jacob Meyer, three of the most respected men in the Rat. Caspar Hedio and Jacob Bedrot, a master of arts and canon of St.

---

16. Kohls, *Die Schule bei Martin Bucer,* pp. 63–64.
17. Engel, *L'Ecole latine,* p. 8.
18. Ernst Anrich, *Zur Geschichte der Deutschen Universität Strassburg* (Strassburg, 1941), p. 23.

Thomas, were appointed visitors.[19] Jacob Sturm's appointment was of central importance. Wimpfeling's tutee, he had grown up under the direction and guidance of the great pedagogue, and thus he represented a continuity between the humanists and the Reform.

Late that summer the Scholarchen reported that they had made arrangements for one Latin school to be quartered in buildings that had been part of the Dominican convent. On November 7, they presented two candidates for the post of schoolmaster to the Ratsherren. The appointment was given to the lowest bidder, so Johann Sapidus, formerly director of the Latin school at Sélestat, now became principal of Strasbourg's new municipal Latin school.[20] Two years later Otto Brunfels voluntarily placed his school under the Scholarchen; his pupils were installed in the old Carmelite convent, and the city had two Latin schools. Brunfels departed after his hearing before the synod of 1533, but the Scholarchen immediately appointed Peter Dasypodius to fill his place. These schools were needed. They were successful and grew rapidly; by 1535 both Sapidus and Dasypodius required two assistants.[21]

Meanwhile, Bucer's original lecture program had expanded, and courses were being offered just below the university level. Early in 1524 instruction in Greek and Hebrew was added to the theological lectures, and instructors were brought in from outside.[22] In 1526 the Scholarchen assumed supervision of the classes as a part of the municipal system. By 1528 the lectures had lost their original adult-education, extension-course flavor and were focused on training theologians. The Scholarchen augmented the courses, adding

19. Engel, *L'Ecole latine*, p. 9.
20. Ibid., p. 11.
21. Ibid., p. 12.
22. Hebrew was first taught by a former Jew, Antonius, then, after August 1524 by Gregor Caselius, and then by Bonifatius Wolfhart and Michael Delius. Greek instruction was started by Johannes Lonicer in 1524 and continued by Jacob Bedrot. See Kohls, *Die Schule bei Martin Bucer*, p. 59.

new fields. Their goal was to supplement the Latin schools, providing young burghers with a broader preparation before they went on to universities.[23] In the early years the lectures had been given in the choir of the cathedral, but by 1528 they, too, were moved to the Dominican convent,[24] which now housed this activity in one wing and the Latin school in another. The offerings were comprehensive. Bucer lectured on the New Testament; Capito, on the Old; Hedio gave courses in theology and history; to these were added rhetoric, mathematics, and geography.[25] In 1529 the Scholarchen arranged for lectures on the *Institutes* by the city jurist,[26] and the first medical courses were given.[27] The school committee had provided not only for the needs of the church but had also opened up the fields of law, medicine, and administration to the youth of the town.

The Magistrat was proud of the new system; indeed, when Jacob Sturm was required to justify the city's defection from the old religion before Charles V at the Diet of Augsburg, part of his defense was that the stature and reputation of the city had been enhanced by new educational institutions.

> First, we provided two schools for young boys wherein two languages, Greek and Latin, are taught besides discipline and virtue.
>
> Second, lectures are paid for and established in the Dominican cloister for the learned and eager priests who wish to learn more, in the Greek and Hebrew languages, in mathematics, in poetry, in rhetoric, and in the law of the world.
>
> Third, every day the books of the Bible and the scriptures are read in the Chapter of St. Thomas, and this, instead of church exercises, is for the good of the God-

23. Engel, *L'Ecole latine*, p. 14.
24. Kohls, *Die Schule bei Martin Bucer*, p. 60.
25. Ernest Höpffner, "Jean Sturm et l'enseignement supérieur des lettres a l'école de Strasbourg," in *L'Humanisme en Alsace*, p. 84.
26. E. Anrich, *Deutschen Universität Strassburg*, p. 27.
27. Kohls, *Die Schule bei Martin Bucer*, p. 59.

fearing and learned priests and to give them an opportunity to improve themselves. A bell is rung as a sign
that the lectures will begin.[28]

Once higher education was well provided for, the Scholarchen turned their attention to the elementary schools for
boys and girls that had been a part of Bucer's original
recommendation. In 1529 the Rat voted to establish an elementary school in each of the nine parishes of the city.[29]
They directed the Scholarchen to draw up plans, which were
carefully considered and discussed, and in 1531 the schools
were instituted with a dual objective—"to habituate the
youth to the fear of God and to study." [30] The new schools
were attached to the parish churches, served the children
of that particular district, and bore the name of the parish.[31]
The Scholarchen appointed the teachers and supervised the
schools through frequent inspections by themselves or by
the visitors. With the establishment of these elementary
schools, the city had achieved a coordinated system of education from the primary classes up to the university under
centralized supervision and control. The chapter schools
were replaced by the Latin schools, and the small private
schools by the new elementary units. And the new public
control was thorough. In 1537 Frau Gregorien Edelman
opened a school near Old St. Peter without authorization
from the school committee; it immediately moved to visit
and inspect her classes, and since nothing further is recorded,
they were probably suspended.[32]

New facilities were also added. In 1531 the Rat voted to
establish a library for the schools. Neither the chapters nor
the convents were willing to let the reformed preachers

28. Text in Joseph Knepper, *Das Schul-und-Unterrechtswesen in
Elsass* (Strassburg, 1905), p. 196.
29. Archives de la ville, Série VI, 695, 21, Mémoire sur les écoles
élémentaires, unpaginated.
30. Ibid.
31. Ibid.
32. A.S.T., 324, Rapport des visiteurs de l'école, Mar. 27, 1537.

or teachers consult their books, so the Rat instructed the Scholarchen to install a library in the choir of the Dominicans' church. When the room was ready, Jacob Sturm sent over his own books, later bequeathing them to the schools.[33]

Bucer's next ambition was to establish a theological school in one of the upper German cities to provide a common education for future theologians.[34] Correspondence went back and forth between him and the Swiss reformers, particularly Ambrosius Blaurer in Constance, until finally the latter reported an offer from Peter Buffler, a merchant of Isny, to underwrite the tuition for one theological student from each of the four cities, Constance, Lindau, Biberach, and Isny if the cities themselves would agree to support other students.[35] The Magistrat of Constance then wrote to the Strasbourg reformers, in April 1534, requesting them to accept these new students. The ministers went through the proper channels and referred the letters to the Scholarchen, stating that they supported the move. The Scholarchen reported to the Rat that they were willing to assume responsibility for such an enterprise but suggested that the city, for its part, should support four theological students from Strasbourg. The group could be lodged in the Dominican convent, with one room for a dormitory, a cell for the instructor, and one room to serve as a study hall. The Magistrat accepted the proposal, agreeing to furnish food and lodging for the students for thirty florins a year.[36] The new institution was called the Collegium Praedicatorum, and very soon the burghers of Strasbourg were petitioning to have their sons admitted on payment of a fee. Opposed to mingling rich students with scholarship students, the director of the school refused the requests, and the Rat accepted his de-

33. Engel, *L'Ecole latine*, p. 16.
34. Stupperich, *Bucers Deutsche Schriften*, 7, Bucers Vorschlag zum weitern Ausbau der Strassburger Schul-und Vorlesungeswesens, p. 522.
35. Ibid., Der Stifftbrief wie die vier stett Constanz, Lindow, Bibrach unnd Isni sampt Petern und Josen den Buflern ain Schulstifft habent uffgericht, p. 539.
36. Engel, *L'Ecole latine*, 17.

cision. On March 29, 1535, they voted to limit the Collegium Praedicatorum to scholarship students, all future theologians, and to open a second school, a Paedogogium for Strasbourg students who could pay the fees.[37]

The arrangements had become complicated. There were the elementary schools, the Latin schools, the Collegium Praedicatorum, and the Paedagogium as well as the lectures and courses at the Dominican convent, and the interrelationships of these units were not clearly defined. Inevitably there was duplication and rivalry, and Hedio and Bedrot's monthly visits, followed by the Scholarchen's quarterly visit, led to the conclusion, in December 1537, that a consolidation of the Latin schools was essential.[38] The financial arrangements were particularly tangled and complex. Bucer believed that the school system should be based on old chapter and church funds rather than on grants from the Magistrat.[39] Thus he visualized an educational system which would be financially independent of the city authorities, and in this instance he was successful in achieving his goal.

The Rat appointed a special commission to consider consolidation, a group which must have included the Scholarchen, the visitors, Bucer, and Jacob Sturm since the draft of the recommendations is in Bedrot's hand, heavily corrected by Jacob Sturm and Bucer.[40] Their report called for unification of the Latin schools and the Paedogogium. No one of these schools, it was noted, could be divided into six classes because there were not enough teachers. However, if the schools combined, a proper order of classes could be established, with a teacher for each group. The change was especially desirable, because the school committee could not hire experienced teachers at the salaries they could offer. The young men they hired required supervision, and this could be accomplished more efficiently in one school than in three.

37. Stupperich, *Bucers Deutsche Schriften*, 7, Die Statuten des Prediger-Kollegiums (1535), p. 547.
38. Kohls, *Die Schule bei Martin Bucer*, p. 84.
39. Ibid., p. 82.
40. Ibid., pp. 84, 87.

Finally, larger classes in the combined school would also provide better competition for the students and give them greater stimulus to learn.[41]

The Rat probably acted on this report in February 1538.[42] The schools were combined; the Dominican cloister was given over to them, and Jean Sturm was appointed rector of the new Gymnasium.[43] Sturm had arrived in the city only in the previous year, having been called from Paris by Bucer and the school committee to teach rhetoric. His classes were so popular that the Scholarchen had forbidden the teachers of the Latin schools to attend since they deserted their own classes to do so. Brilliant as a teacher, he possessed administrative gifts as well. He combined humanist aspirations toward learning with religious sincerity and created a school that made Strasbourg a center of learning and intellectual influence.

Sturm thought in much the same way as the reformers. He talked of balance and harmony, and his goal for his school was to create an enlightened piety.[44] The mere acquisition of languages and the pursuit of *virtu* were inadequate, for the end of education was to create a Christian man. Yet piety alone was also insufficient. Education must provide that knowledge of things, of nature, and of the mind which had been so fully cultivated by the ancients. Thus Sturm's pupils read the classics not only for grammar and rhetoric, but for their content. Latin was not merely a tool; the ancient authors could reveal the world and its meaning to the students. To achieve this goal, Sturm used novel pedagogical

41. Stupperich, *Bucers Deutsche Schriften,* 7, Vorentwurf des "Ratschalags" zur zusammenfassung der Strassburger Lateinschulen (1538), pp. 558–59.

42. Ibid., Introductory note, p. 554. See also Kohls, *Die Schule bei Martin Bucer,* p. 87.

43. The institution was known by a variety of names. It has become customary, however, to refer to the secondary classes as the Gymnasium and the combined Gymnasium and lectures as the *haute école* or *Hochschule.* See Jean Rott, "L'Humanisme et la réforme pédagogique en Alsace," in *L'Humanisme en Alsace* (Paris, 1939), p. 73.

44. Ibid., p. 75.

methods. The students wrote essays, gave speeches, held disputations, and presented plays as a means of using the language. Each student made his own dictionary, inscribing every new term or phrase and its definition in a great book, which accompanied him through his school course.[45] At the same time, Sturm was restrained in his method of communicating the Christian gospel. He did not attempt to teach religion as an academic discipline; yet it was the focus of the school, conveyed not by formal classes but by example and by the very atmosphere. Christianity was lived, not taught. Only in the higher classes were the students given the privilege of reading the Greek texts of the New Testament.[46]

Although Jean Sturm provided a spirit of dedication and genuine Christian zeal, it was Bucer who continued to concern himself with the financial and administrative arrangements for the school system. From the very beginning, the Magistrat had financed the public lecture system from funds of the chapters and convents originally assigned to educational purposes, and it had used the convents for classroom space. The major problem, however, was salaries for the teachers, and this was solved by the use of canonical prebends for the teachers. Essentially the system allowed the Magistrat to assume the right to make appointments to the prebends that came vacant in uneven months; in other words, they took over the old papal privilege of appointment and gave these salaried positions to men who would then teach in the schools. The arrangement was suggested by the chapter of St. Thomas in 1529. In a memorandum addressed to the Magistrat, the canons wrote that "They proposed to use the Chapter funds for the Glory of God and the good of the city, and to return them to their original use, for the chapters, by origin, had been schools for training men for the ecclesiastical responsibilities." [47] They then invited the Rat to make an appointment to a canonry that

45. Ibid., p. 77.
46. Engel, *L'École latine*, p. 28.
47. Ibid., p. 58.

had come vacant in the month of July. Jacob Bedrot was given the post and taught Greek. Unfortunately only the chapter of St. Thomas, which was largely Protestant, made this arrangement voluntarily. Other chapters were assessed for funds for the school, but little was forthcoming, and they continued to use their canonrys as sinecures. The Scholarchen, in the meantime, were hard pressed to find sufficient revenues to pay the teachers, and the schools were constantly growing; under no circumstances were they permitted to use the public funds in the *Pfennigthurm*.[48]

In 1539 Bucer felt that more adequate and regular financing must be provided, and he presented to the Rat the draft of a law that was later known as the *Municipalstatut*.[49] It was designed to make use of the funds of the chapters for the service of the community and used the device of examination to control appointments. The chapters were permitted to keep their traditional right of appointment in even months; the Rat, however, would make all appointments in uneven months. In each chapter a committee of five canons was to be appointed to examine each candidate, under the supervision of a member of the Rat. Conditions for appointment included legitimacy, impeccable moral character, and a promise of faithful performance of duties.[50]

The act was important to the schools because it freed them from their hand-to-mouth dependence on whatever funds the Scholarchen could scrape together. The new arrangement was strongly opposed by the bishop and those chapters that had remained Catholic, but the provisions were carried out over their protests. In 1540 Dasypodius, a strong Protestant, was appointed to a prebend in the Catholic chapter of Young St. Peter.[51] It was not until the Interim in 1548 that the Catholic church was able to regain its old privileges. It took back its control of the Catholic chapters, but the

48. Ibid., p. 56. The *Pfennigthurm*, literally the "Penny Tower," was the tower where the city treasury was located.
49. Kohls, *Die Schule bei Martin Bucer*, p. 92.
50. Stupperich, *Bucers Deutsche Schriften*, 7, Municipal Statut eins Ersamen Rahts der Statt Strassburg (1539), p. 574–76.
51. Engel, *L'Ecole latine*, p. 59.

revenues of St. Thomas were left undisturbed, so that the schools were able to maintain the majority of their teaching staff.[52] Bucer's plan was successful not only for the immediate moment but also in the long run it provided the schools with stable, guaranteed revenues. It also represented the rare instance in which the Rat accepted one of Bucer's recommendations. Its assent may have stemmed from the fact that it was thus relieved of paying the teachers' salaries.[53]

The schools were perhaps the only area where the reformers maintained a degree of leadership right through the whole period. It also provided one of the few examples of close, relatively amicable cooperation between the Magistrat and the ministers.[54] As visitors, clergymen like Hedio and Bedrot played an important part in administering the system. They carried the main burden of supervision, and their reports indicate that they maintained a strict watch over the teachers, the teaching, and the students.[55] Funds for the system came from the chapters, but final controls, involving appointments and salaries, lay with the Scholarchen.[56] Here, then, was an effective sharing of responsibility,

52. Ibid., p. 60.
53. Kohls, *Die Schule bei Martin Bucer*, p. 94. Kohls feels that Bucer conceived of the Municipal Statut as a means of tying the schools more closely to the reformed church since it made the teachers independent of the city. Since the city had never assumed the responsibility for their salaries and since control of the schools still rested in the *Scholarchen*, it would seem to be premature to speak about independence.
54. See Walter Sohm, *Die Schule Johann Sturms und die Kirche Strassburgs in ihrem gegenseitigen Verhältnis, 1530–1581*. Historische Bibliothek, 27 (München und Berlin, 1912). A struggle between the Magistrat and the schools did develop, but this was mainly after the Interim and therefore does not fall within the compass of this study.
55. Some of these reports are available in A.S.T., no. 324. The visitors seem to have kept a particularly close eye on the morals of the school teachers and on the example they set for the pupils.
56. For an excellent résumé of the assignment and utilization of chapter funds for the schools, see Jean Rott, "Documents Strasbourgeois concernant Calvin," *Revue d'histoire et de philosophie religieuses, 44* (1964), pp. 312–20.

and under the joint command, the schools flourished.

Even more significantly, the reformers had instituted a new educational aim with their criterion of *gemeyn nutz*.[57] They talked in terms of education for the common needs of the ordinary burgher. In practice the training they offered remained fundamentally theological, but even so, they were thinking in broader terms. If common men were educated so that they themselves could read and understand the Bible, then they would be open to the Word and a true reformation of men and society could take place. Thus their schools were an essential element in creating the Christian community.

The other important area of innovation was in public welfare. Here the Reformation served to accelerate developments already in process, facilitating the establishment of a centralized system of poor relief controlled by the municipal authorities. It will be remembered that the Magistrat had taken over the direction and administration of certain welfare institutions well before the Reformation. Beginning in 1263, they had brought the major hospitals and the distribution of certain alms under their own supervision, and various Ratsherren served as *Spitalpfleger, Waisenpfleger,* or *Blatterhauspfleger,* responsible for the revenues and administration of these hospitals and asylums for the poor. Furthermore, the status of practice of begging and almsgiving had begun to be seriously questioned. Traditionally, in medieval thought, the beggar was a privileged person, sanctified in a sense by the piety of men like St. Martin. Through his want a Christian could achieve salvation by giving alms, for had not Christ Himself said, that which you do for the least of my brethren, you do also for me?

During the course of the fifteenth century, however, new attitudes had taken shape. Begging began to be recognized as a public burden, and the Magistrat of Strasbourg had attempted to regulate the practice, hoping to limit beggars to those in real need, preventing solicitation of alms by persons

57. Kohls, *Die Schule bei Martin Bucer,* p. 76.

capable of supporting themselves in other ways. As early as 1411, the Rat specified that the poor had a responsibility to work if they could; only those who could not work because of illness or some other calamity should beg.[58] This attitude toward work represented a definite break with the past. The medieval church's emphasis on asceticism had stigmatized labor; work was an evil, the burden man bore for Adam's original sin. In the fifteenth century ideas changed. Disilllusioned with the mendicant friars, dissatisfied with the old practices of almsgiving, and attracted by a new urban culture, men began to feel that work was respectable.[59] In 1414 the Strasbourg Rat promulgated a second ordinance prohibiting the solicitation of alms by the able-bodied.[60] The break with the past had already begun.

The overlapping system of poor relief and haphazard distribution of alms was also subject to criticism and needed reorganization. For centuries individuals had left money and property to a profusion of agencies and provided explicit and particular instructions for gifts to the needy. One will might provide that bread should be distributed to twenty-five beggars on Christmas Eve, another that a penny should be given to sixteen poor men on St. Martin's Day. Each individual bequest had to be carried out, and the parishes, monastic houses, and the city, itself, all had different obligations and responsibilities. By the fifteenth century there was pressure on the city to reorganize the mass of gifts, purses, and donations into a coherent system.[61]

58. Except for a few incidental documents the major materials on welfare in Strasbourg are available in print in Winckelmann, *Das Fürsorgewesen der Stadt Strassburg.* Winckelmann was one of the great archivists of Strasbourg, and the book constitutes a major contribution to the publication of source materials. The volume actually comprises two in one, a first section of text (1) followed by the documents (2). Rather than use a long string of ibid.'s, I will simply use the designation 1 or 2, followed by the page number, and, in the case of documents, the document number. 1, p. 67.
59. Ibid.
60. 1, p. 70.
61. 1, p. 63.

Even Geiler von Kaysersberg, who stubbornly resisted the extension of the magistral authority in most areas, urged the Magistrat to establish a new order of poor relief and in his XXI Articles had proposed that all beggars who were in sound health should work; only those incapable of work should receive relief.[62]

During the decades of the Reform the problems of poor relief were intensified. The bad harvest and high prices of 1517–18 brought a great number of foreign beggars to Strasbourg. Peter Wickgram wrote to a friend that 2,200 persons received alms, while Gebwiler wrote that one thousand beggars were capable of working. The city met the immediate crisis by distributing grain from its warehouses at cheap prices to the poor residing in the hospitals, the poor house, or hostel.[63] These years were followed by others just as depressed. Bad harvests and high prices were the pattern from 1526 to 1530 and again from 1532 to 1535, so that poverty was a grim reality throughout the period, and action was essential.

Initial efforts to extend and reorganize the welfare system were made in November 1522. The Magistrat appointed a committee, which included Daniel Mueg, Mathis Pfarrer, Jacob Meyer, Jacob Spender, and Melchior Zuckmantel, to consider the problem of the poor and the indigent.[64] Pfarrer and Mueg may even then have been drawn to Lutheranism, but neither Capito nor Bucer had arrived in the city at this point, and Zell had only begun to preach. The reform of public welfare was not, then, linked directly to the Reformation. It was a normal outgrowth from preceding developments. The Reformation facilitated the emergence of a new system because it provided an effective ideological formulation and because the breakdown of the monastic units made it easier to institute new agencies. But the demand for change was not a result of the religious crisis. This had oc-

62. Ibid.
63. 1, pp. 73–74.
64. 1, p. 80.

curred separately. It was a coincidence, albeit a fortunate one, that the major ordinances with regard to poor relief were drawn up between 1522 and 1524 when the convents and monasteries were being dissolved. From 1522 the Magistrat ignored the traditional relationship between almsgiving and the church and quietly assumed control of the distribution of all forms of alms and relief in the city by placing them under the usual committee of Ratsherren. There was never any question of giving the reformers any representation on this committee or of consulting them with regard to the welfare ordinances. The Ratsherren believed that the distribution of poor relief was the responsibility of the civil authority.[65] Consciously and deliberately they took control. Mathias Pfarrer provided a clear statement of their intent, in a draft of an ordinance dated 1523.

> First, all the established funds for alms should be requisitioned, and these alms should be delivered over to the *Rat*, whether [collected] by spiritual or worldly persons, *pfleger* or others, so that no one will manage such alms subsequently, and thus that alms will be divided among the poor who are in need, as has been ordered. And so that such alms shall be delivered over to the *Rat*, as it has been drawn up in writing, it is necessary to assign a house where the revenues can be collected . . . and kept.[66]

In final form the ordinance provided that all gifts to the poor were to be given over directly to the city authorities, to be administered by them. Alms boxes were to be placed by the Rat in all the churches, and the citizen was to give his money there. Persons who wished to give flour, wine, clothes, or other gifts should take them to Lucas Hackfurt, the welfare administrator, for distribution by properly delegated authorities. A final section specified that all chapters, cloisters, and burghers who had formerly contributed their

65. Ibid.
66. 2, pp. 88–89, no. 40.

alms to foundations for the poor would henceforth give these monies to the civil authorities.

The ordinances gave broader powers to the civil authority. This assumption of power was, in turn, supported by certain teachings of the reformers. Alms giving was not a good work through which merit and salvation was achieved, but it was a Christian duty arising from a Christian concern for one's neighbor. Charity was an expression of the individual's faith in God and his love for his fellow man. Thus each citizen should give freely and willingly of his own wealth to the poor. The Magistrat incorporated these tenets in the ordinances but, at the same time, it did not dismiss all promise of a heavenly reward. The edict providing for alms boxes in the churches read:

> Each person can put his alms therein, to share with the poor and show his compassion, as God has admonished. And as he wishes to obtain mercy from God, then each person who in the situation of this disrupted world is concerned for his needy neighbor and gives to his help, must, on the day of Judgment, be given a true recompense, and for the earthly, the eternal will be obtained.[67]

Thus, there was a mingling of ideas; one held on to the old, while reaching out for the new.

The legislation of 1523–24 climaxed the campaign against mendicancy and provided a new system of home relief. Begging was abolished by law; any person who had been dependent on begging was to live at home, in his own house, receiving public funds for his support. These funds were to be collected by a committee of the Magistrat called *Almosenherren* and then given to the administrator of poor relief and his nine *Almosenpfleger*, each one responsible for a parish. The latter group would divide the available monies according to the requirements, and four young men would deliver the weekly allowance to each needy home, identified by a

67. 2, p. 106, no. 48.

red and white shield. To guarantee that the allowance was properly spent, the recipients wore similar shields on their clothing, and no one could serve them beer in a tavern or permit them to gamble. In addition, the administrator of welfare and the Almosenpfleger visited the homes of the poor to supervise their activities and their moral behavior.[68]

On August 14, 1523, the Magistrat appointed as the first welfare administrator, Lucas Hackfurt, an early protagonist of the Reform, later the principal of one of the Latin schools. Never a leader in the reform movement, he was an idealist with a genuine desire to create a more Christian community —for a short period later on he would be drawn to Anabaptism. His decision to become supervisor of the poor stemmed from a zeal to put his religious convictions into action. He saw the task as a form of Christian service, and his reports and administrative directives were suffused with Christian concern for his neighbors. He tried to awaken this same spirit in his fellow citizens but was met with indifference. His failure indicates that the ideas preached by the reformers were by no means fully understood or accepted by the average citizen.

He confronted a task of Sisyphus. The major problem was to procure adequate ways and means, for although the number of poor and needy rose throughout the period of the Reform, the new system never provided the previous revenues. Voluntary contributions, given in faith and love, never yielded the same quantity of revenue as that obtained when the donors believed their gifts would guarantee a better life in the world to come. Hackfurt was constantly in search of money. On March 8, 1527, he asked the Magistrat to make available additional funds from the chapter and the convents.[69] On March 27 he suggested that the treasures from two or three of the convents could be sold to provide needed cash.[70] On September 4, 1529, he proposed that the precious

68. 2, p. 98, no. 43.
69. 2, p. 113, no. 67.
70. 2, p. 114, no. 68.

goods, monstrances, and chalices of the churches could be sold and the proceeds used for alms.[71] The following week (Hackfurt was nothing if not persistent), he asked that the Almosenherren be given one or two of the largest monastic buildings so that they could have sufficient revenues and adequate space. They could use the buildings for storage of wheat and flour and could thus run their own bakery. The monasteries had originally been built for the sake of charity, he reasoned, and they should be returned to this purpose.[72] Later he attempted to limit the number of welfare cases by confining the city's responsibility to those who had been burghers for at least five years, and by providing work for the poor, thus removing them from the relief rolls.[73] But he was never able to arouse his fellow citizens to the overwhelming needs of the poor and the homeless.

The reformers encouraged and supported the work of the Almosenherren and of Hackfurt in particular, but they were in no way directly involved in the administration of relief. Their contribution was limited to offering advice and support to Hackfurt or to urging the Rat to enforce more rigorously existing ordinances. In a memorandum dated March 1531, Capito requested the Rat to take action against those who still begged in the streets, suggesting that if the beggars persisted in their habits, they should be deprived of their Bürgerrecht.[74] It was a far cry from the concept of the holy beggar.

Perhaps the major effect of the Reformation on the development of the system of public welfare was the arrival of streams of religious refugees from other cities and rural districts who compounded the problems of the Almosenherren. In a memorandum of 1529, directed to the reformers, Hackfurt outlined a plan for caring for the refugees. He noted first the basic problem of inflation and high prices,

71. 2, p. 118, no. 76.
72. 2, p. 120, no. 77.
73. 2, p. 138, no. 102.
74. A.S.T., 167, Von Bettlen uf den Gassen abzunstellen, Mar. 1531.

conditions sent by God as retribution for the sins of man. Everyone was struggling under these conditions, but it was made harder for Strasbourg because of the arrival of refugees from Germany and France. Because these persons had fled their homes for their religion, it was particularly necessary that the city manifest itself as merciful and eager to help. Every citizen of Strasbourg should give what he could, for each person was only the steward of his property—it was not really his own—and certainly no one would knowingly permit a stranger to be homeless. To make it easy for people to contribute, the Almosenpfleger would send carts around three times a week from house to house, to collect the necessaries of life for the refugees. People should bring out flour, bread, cheese, eggs, apples, vegetables, fish, meat, old shoes, clothes, hats, pillows, blankets, wood—in short, everything that was necessary.[75]

That the plan was not altogether successful is indicated by a later document in which Hackfurt complained in the name of the misery of all the poor. People had not put in the alms boxes the same amount of money they had given to the priests and monks, nor had they acted toward the refugees according to the example of the early church—sharing and offering their help to those in need. The citizens of Strasbourg were only interested in themselves and their own needs—giving gifts to their own family and friends who did not need them—giving only old clothes and junk, which could not even be sold in the secondhand market, to the refugees. They were unwilling to help them find work or employment, which was especially necessary for the young men and women. Hackfurt implored that for the love of God the burghers should think of the needs of the refugees during the hard winter to come.[76]

Welfare provides a particularly interesting example of the

75. A.S.T., 174, Gedechtniss für die Predicanten von der frembden Armen wegen, Dec. 159.
76. A.S.T., 174, Der Schaffner des gemeinen Almustens beklagt sich in Namen aller Armen, Dec. 1534.

impact of ideological change. In this case the new concept of Christian responsibility was not readily accepted. The average burgher had given when he thought it was a matter of assuring his eternal life. Now that he knew money would make no difference at the Last Judgment, he was less generous. The city had assumed a function it had coveted for years, only to find that it had insufficient revenues to meet these new responsibilities. The Reformation had attempted to provide a new concept of social responsibility. In actual fact it gave ideological support for the civil assumption of the welfare function. Indirectly it helped to make available monastic revenues and facilities, but even these were insufficient for a practicable system of indoor poor relief. The Reformation and the urban economy destroyed the myth of the holy beggar, but they did not destroy his need, nor were the reformers able, in so short a time, to establish a new ethic of charity, a new awareness of man's responsibility to his fellow man.

CHAPTER 15

ECONOMIC, SOCIAL, AND POLITICAL CONDITIONS AFTER THE REFORM

HE Reformation had little effect on the economic life or on the economic institutions of Strasbourg. These depended on the broader factors of European trade—the opening of the new Atlantic sea routes, the price rise, and the changes in the money market—the religious changes were external to them. In general, economic conditions were remarkably stable in these particular decades: The patterns of commerce and the flow of trade were not disturbed; Strasbourg continued to be a flourishing commercial center.

Data on economic conditions in other German cities reflect a similar pattern, with no particular change in the period of the Reform.[1] The major development was the steady upward movement of prices from 1500 until the Thirty Years' War.[2] This was a manifestation of the sixteenth-century price revolution, and existing records indicate consistently higher agricultural prices, with wages held at a relatively constant rate. Registers for individual German cities indicate poor agricultural conditions in the early thirties. Thus, the record for Augsburg shows a good harvest for 1525, famine in 1526, and high prices for grain, wine,

1. M. S. Elsas, *Umriss eine Geschichte der Preise und Löhne in Deutschland* (Leiden, 1936). See tables on pp. 34–35, 41–42, 48–49.
2. L'Abbé A. Hanauer, "Denrées et salaires," in *Études économiques sur l'Alsace ancienne et moderne* (2 vols. Strasbourg, 1878). See charts for prices of poultry, p. 209; saltwater fish, p. 221; dried vegetables, p. 237.

salt, and wood throughout Bavaria and Swabia in 1529. High prices and famine conditions are recorded for 1531 to 1534, and not until 1536 is there a surplus of wine and grain.[3] Munich records also indicate famine conditions for grain in the period from 1530 to 1532. In Strasbourg there is no record for 1528 to 1530, but in 1531 the price was 162 deniers per rezal of wheat, as against a usual price of around 60 or 70.[4] Bad harvests and famine conditions were again general from 1540 to 1542; the price of wheat per rezal rose to 192 deniers in Strasbourg in 1545.[5] Prices fluctuated, but daily wage rates were relatively stable for the period from 1525 to 1548. The Augsburg record shows an unchanging daily rate of 10.5 dinar for a strawcutter;[6] the plasterer's wage stood at 18 dinar,[7] and the bricklayer's at 28 dinar.[8] In Strasbourg, the carpenter's wage was stable at 24 shillings from 1525 to 1548; the mason's wage fluctuated slightly between 24 and 28 shillings.[9]

Trausch's record of agricultural prices in Strasbourg reflects conditions similar to those described by Elsas and Hanauer—a scarcity of food products which began in 1528. The price of grain rose from two to six florins (for an unstated measure), while Italian grain merchants were buying heavily in the Alsatian market. The people in Swabia had nothing to eat, and 1,400 peasants were housed and fed in the former Franciscan convent in Strasbourg.[10] The scarcity continued in 1529 and 1530, and prices were very high. An eight-ounce loaf of bread cost 1 pfennig; four eggs cost 2 pfennigs.[11] In 1535 the ten-year period of famine ended with a warm summer. Both 1539 and 1540 were particularly good wine years. The only poor year thereafter was 1544, when

3. Elsas, *Preise und Löhne*, pp. 186–87.
4. Hanauer, "Denrées et salaires," p. 94.
5. Ibid.
6. Elsas, *Preise und Löhne*, p. 724.
7. Ibid., p. 728.
8. Ibid., p. 731.
9. Hanauer, "Denrées et salaires," pp. 418–19.
10. Trausch and Wencker, *Chroniques*, p. 62.
11. Ibid., p. 63.

a great hailstorm in early May destroyed the fruit and vegetable plantings.[12]

In at least one of Strasbourg's major industries, weaving, conditions improved in this period. The depression the textile industry had suffered because of customs barriers of 1500 reached its lowest ebb between 1514 and 1520,[13] and this was followed by a period of recovery. Between 1525 and 1528 the Magistrat promulgated new regulations to maintain the quality of local textiles, making provisions for sealing and stamping the cloth in an attempt to restore the weaving industry to its former position.[14] This was followed in 1529 by a detailed edict minutely regulating cloth manufacture.[15] The new regulations were apparently successful, for although the industry had to struggle to compete with English goods and imports from the Low Countries, it reached a relatively stable position in 1550, lasting until the crisis of the Thirty Years' War.[16] The period of the Reformation was a time of relative stability, marked only by the recurrence of the same problems the industry had experienced in the fifteenth century: the division of labor among the various groups concerned with producing and selling cloth, the supervision of the measurement of finished materials, and the regulation of the manufacture of inferior goods. No major changes took place either in the organization of production or in the general level of economic activity.

Unfortunately, the lack of guild records for this period makes it impossible to analyze activity trade by trade, but detailed study of the furriers, locksmiths, and tailors reveals that the conditions of the previous period gradually congealed. The masters continued to extend disciplinary and regulative controls over the journeymen and apprentices.[17] This had started, however, well before the Reform. There is

12. Ibid., p. 64.
13. Schmoller, *Tucher und Weberzunft*, p. 514.
14. Ibid., pp. 136–38.
15. Ibid., pp. 138–42.
16. Ibid., p. 518.
17. Rott, "Artisanat et mouvements sociaux," pp. 153–54.

no evidence that the religious crisis of the twenties and thirties resulted in economic dislocation, and only a few documents indicate hardship or disruption. The sculptors and stonecutters addressed a petition to the Rat, complaining that they could no longer earn their living since the introduction of the Reform.[18] The apprentice tailors asked for a raise in wages in 1526 because of the abolition of saint's-day holidays. Wages had been fixed to include a certain number of holidays, and now the workers spent more days at work but received the same pay as before. They demanded, therefore, a higher wage and a day off every two weeks to take a bath. The Rat agreed that at least the chief journeymen should receive an extra *sou* a week and that the master was to provide food on bath days.[19] The apprentice furriers fared less well, the masters during this period consistently attempted to limit the number of workers in each shop. The workers objected strongly, saying that it went against the scriptures, which gave the right to work to every man, for man was made to work, as a bird was made to fly. Furthermore, the workers stated, the restrictions made it difficult for refugees from other cities to come to Strasbourg in pursuit of freedom to practice the gospel.[20]

While these indicate problems with the work week and wage adjustment, there is nothing in the records to indicate that any group suddenly came into possession of new wealth, or, conversely, that any group lost its wealth. Those who had money and economic power in 1520 still had it in 1548.[21]

18. Archives de la ville, Série V, 1, Folio 12.
19. Rott, "Artisanat et mouvements sociaux," p. 153.
20. Ibid., p. 154.
21. This statement is based on conversations with M. Joseph Fuchs, the archivist of the Strasbourg Archives. M. Fuchs' particular field of interest is economic and social history. He has scoured the Archives for pertinent materials, but they do not exist for the sixteenth century. M. François Wendel, the Professor of Protestant Theology at the University of Strasbourg, noted that a quantity of raw economic material exists in the records of notarial contracts. The notarial oath was administered by the city, and all contracts—marriages, loans, buying and selling—had to be sworn before an official notary. The complete records of notaries exist for the period from 1450 to 1680. A careful

Even the population and the size of the labor force seems to have been relatively stable. A rough estimate of the number of persons in the guilds before the Reform, in 1537 during the Reform, and again in 1545–46 may be obtained from rosters that appear in the city ordinances. It is impossible to arrive at any precise figures from these lists, but it does appear that despite the ravages of plague years the population maintained itself at a relatively constant level and may have even increased.[22]

The Reform did have a profound effect on the social structure of the city and on specific social groups. Medieval urban society was marked by its dualism. A relatively complete social ladder, ranging from the urban nobility down to the lowest apprentice, existed side by side with the ecclesiastical hierarchy, which ranged from the bishop and his administrative staff down to the parish priest's helper. There was little contact between the two groups. Living within the same walls, they lived separate lives. The legal division between the two was ended by the Magistrat's edict of 1525, which required all the clergy to purchase Bürgerrecht. Whether they lived closely with their fellow citizens or not, even the most arrogant *Chapterherr* was technically a citizen of Strasbourg and had sworn obedience to the Rat.

The reformers consciously tried to break down the ancient customs separating the burghers and the clergy. Casting off their clerical robes, they assumed the less conspicuous academic dress. They regarded it as their duty to marry, feeling that this would bring them closer to the lives and problems of their people. Similarly, they felt morally obliged to acquire Bürgerrecht.[23] Capito explained this carefully in a

analysis of these documents would provide a record of the approximate wealth of various individuals and families and would reflect any changes in their economic position.

22. See Appendix C.

23. The acquisition of burgher status was not an entirely new phenomenon, and it had always been encouraged by the Magistrat. However, as it became a matter of conscious policy on the part of the re-

pamphlet written in 1524. The scriptures taught that every man must submit to the secular authority and that it was therefore God's commandment that the clergy accept the responsibility of citizenship. In addition, citizenship provided a means by which a man could serve his neighbor and his neighbor's needs.[24] In his *Entschuldigung* before the bishop's Fiskal, Capito explicitly asserted his desire to establish better relations between the clergy and the burghers —the clergy had enjoyed a privileged status for too long and had used these advantages, not for the common good, but for their own enrichment and comfort. Instead of demanding a special status for itself, the clergy should set a good example to the burghers by sharing the burdens and responsibilities of the other citizens. This was Christian neighborliness.[25]

Having stated a new social ideal, the reformers put it into effect. They identified themselves with the Gemeinde and were accepted by them as leaders, and the old anticlerical feelings gave way to genuine respect and affection. Yet the ministers were not totally successful. They were never given the same degree of recognition, nor were they accepted as equals by the upper middle class, particularly by the Magi-

---

formed ministers, there were as many clerical purchasers of Bürgerrecht in one year as there had been before in ten. In 1525 the edict requiring purchase was passed, and thereafter the figure represents new clergy arriving in town. Number of Persons of Clerical Status Purchasing Bürgerrecht in Strasbourg (based on figures taken from the Archives de la ville, E.5, *Livres de bourgeoisie*, 1, 1480–1530).

1451–60	11	1523	22
1461–70	44	1524	22
1471–80	20	1525	172
1481–90	22	1526	21
1491–1500	12	1527	6
1501–10	25	1528	14
1511–20	11	1529	9

24. Röhrich, *Geschichte der Reformation*, 1, 189. The pamphlet was entitled: *Das die Pfaffheit schuldig sey burgerlichen Eyd zu thun on Verletzung irer Eeren.*

25. Capito, *Entschuldigung an den Bischoffen*, p. 4.

strat. The latter never granted them the deference and re-spect it showed to the bishop or the Chapterherren, indeed it was never quite sure where to place the ministers socially —higher than a priest, but somehow lower than a canon. The reformers did not fall heir to the political power of their predecessors either. The Rat was manifestly unwilling to treat them as political equals or to grant them supervisory powers even within their own sphere—the church. Thus, by attempting to bridge the ancient gap between clergy and laity, the reformers had created a new class, respected by the lower classes but separated from the seats of power.

The schism between the burgher and the clergy no longer existed legally. One whole group of clerical persons—the monks and nuns—had disappeared except for a few elderly nuns and a handful of monks. Both the reformers and the civil authorities had believed that secularization of the clergy would result in a new unity, in a stronger, corporate society. Instead, the Reform created within the city a series of sepa-rate groups, each one loyal to its own ideology. On the one hand there was the group of nuns still clustered in the con-vents, refusing to listen to the evangelical clergy who preached to them on Sunday, and the canons of the ca-thedral, Old St. Peter, and Young St. Peter still singing their services—all maintaining their loyalty to the bishop and the Roman church. While it is impossible to know how many citizens remained faithful to Rome, there were enough so that the Rat tried to control the numbers who went out to hear Mass in the villages. There always remained a handful of Lutherans, manifestly unsympathetic to the reformers and the Rat. After 1528 the majority, covering all classes from Ratsherren to apprentice, accepted the Reform. And then there were the Anabaptists.

No group reveled in their separateness more than the Ana-baptists. Their difference, their special election, their alien-ation from the main body was a major element of their at-traction. They drew their major support from the lower echelons of society, artisans, and craftsmen.[26] One can only speculate as to whether their espousal of sectarianism indicated a search for identity. This group had lost its original position in the economic hierarchy. They could exercise little influence in their guilds, a journeyman could no longer move easily up the ladder to become a master craftsman. Denied the opportunity to acquire economic status or security, Anabaptism offered its adherents assurance of their superiority. Held together as a disciplined elite, armed with a convincing doctrine, militant in their demands, and intolerant of all opposition, the sects were a new type of group, consciously refusing integration. The reformers had offered

26. The composition of the sectarian groups is indicated in the lists of those appearing before the Rat accused of Anabaptist activity. A list (from Krebs and Rott, *Elsass, I*, no. 224, 270–72) in October 1530 included the following persons:
A butcher's wife
A clockmaker
A shepherd
An armorer
A cutler
A maker of tiles for stoves
A tailor
A teacher, the brother of the cathedral organist
A carpenter (from Vienna)
A butcher
Lukas Hackfurt, the supervisor of poor relief
Depositions made by individual Anabaptists in prison, taken as a means of acquiring samples of their handwriting (also from Krebs and Rott, *Elsass, I*, no. 175, 228–31), give further occupational information:
Dees Nelle, from Staufenberg, I cannot write, am a vine-dresser.
Jerg Nespitzer, from Layinger, cannot write, a weaver at Han's Berts.
Jorg Walter, also a weaver.
Linkhart Vonk from Ehrstätt, an apprentice with Kristoff the shoemaker, cannot write.
Heynrich Groman, a brickmaker from Wörms.
Anders Huber from Lahr, a canon.
Hans Franck from Milttenbrugek, the tailor in the Kuorbengassen.
Lorenz Liesch, furrier from Nördlinger.
Peter from Ladenburg, a rummage dealer.
Hans from Strassburg, a rummage dealer.
Contz from Wissbaden, a player.
Eighteen persons listed as beggars.

as an inherent part of their doctrine a new concept of community, of Christian responsibility. Each group, however, tended to interpret this message differently, and it led, even within the first ten years, to increasing social fragmentation. The old dichotomy was replaced by a series of smaller divisions.

The social class most closely caught up in the Reform was the populace, the Gemeinde. The earliest response to the preaching of Zell came from the anonymous mass of *Leute* who crowded in to the cathedral, individualized only by the two carpenters who made him a portable pulpit which they carried back to their homes at night. The parish, sturdy working-class folk, supported Anton Firn when he married and was dismissed by the bishop. The congregation of Young St. Peter, composed of stonecutters, carpenters, and tailors, assembled in the aisles, armed, to enforce their selection of an evangelical preacher. It was handworkers and "a variety of trash" who gathered in the Horse Market and rioted at the Augustinian and Carthusian monasteries.[27] Furthermore, the threat of unrest on the part of this group led the Magistrat, step by step, to close down the convents, to support the married priests, and, finally, to abolish the Mass.

The zeal of this group did not flag after the enthusiasm of the first few years. It is often assumed that the failure of the Peasants' Revolt broke the support of the lower classes for the Reform. This was not the case in Strasbourg. In the first place, the Gemeinde of the guilds did not actively support the peasants; this was made quite clear in the individual hearings held by the Rat, in which each guildsman was questioned on his attitude. After the Peasants' Revolt when the major campaign to abolish the Mass was mounted, numerous petitions addressed to the Magistrat were written and signed by the Gemeinde themselves. Fifteen of the twenty guilds directly petitioned the Rat to abolish the Mass, although we have no way of knowing whether these requests reflected the decision of the entire guild. The ac-

27. Büheler, *Chronique,* p. 73.

cumulated evidence indicates broad popular support for the reformers at this period, but less enthusiasm on the part of the governing class. The fact that it is impossible to uncover any evidence of a major Anabaptist congregation of Strasbourg burghers is another testimony to their loyalty to the reformers. While individuals may have flirted with the sectarian doctrines, the majority of the citizens remained in their parish churches with their reformed preacher. A decisive indication of the continued devotion of the populace to the Reform is reflected in the short-lived experiment with a system of Christian discipline in 1547–48. The congregations of St. Nicholas and Young St. Peter, both largely working class parishes, voluntarily accepted the idea of discipline and took the initiative, in the face of stiff opposition from the Rat, to call the parish together and submit to self-examination and criticism. When the minister Fagius was afraid to attend such a meeting because of magistral disapprobation, three stalwart members of the parish went to his house and brought him to the church.[28] It was the parishioners who supported the establishment of the Christian community.

The support of the populace for the new movement extended through the period under consideration. Furthermore it should be recognized that their interests were not betrayed by the Reform but that they received specific social and economic advantages from it, such as reassignment of the tithes. The tithes collected by the medieval church were disliked by all urban classes. From the viewpoint of modern tax policy, as a fixed tax they constituted an especially heavy burden on the lower-income groups. At the very dawn of the Reformation, groups of parishioners took action to rid themselves of the levy or to turn it to parish needs. In 1523 the gardeners of St. Andreas protested against the collection of tithes because their priest was old and refused to preach the Gospel. In early 1524 the gardeners of St. Aurelie asked the chapter of St. Thomas for an evangelical preacher and offered to pay his stipend from

28. Bellardi, *"Christlichen Gemeinschaft" in Strassburg*, pp. 50–51.

their own pockets. When the chapter was slow in assenting to the plan, the parish, with the assent of the Rat, decided in May to requisition the tithes for this purpose.[29] Although the Magistrat did not abolish the tithes after it had assumed the direction of the parish churches in 1525, the funds were administered by civil officials and were used mainly to support the parishes. There was no longer a feeling that the laity were being gouged to support the lazy and indolent clergy. Furthermore, by 1525–26 the majority of the monastic properties and much of the property and revenues of the chapters were being used for public purposes. The reorganization of welfare, the expansion of the hospital, the new school facilities, scholarships, teacher salaries—all were dependent on former ecclesiastical funds and were available to all the citizens. Although this did not involve distribution of the wealth among individuals, goods and services were made available on a broad scale.[30] There was never any attempt by the Rat to limit the schools or the hospitals to the upper classes; indeed it made every effort to establish scholarship funds for the poor and maintained a large refugee center as well as a church for persons who were not even citizens.

Besides the reassignment of ecclesiastical revenues, the Magistrat created legislation to abolish the use of perpetual leases, again mainly involving church property. Attempts to control this practice reached back to the fifteenth century, and in 1502 the Rat had tried again. In 1523 an act was passed providing for redemption of current leases and forbidding this arrangement in the future. While this, in most cases, freed property leased by the patriciate, it also affected the lower classes, for they too leased houses owned by the church, particularly in the parishes of St. Stephen and St. Aurelie, where the gardeners rented their lands from the nearby convents.[31] Abolition of the lease in perpetuity was

29. Rott, "Artisanat et mouvements sociaux," p. 144.
30. Ibid., p. 150.
31. Ibid., pp. 150–51.

one more means of moving property out of the control of the church and making it available to the citizens.

In addition to these material and tangible benefits the Reform also created a new self-confidence among the workers, arising from a sense of the dignity and worth of their labors. The reformers' sermons criticizing the monastic clergy taught that God respected and honored the working man, the laborer in the vineyard, and manual work for the first time was raised to the same level of importance as prayer and intellectual activity.[32] Thus the Reform resolved some of the traditional problems and dissatisfactions of the workers, and they were given a meaningful ethic. The ministers spoke of doing one's job well, of being a good Christian neighbor, of fulfilling one's duty to the city—all this gave the workers a sense of integrity.[33]

If the Reform gave fresh meaning to the lives of the common people, the patriciate made proportional gains. This stable group, composed of men of position or power, had little need for the social message of the new ideology. In the early years their response to the Reform was not enthusiastic. Gradually they did accept the Reformation, but as they did so, they modified and changed its original emphasis. It is perhaps more accurate to say that they absorbed the Reform, fitting it into and adapting it to their particular objectives. These objectives were primarily political. From the time of the foundation of the city the burgher officials had always had to struggle with the pragmatic realities of the dual jurisdiction. The state-within-a-state structure of the city made it difficult for them to assess and collect taxes, to muster and assign the militia, and to bring citizens to court and see that justice was done. Now, after four centuries, they could emerge as victors in this ancient struggle for primacy. The Roman clergy and church had been reduced to political impotency, and the magistral class could assume full control.

32. Ibid., p. 152.
33. Ibid., p. 151.

Assumption of control did not, however, entail a change in the constitution or in the power structure of the city. The constitution of Strasbourg remained unaltered from 1480 to 1789—the major committees of the Magistrat maintained their same form and functions; the Ratsherren stood outside the door of the cathedral every January to exchange their oaths of obedience and mutual responsibility with the citizens. Significantly, in the period of the Reformation the membership of the Rat itself showed a high degree of stability and continuity. The same men were elected and re-elected for periods of ten to twenty years.[34] Political power remained in the same hands. No new members were elected purely because they accepted the reformed religion: no new group emerged to grasp authority. The traditional, constitutional electoral process continued to place the same experienced veterans in the magistral offices. After 1528 the majority of these men had acknowledged the Reform, but this did not mean that the Magistrat had been infiltrated by protagonists of the new religion. Instead, it meant that the magistral class, as a whole, had adopted the Reform and would proceed cautiously and deliberately to make the necessary changes. In this process, however, it consciously eschewed novel political forms. The reformers offered them a new concept of the state, the idea of a unified corporate entity in which the magistrates, the clergy, and the citizens would work together to achieve a common end. The Magistrat refused this solution to the old problem of dichotomy and instead created unity by keeping its recently acquired functions exclusively to itself.

They did not develop new institutions or forms of organization either; instead they resorted to standard, tried techniques of administration and control, and their activities resulted in further proliferation of the standing committees, boards, and commissions which characterized the Magistrat. As a new function was acquired, a new set of Pfleger

34. See Appendix D.

was established to take care of it. Composed of three, four, or five Ratsherren, appointed for life, the Pfleger were responsible for prudently administering the funds involved and for reporting to their fellow Ratsherren from time to time. Four new major committees were thus added to the Rat—the *Klosterherren,* the *Scholarchen,* the *Almosenherren,* and the *Kirchenpfleger.* The result was an extensive increase in the functions and authority of the Magistrat, an increase that was particularly significant because the balancing elements of the medieval corporate state were weakening. The Roman church had been destroyed as a separate entity; the Reformed church was far too weak to be able to assert itself; and the guilds, well before the Reform, had ceased to play their self-governing, semi-autonomous role in the city. Thus the traditional medieval system, involving a division of power among several equal or relatively equal elements, was replaced by a concentration of authority in the hands of one group. The process had begun in the thirteenth century, and the crisis of the Reform provided the opportunity for its consummation.

The final effect of the Reformation was thus clearly related to the institutional and social structure of the society it had sought to influence. It achieved its initial success with marginal institutions and marginal groups. Weak and outdated institutions such as the monasteries and the liturgical activities of the chapters fell rapidly under the attack of the vital, fresh ideological formulation. The Gemeinde, who were only beginning to be conscious of themselves, found a rallying point in the new preaching and were drawn to the new religion. As the idea moved out from these groups, to meet the stronger, more stable elements in the city, however, a significant change took place. The reformers were not able to exert the same degree of influence but were replaced by the traditional leaders—the Magistrat. The change occurred in the process of holding the synod—after 1533 the new religion lost its initial force of discovery and revelation.

It was no longer able to change institutions by the force of its novelty; instead, it was adapted by traditional forces to serve their particular ends.

The Reform was not like a pebble thrown into the water whose influence spread out in precise, concentric, ever-widening circles. It achieved its greatest force at the moment of impact. For a brief period it was able to shatter old customs and create new directions. After this initial moment, however, a process of interaction set in, and the Reform was adapted and absorbed to fit the existing social and institutional pattern. It could transform certain institutions but was itself changed by others. Thus the revolutionary force of the idea was deflected by the political stability of the city and the strength of its traditional institutions.

APPENDIXES

APPENDIX A-1

Catholic and Protestant Sermons Published in Strasbourg, 1480–1548

	1480–84	1485–89	1490–94	1495–99	1500–04	1505–09	1510–14
Catholic sermons	8	15	12	12	8	12	16
Protestant sermons	0	0	0	0	0	0	0

	1515–19	1520–24	1525–29	1530–34	1535–39	1540–44	1545–48
Catholic sermons	25	8	0	0	0	0	0
Protestant sermons	3	21	6	1	0	1	2

APPENDIX A-2

Lutheran Tracts and Reformed and Catholic
Controversy Published in Strasbourg, 1518–1528

	1518	1519	1520	1521	1522	1523	1524	1525	1526	1527	1528
Books, sermons and tracts by Luther	0	4	17	8	8	14	6	10	3	3	0
Protestant polemic controversial works defenses vs. the Catholics	0	0	4	8	5	2	24	15	9	2	0
Catholic polemic	1	0	6	7	9	15	17	3	1	2	0

APPENDIX B-1

Summary of the Principal Professions Recorded in Three Parishes Requesting Reforming Preachers

The figures that follow give some indication of the social and economic composition of those parishes which were the first to involve themselves in the Reformation. Unfortunately no parish records for the years 1520–39 have survived. The very earliest available begin with 1540. I have used the years 1540–60 in making this analysis. The parish register for St. Stephen begins only at 1561. In this case I took the first register, which covers 1561–68, not wishing to extend the figures too far beyond the others.

The special nature of the medieval economy gives the analysis some validity since, by and large, sons tended to follow their father's profession. The children born in 1524 may be the very persons who are appearing on the registers in 1540–60. Furthermore, the town did not undergo any significant growth. No new quarters were developed during the Reform, and property tended to stay within a family. A final problem with regard to the data is that the profession is not given with every entry. In general it would seem to appear only one in four entries, somewhat at the whim of the pastor. There will be two pages in which every father is given a profession, then two pages with none. The figures thus actually provide a sample of approximately one quarter of the parish. Since St. Martin had disappeared by 1540 and St. Laurence was absorbed into the larger unit of the cathedral, I prepared figures only for the three parishes which remained the same.

	St. Aurelie	Young St. Peter*	St. Stephen
Gardener	108	80	80
Ropemaker	52	2	0
Domestic servant	64	24	5
Day laborer	40	10	0
Clothing trade	108	101	0
Woodworker	56	69	0
Fisherman	0	1	144
Boatman	0	0	119
Metalworker	13	36	3
Stoneworker	17	15	0

* It must be remembered that these figures cover only a seven-year period in the case of Young St. Peter, as against twenty years for the other two.

APPENDIX B-2
Register of the Professions Recorded in the
Parish Register of St. Aurelie
1540–1560

Gardener	108
Ropemaker	52
Domestic servant	64
Day laborer	40
Tailor	68
Customs collector	8
Miller	24
Cooper	28
Carpenter	28
Baker	28
Weaver	20
Furrier	20
Innkeeper	32
Strawcutter	12
Stonecutter	16
Locksmith	12
Shearer	3

Miscellaneous   2 each: Mercenary soldier, midwife, papermaker, butcher, oilmaker, teacher, doctor, wagoner

1 each: Groom, messenger, grocer, mason, cutler, stovemaker, harnessmaker, grain measurer, dollmaker, tiler, draper, soapmaker, fisherman, bather, forest-warden, hempmaker, veterinarian (known by the medieval term of the nunmaker), trumpeter in the cathedral

APPENDIX B-3
Register of the Professions Recorded in the
Parish Register of Young St. Peter
1561–1568*

Gardener		80
Day laborer		10
Domestic servant		24
Clothing trades		101
Weaver	22	
Tailor	39	
Hatmaker	12	
Furrier	16	
Shoemaker	11	
Dyer	1	
Woodworker		69
Cooper	23	
Carpenter	46	
Metalworker		36
Smith	12	
Locksmith	9	
Mintworker	2	
Armorer	10	
Cutler	2	
Coppersmith	1	
Mason and stonemason		15
Printer and bookbinder		4
Scribe and notary		4
Doctor-surgeon		3
Teacher		5
City official		8
Wagoner		9

Miscellaneous   1 each: Torturer, ropemaker,
basketmaker, glazier,
ragman, fisherman,
organmaker

* Parish Register begins only at 1561.

APPENDIX B-4

Register of the Professions Recorded in the
Parish Register of St. Stephen
1540–1560

Fisherman	144
Boatman	119
Gardener	80
Baker	61
Bather	6
Brewer	4
Draughtsman (for beer)	6
Gunsmith-armorer	3
Bridgemaster	1
Tanner	6
Wagoner	3
Apothecary	1
Crossbowman for the city	1
Doctor	4

APPENDIX C
Roster Lists of Strasbourg Guilds
1444–1551

The following lists provide the only available enumerations of the guilds. Located in the city archives, they are based on periodic musters made for the purpose of training or for inspection of the arms of those burghers required to give military service or to stand watch. Comparable lists are available for 1444, 1507, 1537, 1545/46, and 1551. A list for 1520 involves only a partial review and is not useful since there is no way of knowing the percentage of each guild present. A list for 1551 is too late for this study.

Even the four lists presented can give only a very general idea. The 1444 roster provides a basis of comparison. The others indicate that despite plague years, the population maintained itself at a relatively constant level over a long period of time and the traditional trades continued to employ about the same number of men. The lists also give an indication of the comparative size and importance of the different trades or activities, although it is always necessary to remember that the guilds, for military and voting purposes, included persons outside that particular trade.

Note that several of the guilds were still known by the name of the house where they met: Thus the Anchor was the boatmen, the Flower the butchers; the Friburger the innkeepers; the Lucern the millers. The Spiegel (Mirror) included the most important merchants, while the Möhrin (the Moor) was made up of the poorer trades—ropemakers, merchants of saltfish, carters, secondhand dealers, old clothes merchants and a pot-pourri of miscellaneous activities. During the Reformation most of the clergy who became burghers preferred to be placed in the Spiegel, the Friburger, the tailors, or the gardeners.

In the totals listed for 1444 I have done some regrouping. In the original list certain guilds appeared as independent entities which, by 1507, had been joined in the process of rationalization of the guilds. Since I am primarily interested here in total numbers, I have placed these trades with their later unit:

1. Secondhand dealers, fruit merchants, ropemakers, in the Möhrin.
2. Weavers, clothmakers, and wool shearers under Clothmakers.
3. Hawkers of wine and wine gaugers with the Winetasters.
4. Millers, grain merchants, and oil merchants in the Lucern.
5. Porters of barrels together with the coopers.
6. Carpenters and wheelwrights together.

Roster Lists of Strasbourg Guilds

	1444	1507	1537	1545/46.
Anchor (boatmen)	262	83	112	126
Spiegel (merchants)	265	129	226	235
Flower (butchers)	152	116	130	152
Friburger (innkeepers)	118	58	89	101
Clothmakers	264	141	210	259
Lucern (millers)	122	140	110	138
Möhrin (tradesmen)	165	70	368	587
Goldsmiths	142	126	136	241
Bakers	160	214	108	102
Furriers	93	70	80	80
Coopers	223	163	103	161
Tanners	77	68	67	73
Winetasters	128	75	160	190
Tailors	293	235	173	280
Smiths	163	226	146	209
Shoemakers	222	120	87	107
Fishermen	234	110	201	226
Carpenters	200	120	213	273
Gardeners	690	?	714	803
Masons	114	100	265	248

The lists for 1520 and 1537 were published by Schmoller in *Die Strassburger Tücher Und Weberzunft*, 1879, p. 515. The originals may be found in the Archives de la ville R 29, Folios 262 and 102, respectively. As indicated the 1520 list is too fragmentary to be very useful. The list for 1444 was published by M. Dollinger in his article "Le Premier Recensement et le chiffre de population de Strasbourg en 1444," *Revue d'Alsace*, 94, 1955 and may be consulted in its entirety there. The article is important because it definitively dates this list as 1444 rather than 1474–76 as had been suggested by Eheberg, making it one of the earliest examples of a city census, five years earlier than that of Nuremberg and contemporary with that of Fribourg in Switzerland.

The lists for 1507, 1545/46 and 1551 were found by M. Rott and M. Fuchs in the course of work on the catalogue of the Archives. They are listed in *Archives de la ville*, VI, VCG, 591. M. Rott has published a far more detailed breakdown of the lists in "Artisanat et mouvements sociaux à Strasbourg autour de 1525," in *Artisans et ouvriers d'Alsace*, Strasbourg, Librairie Istra, 1965, p. 158.

APPENDIX D-1
Membership of the Magistrat of Strasbourg
1508–1548

Analysis of the membership of the Magistrat at ten-year intervals from 1508 to 1548 shows a high degree of stability and continuity in the membership of the Stettmeister and Rat, from whom all positions in the major committees were filled. The same men were elected and reelected for periods of ten to twenty years. The lists of Stettmeister and Ratsherren elected from the guilds indicate that the majority of the members of the Rat served five or six terms of office. Thus, in 1508, fourteen of the twenty members of the Rat had already served from one to eight terms; five were new members that year; no dates exist for one member. Seventeen of these twenty were reelected after 1508. The Stettmeister showed an even greater degree of continued service. Adam Zorn served five terms as Stettmeister before 1508, and five terms thereafter. Otto Sturm had served fifteen previous terms and would serve three more. Hans von Endigen was elected to three terms before 1508, and to ten terms thereafter. Ludwig Boecklin was the only new Stettmeister; he served eight terms thereafter.

Of the twenty representatives from the guilds serving in 1518, thirteen had seen prior service, seven were new members, and thirteen were reelected after 1508. Glad Boecklin, one of the Stettmeister, served only two terms: 1517 and 1518. Hans Bock spent six terms in office before 1515, and fourteen terms thereafter. Peter Elhart had three terms before 1518, and seven thereafter. Egenolff Roeder, newly elected in 1518, would serve fourteen terms thereafter.

The Magistrat of 1528 is of particular interest since these men were in office at the time of the final decision to abolish the Mass. Two men had been elected for the first time in 1513 and 1515, respectively. Five had been first elected between 1520 and 1523; eight had served their first term after 1524; and five were serving their first term in 1528. Thus, thirteen of the Rat had served their first term after the Reform movement was well under way. The pattern of stability and repeated service did not change. Seventeen of these men were reelected after 1528. Of the Stettmeister, Jacob Zorn zum Riet had had two terms before 1528, two thereafter; Peter Elhart, eight before 1528, two thereafter; Jacob Sturm, one before 1528, eight thereafter. Hans Jacob Zorn served only in 1527 and 1528.

In 1538 the guild representatives included fourteen members with previous service, six who were serving their first term. There is an unusually high proportion of men, seven of the twenty, serving only two terms. This may be at least partially explained by the fact that

1538 was a bad plague year with a large number of deaths. The Stettmeister included: Egenolff Roeder von Diersperg, with eleven terms before 1538, three thereafter; Hans Bock, with seventeen terms before 1538, three thereafter; Ulman Boecklin, with four previous terms and six thereafter. Hiltbrandt von Mülnheim had served his first term in 1537 and completed thirteen more after 1538.

The figures for 1548 returned to the usual pattern. Sixteen members had had prior service, and four were serving their first terms. Even with the Schmalkaldic War and the establishment of the interim religion, sixteen would go on to reelection. The Stettmeister, however, did not have quite the same record of continuous service as before. Wolfgang Boecklin served only in 1547 and 1548; Claus Zorn zum Riet had only five terms: 1542, 1543, 1545, 1546, and 1548. Peter Sturm had served six terms before 1548 and would continue for six terms thereafter.

As far as the Ammeister were concerned, as Ford has pointed out, the position was simply rotated between six men. The law provided that a former Ammeister could be reelected after a five year interval. As a result, each former Ammeister simply awaited his turn (meanwhile still retaining the title, if not the functions, of Ammeister).*

Although the figures do not disclose the political or religious views of the Magistrat, they do indicate the stability of the political authority. As a general rule, two thirds of the members had seen prior service, and only one third of the membership was new—thus the majority were always repeaters. These particular years were selected as a relatively random choice, the octaval years were used because they included both 1528 and 1548, the years that saw the greatest changes. The figures for the intervening years reflect the same pattern. At no time in the period from 1520 to 1548 was there a sudden change in the composition of the Rat or in the Stettmeister. It is invariably the same general proportion of thirteen to sixteen old members, with four to seven new members. The evidence of continuity and stability is paramount.

* See Franklin Ford, *Strasbourg in Transition,* p. 12.

APPENDIX D-2

RATSHERREN, WITH TERMS OF SERVICE

1508

Ammeister

Jacob Wisebach, deceased, succeeded by: Heinrich Ingolt.

Stettmeister*

Adam Zorn, 1478, 1479, 1481, 1505, 1506, 1508, 1509, 1511, 1512, 1514, 1515.
Otto Sturm, 1484, 1485, 1487, 1488, 1490, 1491, 1496, 1497, 1499, 1500, 1502, 1503, 1505, 1506, 1508, 1509, 1511, 1512.
Ludwig Boecklin, 1508, 1510, 1511, 1513, 1514, 1516, 1517, 1519, 1520.
Hans Ludwig von Endigen, 1504, 1505, 1507, 1508, 1510, 1511, 1513, 1514, 1516, 1517, 1519, 1520, 1522, 1523.

Constoffler

Claus Berer
Martin Sturm
Reimbolt Spender
Jacob Zorn zum Riet
Melchior Zuckmantel
Peter Elhart

Representatives from the Guilds

Boatmen	Peter Arge, 1498, 1499, 1502, 1503, 1508, 1509.
Spiegel	Heinrich Ingolt, 1491, 1492, 1501, 1502, 1507, 1508, 1511, 1512.
Butchers	Gotpfrydt von Hohenburg, 1504, 1505, 1508, 1518, 1519.
Innkeepers	Claus Werlin, 1495, 1496, 1507, 1508.
Clothmakers	Ludwig Müge, 1503, 1504, 1507, 1508, 1513.
Millers	Hans von Burgheim, no entry for this name.
Möhrin	Diebolt Hiltbrant, 1500, 1501, 1504, 1505, 1508, 1509, 1512, 1513.
Goldsmiths	Hieronymus von Frankfurt, 1503, 1504, 1507, 1508, 1511, 1512.

* No distinction was made in the year 1508 between service in the Rat and service as a Stettmeister.

Bakers   Claus Swenck, 1508, 1509.
Furriers   Hans Slappe, 1474, 1479, 1480, 1507, 1508, 1515, 1516.
Coopers   Veltin von Dürningen, 1504, 1505, 1508, 1509, 1512, 1513, 1516, 1517, 1520, 1521, 1524, 1525.
Tanners   Vix Kintwilr, 1504, 1507, 1508, 1513, 1514, 1519, 1520.
Winetasters   Hans von Adertzheim, 1508, 1509.
Tailors   Mathis Meiger, 1508.
Smiths   Joste von Friburg, 1492, 1493, 1496, 1497, 1500, 1501, 1504, 1505, 1508, 1509.
Shoemakers   Herman Hess, 1501, 1504, 1508, 1509, 1512, 1513, 1518, 1519.
Fishermen   Hans Ulrich, 1507, 1508, 1515, 1516, 1519, 1520.
Wagoners   Marx Rebestock, 1481, 1482, 1487, 1488, 1489, 1499, 1500, 1507, 1508, 1513, 1514, 1519, 1520, 1523, 1524, 1529, 1530, 1533, 1534.
Gardeners   Asmus Hirt, 1508, 1509.
Masons   Hans von Wasselnheim, 1508, 1509, 1512.

RATSHERREN, WITH TERMS OF SERVICE

1518

Ammeister

Andres Trachenfels

Stettmeister

Gladi Boecklin, Senat, 1510, 1511, 1513, 1514.
                Stettmeister, 1517, 1518.
Hans Bock, Senat, 1512, 1513.
                Stettmeister, 1506, 1507, 1509, 1510, 1512, 1513, 1515, 1516, 1518, 1522, 1523, 1525, 1526, 1529, 1530, 1532, 1533, 1535, 1536, 1538, 1539, 1541, 1542.
Peter Elhart, Senat, 1494, 1495, 1500, 1501, 1505, 1506, 1508, 1509, 1511, 1512.
                Stettmeister, 1514, 1515, 1517, 1518, 1521, 1523, 1524, 1525, 1528, 1529, 1531.
Egenolff Roeder, Senat, 1515, 1516, 1519.
                Stettmeister, 1518, 1519, 1523, 1524, 1526, 1529, 1530, 1532, 1535, 1536, 1538, 1539, 1549, 1550.

Appendix D

Constoffler

Claus Berer
Heinrich Hüffel
Ludwig Zorn zum Riet
Heinrich Bertsch
Ulrich Büchssener
Philips Boecklin

Representatives from the Guilds

Boatmen	Ludwig von Rotwil, 1510, 1511, 1514, 1515, 1518, 1519.
Spiegel	Herbert Hetter, 1517, 1518.
Butchers	Gotpfrydt von Hohenburg, 1504, 1505, 1508, 1518, 1519.
Innkeepers	Claus Ingolt, 1518.
Clothmakers	Bastian Erbe, 1517, 1518, 1525, 1526, 1531, 1532, 1539, 1540.
Millers	Caspar Rumler, 1517, 1518.
Möhrin	Hans Lyndenfelss (Lindenfelss), 1518, 1519, 1523, 1526, 1527.
Goldsmiths	Bartholemis Kysteler, 1517, 1518.
Bakers	Hans Becke, 1518, 1519, 1522, 1523.
Furriers	Hans Schott, 1518, 1521, 1522.
Coopers	Wernher von Westhoffen, 1514, 1515, 1518, 1519.
Tanners	Hans von Ettlingen, 1517, 1518.
Winetasters	Jacob Kochersperg, 1510, 1511, 1514, 1515, 1518, 1519.
Tailors	Philips von Otenheim, 1518, 1523, 1524.
Smiths	Hans von Schuffoltzheim, 1518, 1519.
Shoemakers	Herman Hesse, 1501, 1504, 1508, 1509, 1512, 1513, 1518, 1519.
Fishermen	Heinrich Paltener, 1517, 1518.
Wagoners	Peter Trum, 1517, 1518, 1521, 1522.
Gardeners	Clauss Wolff, 1494, 1495, 1502, 1503, 1510, 1511, 1518, 1519.
Masons	Leohart von Mutzich, 1518.

RATSHERREN, WITH TERMS OF SERVICE

1528

Ammeister

Martin Herlin, 1522, 1528, 1534, 1540, 1546.

Stettmeister

Jacob Zorn zum Riet, Rat, 1507, 1508, 1514, 1519.
　　　　Stettmeister, 1525, 1526, 1528, 1529, 1531.
Peter Elhart, Rat, 1494, 1495, 1500, 1501, 1505, 1506, 1508, 1509,
　　　　1511, 1512.
　　　　Stettmeister, 1514, 1515, 1517, 1518, 1521, 1522, 1524,
　　　　　　　　1525, 1528, 1529, 1531.
Jacob Sturm, Rat, 1524, 1525.
　　　　Stettmeister, 1527, 1528, 1530, 1531, 1533, 1534, 1536,
　　　　　　　　1537, 1549, 1550.
Hans Jacob Zorn, Stettmeister, 1527, 1528.

Constoffler

Jerg von Mülnheim	Peter Sturm	Jerg Berer
J. Wurmser		
Hans Sturm		

Representatives from the Guilds

Boatmen	Erhard Rotwil, 1524, 1525, 1528, 1529, 1546, 1547, 1549.
Spiegel	Frantz Bertsch, 1527, 1528, 1532, 1541, 1542, 1544.
Butchers	Bernhart Hasse, 1523, 1528, 1529, 1534, 1535, 1542, 1543.
Innkeepers	Lux Mesinger, 1527, 1528, 1535, 1536, 1541, 1542, 1545, 1546.
Clothmakers	Lasarus Bernher, 1515, 1516, 1527, 1528, 1561, 1562, 1565, 1566, 1569, 1570, 1575, 1576.
Millers	Sigfridt von Biettenheim, 1523, 1524, 1527, 1528, 1531, 1532, 1535, 1536, 1542.
Möhrin	Jerg Burghäusen, 1524, 1525, 1528, 1529, 1532, 1533.
Goldsmiths	Jost Louchberger, 1521, 1522, 1527, 1528, 1531, 1532.
Bakers	Heinrich Münch, 1528, 1529, 1532, 1533, 1536, 1537, 1540.
Furriers	Heinrich Holcher, 1527, 1528.
Coopers	Hans Meigel, 1528, 1529, 1532, 1533, 1536, 1537.
Tanners	Lorentz Schott, 1523, 1524, 1527, 1528.
Winetasters	Hans Hug, 1528, 1529, 1532, 1533.

Appendix D

Tailors	Ludwig Binder, 1527, 1528, 1537, 1538.
Smiths	Bastian Württemberg, 1528, 1529, 1534, 1535, 1540.
Shoemakers	Hans Schütz, 1520, 1521, 1524, 1528, 1529, 1530, 1531.
Fishermen	Diebolt Lamp, 1527, 1528.
Wagoners	Caspar Romler, 1527, 1528, 1537, 1538.
Gardeners	Mathis Rodt (Roth), 1513, 1520, 1521, 1528, 1529.
Masons	Hans Wundermacher, 1528, 1529.

RATSHERREN, WITH TERMS OF SERVICE

1538

Ammeister

Hans Lindenfals, 1532, 1544.

Stettmeister

Egnolf Roeder von Diersperg, Rat, 1515, 1516.
Stettmeister, 1518, 1519, 1523, 1524, 1526, 1527, 1529, 1530, 1532, 1533, 1535, 1536, 1538, 1539, 1549, 1550.

Hans Bockh, Rat, 1512, 1513.
Stettmeister, 1506, 1507, 1509, 1510, 1512, 1513, 1515, 1516, 1518, 1522, 1523, 1525, 1526, 1529, 1530, 1532, 1533, 1535, 1536, 1538, 1539, 1541, 1542.

Hiltbrandt von Mulnheim, Rat, 1532, 1533.
Stettmeister, 1537, 1538, 1540, 1541, 1543, 1544, 1547, 1549, 1550, 1552, 1553, 1555, 1556.

Ulmann Boecklin, Rat, 1529, 1530.
Stettmeister, 1532, 1534, 1535, 1537, 1538, 1540, 1541, 1543, 1544, 1546, 1547.

Constoffler

Sigmund Wecker von Mittelhausen
Friderich Sturm
Philips von Kageneckh
Heinrich von Mülnheim
Jerg Boecklin
Claus Zorn zum Riet

Representatives from the Guilds

Boatmen	Peter Arg, 1538, 1539.
Spiegel	Hans Ebel, 1523, 1524, 1537, 1538, 1543.

Butchers   Hans Naf, 1538, 1539, 1544, 1545, 1548, 1549.
Innkeepers   Veltin Kips, 1537, 1538.
Clothmakers   Peter Behem, 1529, 1530, 1537, 1538.
Millers   Caspar von Molsheim, 1537, 1538, 1545, 1546, 1549, 1550.
Möhrin   Anthoni Wickler, 1538, 1539.
Goldsmiths   Jost Vetter, 1523, 1524, 1537, 1538.
Bakers   Michael Schaeffer, 1534, 1535, 1538, 1539.
Furriers   Anders Schlapp, 1537, 1538.
Coopers   Symon Franckh, 1534, 1535, 1538, 1539, 1542.
Tanners   Amandus Heusch, 1537, 1538.
Winetasters   Diebolt Gerfalckh, 1538, 1539, 1546, 1547, 1552, 1553, 1556, 1557, 1560, 1561.
Tailors   Ludwig Binder, 1527, 1528, 1537, 1538.
Smiths   Jacob Clein (Klein), 1522, 1523, 1538, 1539, 1544, 1545.
Shoemakers   Eckhart Wertheimer, 1538, 1539.
Fishermen   Anselm Balthner, 1537, 1538.
Wagoners   Caspar Romler, 1527, 1528, 1537, 1538.
Gardeners   Hans Roth, 1538, 1539, 1544, 1545, 1552, 1553, 1560, 1561.
Masons   Hans Kupffer, 1530, 1531, 1538, 1539.

RATSHERREN, WITH TERMS OF SERVICE

1548

Ammeister

Jacob von Duntzenheim, also Ammeister in 1554.

Stettmeister

Wolfgang Boecklin, Senat, 1539, 1540, 1544, 1545.
          Stettmeister, 1547, 1548.
Peter Sturm, Senat, 1524, 1525, 1527, 1528, 1530, 1531, 1533, 1534, 1536.
          Stettmeister, 1539, 1540, 1542, 1543, 1545, 1546, 1548, 1549, 1551, 1552, 1553, 1556, 1557.
Jacob Widergreen von Stauffenberg, Senat, 1541, 1542.
          Stettmeister, 1544, 1545, 1547, 1548, 1550, 1551.
Claus Zorn zum Rieth, Senat, 1538, 1539.
          Stettmeister, 1542, 1543, 1545, 1546, 1548.

316

Appendix D

Constoffler

Steffan Sturm   Mathis Brun von Reichenberg
Bernhardt Goss (von Dreckelstein)   Assmus Boecklin
Adolf von Mittelhausen   Ludwig Bock

Representatives from the Guilds.

Boatmen	Michael Heuss, 1544, 1545, 1548.
Spiegel	Friedrich von Gottsheim, 1547, 1548.
Butchers	Hans Neff (Naf), 1538, 1539, 1544, 1545, 1548, 1549.
Innkeepers	Hans Schell (Schoell), 1547, 1548, 1553, 1554.
Clothmakers	Lorentz von Dalheim, 1547, 1548, 1559, 1560, 1563, 1564.
Millers	Lorentz (Gremp) von Erstein, 1547, 1548, 1553, 1554.
Möhrin	Diebolt Schoell, 1548, 1549.
Goldsmiths	Martin Krossweiler, 1547, 1548.
Bakers	Michael Odenstein, 1544, 1545, 1548, 1549.
Furriers	Barthel Keller, 1547, 1548, 1551, 1552, 1577, 1578.
Coopers	Clauss Kayser, 1544, 1545, 1548, 1549, 1553.
Tanners	Jacob von Duntzenheim, 1541, 1542, 1547, 1548.
Winetasters	Hanss von Odratzheim, 1504, 1505, 1512, 1513, 1520, 1521, 1526, 1527, 1530, 1531, 1534, 1535, 1542, 1543, 1548, 1549, 1554, 1555, 1558.
Tailors	Jörg Christman, 1531, 1532, 1535, 1536, 1539, 1540, 1543, 1544, 1547, 1548, 1551, 1552, 1555, 1556, 1559, 1560.
Smiths	Hanns Lux, 1548, 1549.
Shoemakers	Humprecht Streler, 1548, 1549.
Fishermen	Jacob Mench, 1547, 1548, 1551, 1552, 1555, 1556, 1559, 1560, 1563, 1564.
Wagoners	Thomas Lehen, 1539, 1540, 1543, 1544, 1547, 1548, 1553, 1554, 1557, 1558, 1561, 1562.
Gardeners	Steffan Bruch, 1548, 1549.
Masons	Jacob Kun (Khun), 1536, 1537, 1540, 1541, 1544, 1545, 1548, 1549, 1551, 1554, 1555.

BIBLIOGRAPHICAL NOTE

The major documentary source for the period of the Reformation in Strasbourg is the Archives of the Chapter of St. Thomas. These archives are on deposit with the Municipal Archives and are administered by the same direction but are separately catalogued. The catalogue of Jean Adam, *Inventaire des archives du Chapitre de St. Thomas de Strasbourg* (Strasbourg, Imprimerie Alsacienne, 1937), is available in libraries in this country. The archives include copies of magistral documents, documents pertaining to the chapter itself, and a large collection of Bucer's and Capito's letters. Since several of the parishes in the city fell under the jurisdiction of the chapter, the archives contain parish documents. There are also miscellaneous documents pertaining to the administration of public welfare and the establishment of the schools. There is a wealth of material on the Anabaptists and on the organization and the liturgical forms of the evangelical church. They also contain several volumes, known as the *Varia Ecclesiastica*, a register of various documents concerned with church history made by the archivist Wencker in the eighteenth century. These are invaluable since in many cases the originals have been lost. The contents of the *Varia* are itemized in the archival inventory.

The Municipal Archives are catalogued in a series of volumes beginning with Brucker's *Inventaire sommaire des archives communales de la ville de Strasbourg*, antérieures à 1790, Série AA: Actes constitutifs et politiques de la commune, 4 vols. (Strasbourg, Imprimerie R. Schultz et Cie, 1878–1886). (Volumes 3 and 4 printed by G. Fischbach).

Since World War II new archival indexes have been prepared. Originally the archives were catalogued in terms of the place where the documents had been kept. The new catalogues use numbers instead of these ancient letter designations. They have been printed by the city of Strasbourg. Nine of them are listed below by their serial numbers. I have included page numbers as an indication of the size of the collections.

Fuchs, Joseph, *Inventaire des archives de la ville de Strasbourg antérieures à 1790*, Série I (formerly Inneres Dreizehner

319

Gewölbe) et Supplement de la Série AA, Strasbourg, Mairie, 1954, 1 vol. in 4°, 168 pp.

———, Série II (formerly Vorderes Dreizehner Gewölbe), Strasbourg, Mairie, 1953, 1 vol. in 4°, 193 pp.

Raeuber, Eugène, Série III (formerly Gewölbe unter der Pfalz), Strasbourg, Mairie, 1950, 1 vol. in 4°, 183 pp.

———, Série IV, Strasbourg, Mairie, 1949, 1 vol. in 4°, 218 pp. (in process of revision, to be republished in 1968–69).

Fuchs, Joseph, Série V, Strasbourg, Mairie, 1952, 1 vol. in 4°, 251 pp.

———, Série VI (formerly Verschlossenes Canzleigewölbe), Strasbourg, Mairie, 1960, 1 vol. in 4°, 500 pp.

———, Série VII (formerly Pfennigthurmgewölbe), Strasbourg, Mairie, 1964, 1 vol. in 4°, 234 pp.

———, Séries VIII et IX (Chartreuse, St. Nicholas aux Ondes, Fonds Wetzlar, Ordre Teutonique), Strasbourg, Mairie, 1964, 1 vol. in 4°, 150 pp.

For a careful summary of the history of the Strasbourg Archives and a definitive description of the various archival indexes listed above see the note by Jean Rott, "Chantiers Actifs: Les archives de la ville de Strasbourg" in the section "Archives, Bibliothèques, Musées," *Revue d'Alsace, 96* (1957), 221–29.

In addition to these sources, the *Thesaurus Baumianus,* deposited in the Bibliothèque Nationale at the University of Strasbourg, contains copies, in a nineteenth-century hand, of the major correspondence between the Strasbourg reformers and their colleagues in Swiss and German cities. This is particularly valuable because Bucer's handwriting is especially difficult to read, and the *Thesaurus* makes it possible to use the Bucer material without spending a prolonged period learning his hand.

The Strasbourg chronicles are a story in themselves. Until 1870, the city was rich in chronicle materials. There were five major ones, beginning with the *Koenigshoeven.* At the time of the siege of the city in 1870, M. Reuss, the archivist, recommended to his academic colleagues that special arrangements be made for some of the collections of the library and suggested that each man take home a certain number of rare volumes to be hidden in a safe place. The idea was dismissed as being overcautious. Unfortunately, Reuss's worst fears were realized when shots from the German bombardment burned the library. After the war the chronicles were painfully reconstructed, using the notes taken by various scholars, and these are the versions which must now be used. The chronicles are available in more than one edition. The edition I used, because it was possible to check all the footnote references, is the edition available in the Strasbourg

Bibliographical Note

Archives, published in Strasbourg by the Imprimerie Alsacienne. The chronicles are also published by the Société pour la conservation des monuments historiques d'Alsace. If this latter edition is used, the pagination may be different, but it is not difficult to find the citation since the texts are always in chronological order. The chronicles are not to be dismissed as hearsay accounts but are important records of archival materials no longer available. The following data provide some account of each collection:

Brant, Sebastian, *Les Annales*, Fragments recueillis par l'Abbé L. Dacheux, Fragments des anciennes chroniques d'Alsace, 4 vols. (Strasbourg: Imprimerie Strasbourgeoise, 1892–1901), vols. 3 and 4. Also published in: *Bulletin de la Société pour la conservation des monuments historiques d'Alsace*, IIᵉ série, 19 (1892–1901). These so-called *Annales de Brant* are in fact the work of a member of the Wencker family, chroniclers and historians of Strasbourg. Jacques II Wencker was a director of the Strasbourg Archives and in 1783 published this work with the title: "extractus ex prothocolis D. D. xxi necnon quibusdam ex annalibus Seb. Brandii, auctori Jacobo Wenckero." The work has always gone under the name *Chronicles of Sebastian Brant*. Dacheux, who prepared the modern edition, notes that the work is most useful since Wencker carefully edited the various manuscripts used, and the work may be considered as a résumé of important archival documents which unfortunately were destroyed after 1763.

Büheler, Sebald, *La Chronique Strasbourgeoise*, Fragments recueillis et annotés par l'Abbé L. Dacheux, Fragments des anciennes chroniques d'Alsace, 4 vols. (Strasbourg: Imprimerie Alsacienne, 1892–1901), vol. 1. Also published in: *Bulletin de la Société pour la conservation des monuments historiques d'Alsace*, IIᵉ série, 13 (1888). Originally a chronicle in classic form based on the example of the Koenigshoeven *Chronicle of Strasbourg*, the book started with the creation and came down to the popes, emperors, and finally the bishops of Strasbourg. It was started by Büheler, senior, but the section on the Reformation was written by the son, probably in 1588. Due to its explicitness and detail, modern scholarship concludes that the material from 1530 on is based on actual recollections of the author. Büheler was Catholic, and thus the work is particularly useful as a balance wheel to the Protestant accounts.

Specklin, Daniel, *Les Collectanées*, Fragments recueillis par Rodolphe Reuss, Fragments des anciennes chroniques d'Alsace, 4 vols. (Strasbourg: Librairie J. Noiriel, 1892–1901), vol. 2. Also published in: *Bulletin de la Société pour la conservation des monuments historiques d'Alsace*, IIᵉ série, 14 (1889). Daniel Specklin, born in Strasbourg in 1536, was apprenticed in the textile industry and also was trained as an engraver in wood. He became an architect and practiced in various courts of Germany from 1555 to 1564. In 1564 he returned to Strasbourg, and in 1557 he was made architect of the city, responsible for the fortifications. In 1587 he informed the Council of XIII that he had been writing a chronicle of the city during the last year because he did not have enough official work. The Council was unenthusiastic. They felt that his grammar was poor. The chronicle is important because it is based on the recollections of persons contemporary to the events described. Specklin was Protestant but had spent some time in Catholic countries, working for Catholic princes, and remained until the end of his life on the best of terms with the representatives of the empire and the Catholic princes in the area. The work, while Protestant in feeling, is in no way polemical.

Les Chroniques Strasbourgeoises de Jacques Trausch et de Jean Wencker, Fragments recueillis par l'Abbé L. Dacheux, Fragments des anciennes chroniques d'Alsace, 4 vols. (Strasbourg: Imprimerie Strasbourgeoise, 1892–1901). Also published in: *Bulletin de la Société pour la conservation des monuments historiques d'Alsace,* IIe série, 15 (1892). Jean Wencker was born in 1590 of a magistral family. He was Ammeister of the city and started to write his chronicle in 1637. In his preface he notes that the terrible famines of 1636 and 1637 had made him search through the old authors to see if other periods of war and bad harvests had caused similar shortages. He writes from a Protestant viewpoint. The importance of the chronicle is that as Ammeister, he had all the city archives at his disposal. Trausch was a lawyer and procurer of the Rat at the time.

BIBLIOGRAPHY

Adam, Jean, *Inventaire des archives du chapitre de St. Thomas de Strasbourg*, Strasbourg, Imprimerie Alsacienne, 1937.

Adam, Johann, *Evangelische Kirchengeschichte der Stadt Strassburg*, Strassburg, J. H. Ed. Heitz, 1922.

Allgemeine Deutsche Biographie, 45 vols. Leipzig, Duncker und Humblot, 1875–1900.

Ammon, Friederich Wilhelm Phillipp von, *Geiler von Kaisersberg, Leben, Lehren und Predigen*, Erlangen, J. J. Palm und Ernst Enke, 1826.

Andreas, Willy, *Deutschland vor der Reformation*, Stuttgart, 1932.

——, *Strassburg an der Wende vom Mittelalter zur Neuzeit*, Leipzig, Köhler und Amelang, 1940.

Anrich, Ernst, *Geschichte der Deutschen Universität Strassburg*, Festschrift aus Anlass der Feierlichen Wiederaufnahme der Lehr-und Forschungstätigkeit an der Reichsuniversität Strassburg, Strassburg, *Strassburger Neueste Nachrichten*, 1941.

Anrich, Gustav, *Strassburg und die Calvinische Kirchenverfassung*, Rede bei der Rektorats-Übergabe am 3 mai 1928 im Festsaal der Universität, Tübingen, J. C. B. Mohr, 1928.

——, *Die Strassburger Reformation*, Vortrag zum Reformationsjubiläum 1917, Schriften des Vereins für Reformationsgeschichte, 36, Leipzig, Rudolf Haupt, 1918.

Association Guillaume Budé, *L'Humanisme en Alsace*, Paris, Societé d'édition "Les Belles Lettres," 1939.

Baron, Hans, "Religion and Politics in the German Imperial Cities during the Reformation," *English Historical Review*, 52, 1937.

——, "Zur Frage des Ursprungs des deutschen Humanismus und seiner religiösen Reformbestrebungen," *Historische Zeitschrift*, 82, 1925.

Baum, Adolf, *Magistrat und Reformation in Strassburg bis 1529*, Strassburg, J. H. Ed. Heitz, 1887.

Baum, Johann Wilhelm, *Capito und Butzer*, Elberfeld, 1860.

Bellardi, Werner, *Die Geschichte der "Christlichen Gemeinschaft" in Strassburg (1546–1550)*, Quellen und Forschungen zur Reformationsgeschichte, 18, Leipzig, M. Heinsius Nachfolger, 1934.

Bickel, Ernest, *Wimpfeling als Historiker*, Inaugural-Dissertation, Marburg Universität, Marburg, 1904.

Bopp, Marie-Joseph, *Die Evangelischen Geistlichen und Theologen in Elsass und Lothringen*, Genealogie und Landesgeschichte in Auftrag der deutschen Arbeitsgemeinschaft genealogischer Verbände, ed. Heinz F. Friederichs, 3 vols. Neustadt, a.d. Aisch, Degener und Co., 1959.

Bornkamm, Heinrich, *Martin Bucers Bedeutung für die europäische Reformationsgeschichte*, Schriften des Vereins für Reformationsgeschichte, 169, Jahrgang 58, Heft 2, Gütersloh, C. Bertelsmann Verlag, 1952.

Brant, Sebastian, *Les Annales*, Fragments recueillis par l'Abbé L. Dacheux, Fragments des anciennes chroniques d'Alsace, 4 vols. Strasbourg, Imprimerie Strasbourgeoise, 1892–1901, vols. 3 and 4. Also published in: *Bulletin de la Societé pour la conservation des monuments historiques d'Alsace*, deuxième série, *19*, Strasbourg, 1892–1901.

——, *Das Narrenschiff*, in neuer übertragung von Franz Hirtler, München, Zinnen Verlag, 1944.

——, *The Ship of Fools*, Eng. trans. into rhyming couplets, Edwin H. Zeydel, Records of Civilization, Sources and Studies, 36, ed. A. P. Evans, New York, Columbia University Press, 1944.

Brucker, J., ed., *Inventaire sommaire des archives communales de la ville de Strasbourg antérieures à 1790*, 4 vols. Strasbourg, R. Schultz et cie., G. Fischbach, 1878–86.

Brunfels, Otto, *Von dem Pfaffen Zehenden Hundert unnd zwen und fyertzig Schlussreden*, Strassburg, Johannes Schott, 1524.

Büheler, Sébald, *La Chronique Strasbourgeoise*, Fragments recueillis et annotés par l'Abbé L. Dacheux, Fragments des anciennes chroniques d'Alsace, 4 vols. Strasbourg, Imprimerie Alsacienne, 1892–1901, vol. 1. Also published in: *Bulletin de la Societé pour la conservation des monuments historiques d'Alsace*, deuxième serie, *13*, Strasbourg, 1888.

Butzer, Martin, *An ein christlichen Rath uñ Gemeyn der Statt Weissenburg Summary seiner Predig daselbst gethon*, Strassburg, Johannes Schott, 1523.

——, *Instruction in Christian Love*, 1523, trans. Paul Traugott Fuhrman, Richmond, Va., John Knox Press, 1952.

——, *Ein summarische Vergriff der Christlichen Lehre und Religion die Man zu Strassburg hat nun in die XXViij Jar Gelehret*, Strassburg [no printer's mark], 1548.

——, *Verantwortung auff das in seine Widerwertigen ein Theil mit die Warheit ein Theil mit Lügen zum argsten Zumessen*, Strassburg [no printer's mark], 1523.

Bibliography

Capito, Wolfgang, *Entschuldigung an den hoch wurdigen Fürsten unsern Herren Wilhelmen Bischoffen zu Strassburg*, Augsburg, S. Otmar, 1524.

Clasen, Claus Peter, "Medieval Heresies in the Reformation," *Church History*, 32, 1963.

——, "The Sociology of Swabian Anabaptism," *Church History*, 32, 1963.

Cornelius, C. A., *Die Ruckkehr Calvins nach Genf*. Aus den Abhandlungen der k. bayer. Akademie der Wissenschaft, München, Verlag der k. Akademie, 1888.

Courvoisier, Jaques, *La Notion d'église chez Bucer*, Etudes d'histoire et de la philosophie religeuse de la Faculté de Théologie de l'Université de Strasbourg, 28, Paris, Alcan, 1933.

Cowie, Murray A., and Cowie, Marian L., "Geiler von Kaysersberg and Abuses in 15th Century Strassburg," *Studies in Philology*, 58, 1961.

——, "Rudolph Agricola and Peter Schott," University of North Carolina Studies in the Germanic Language and Literatures, 26, 1959.

——, eds., *The Works of Peter Schott (1460–1490)*, University of North Carolina Studies in the Germanic Languages and Literatures, 41, Chapel Hill, The University of North Carolina Press, 1963.

Crämer, Ulrich, *Die Verfassung und Verwaltung Strassburgs von der Reformationszeit bis zum Fall der Reichsstadt (1521–1681)*, Schriften des Wissenschaftlichen Instituts der Elsass-Lothringer im Reich an der Universität Frankfurt, Frankfurt am Main, 1931.

Dacheux, L., *Un Reformateur catholique, Jean Geiler*, Paris, C. Delagrave, 1876.

Eells, Hastings, *Martin Bucer*, New Haven, Yale University Press, 1931.

Eheberg, Karl Theodore von, *Verfassungs-, Verwaltungs- und Wirtschaftgeschichte der Stadt Strassburg bis 1681*, Strassburg, J. H. Ed. Heitz, 1899.

Elsas, M. S. *Umriss eine Geschichte der Preise und Löhne in Deutschland*, Leiden, A. W. Sijthoff, 1936.

Engel, Charles, *L'Ecole latine et l'ancienne académie de Strasbourg, 1536–1621*, Strasbourg, Schlesier et Schweikhardt; Paris, Fischbacher, 1900.

Ficker, Johannes, *Die Anfänge der akademischen Studien in Strassburg*, Rektoratsreden der Universität Strassburg, Strassburg, Universitäts-Buchdruckerei von J. H. Ed. Heitz, 1912.

——, *Thesaurus Baumianus*, Verzeichnis der Briefe und Aktenstücke, Strassburg, Selbstverlag der Bibliothek, 1905.

—— und Otto Winckelmann, *Handschriftproben des sechzehnten*

Jahrhunderts nach Strassburger Originalen, 2 vols. Strassburg, Karl J. Trübner, 1905.

Ford, Franklin L., *Strasbourg in Transition, 1648–1789,* Cambridge, Mass., Harvard University Press, 1958.

Fuchs, E., "Die Belesenheit Geilers von Kaisersberg," *Zeitschrift für Deutsche Philologie, 52,* 1927.

Fuchs, [François] Joseph, "Le Droit de bourgeoisie à Strasbourg," *Revue d'Alsace, 101,* 1962.

——, *Inventaire des archives de la ville de Strasbourg, anterieure à 1790,* Série V, Strasbourg, 1952.
Série II, Strasbourg, 1953.
Série I, Strasbourg, 1954.
Série VI, Strasbourg, 1960.
Série VII, Strasbourg, 1964.
Série VIII et IX, Strasbourg, 1964.
(See Bibliographical Note for full entry.)

——, "Les Prechter de Strasbourg, une famille de négociants banquiers du XVI siècle," *Revue d'Alsace, 95,* 1956.

Geiler, Johann, *Das Evangelibuch,* Strasbourg, Johannes Grieniger, 1515.

Genschmer, Fred, *The Treatment of the Social Classes in the Satires of Brant, Mürner and Fischart,* An Abstract of a Thesis in the Graduate School of the University of Illinois, Urbana, Illinois, University of Illinois Press, 1934.

Gerbert, Camill, *Geschichte der Strassburger Sectenbewegung zur Zeit der Reformation, 1524–1534,* Strassburg, Heitz und Mündel, 1889.

Gilbert, William, "Sebastian Brant: Conservative Humanist," *Archiv für Reformationsgeschichte, 46, Heft 2,* 1955.

Goldberg, Martha, *Das Armen und Krankenwesen des Mittelalterlichen Strassburg,* Inaugural-Dissertation, Universität Freiburg, Strassburg, 1909.

Hahn, Karl, *Die Katholische Kirche in Strassburg unter dem Bischof Erasmus von Limburg, 1541–1568,* Frankfurt am Main, Moritz Diesterweg, 1940.

Hanauer, L'Abbé, "Denrées et Salaires," in *Études économiques sur l'Alsace ancienne et moderne,* 2 vols. Strasbourg, Hagemann, 1878.

Hatt, Jacques, *Liste des membres du Grand Sénat de Strasbourg, des stettmeistres, des ammeistres, des conseils des XXI, XIII et des XV du XIIIᵉ siècle à 1789,* Strasbourg, Mairie, 1963.

——, "Les Métiers Strasbourgeois du XIIIᵉ au XVIIIᵉ siècle," *Revue d'Alsace, 101,* 1962.

Bibliography

——, *Une Ville du XVe siècle, Strasbourg*, Strasbourg, 1929.

Haug, Hans, *L'Art en Alsace*, Arthaud, 1962.

Hedio, Caspar, *Von dem zehenden zwo trefflicher predig Beschehen im Munster zu Strassburg*, Strassburg [no printer's mark, ca. 1524].

Heitz, Friedrich Carl, *Das Zunftwesen in Strassburg*, Strassburg, F. C. Heitz, 1856.

Herzog, Anton, *Die Lebensmittelpolitik der Stadt Strassburg in Mittelalter*, Abhandlungen zur mittleren und neueren Geschichte, 12, Berlin und Leipzig, Dr. Walther Rothschild, 1909.

Höpffner, Ernest, "Jean Sturm et l'enseignement supérieur des lettres à l'école de Strasbourg," in *L'Humanisme en Alsace*, Etudes de l'Association Guillaume Budé, Paris, Societé d'édition, "Les Belles Lettres," 1939.

Holborn, Hajo, "The Social Basis of the German Reformation," *Church History*, 5, 1936.

Hommage à Lucien Febvre, 2 vols. Paris, A. Colin, 1953–54, vol. 2.

Huizinga, J., *The Waning of the Middle Ages*, London, E. Arnold & Co., 1948.

Joachimsen, Paul, "Der Humanismus und die Entwicklung des Deutschen Geistes," *Deutsche Viertaljahrsschrift für Literaturwissenschaft und Geistesgeschichte*, 8, 1930.

——, *Geschichtsauffassung und Geschichtschreibung in Deutschland unter dem Einfluss des Humanismus*, Teil 1, Leipzig, B. G. Teubner, 1910.

Kantzenbach, Friederich Wilhelm, *Das Ringen um die Einheit der Kirche in Jahrhundert der Reformation*, Stuttgart, Evangelische Verlagswerk, 1957.

Kiessling, Elmer Carl, *The early sermons of Luther and their relation to the pre-reformation sermon*, Grand Rapids, Mich., Zondervan Publishing House, 1935.

Knepper, Joseph, *Das Schul-und-Unterrichtswesen in Elsass*, Strassburg, J. H. Ed. Heitz, 1905.

Knobloch von, J. Kindler, *Das Goldene Buch von Strassburg*, Wien, Carl Gerolds Sohn, 1886.

Knod, Gustav Carl, *Elsässische Studenten in Heidelberg und Bologna*, Separat Abdruck aus *Zeitschrift für Geschichte des Oberrheins*, N. F. 7 (1892), 2.

Kohler, Walther, *Zwingli und Luther, ihr Streit über das Abendmahl nach seinen politischen und religiösen Beziehungen*, 2 vols. Quellen und Forschungen zur Reformationsgeschichte 6–7, Leipzig, M. Heinsius Nachfolger, 1924–53.

Kohls, Ernst-Wilhelm, *Die Schule bei Martin Bucer in ihrem Ver-*

hältnis zu Kirche und Obrigkeit, Pädagogische Forschungen, Veröffentlichungen des Comenius-Instituts, 22, Heidelberg, Quelle und Meyer, 1963.

Köpcke, Hermann, *Johannes Geiler von Kaisersberg, Ein Beitrag zur religiösen Volkskunde des Mittelalters,* Inaugural-Dissertation, Universität zu Breslau, Breslau, 1926.

Krebs, Manfred and Rott, Hans George, *Elsass I, Stadt Strassburg 1522–1532, Elsass II, Stadt Strassburg 1533–1535,* Quellen zur Geschichte der Täufer, 7–8, Gütersloh, Verlaghaus Gerd Mohn, 1959–60.

Kreider, Robert, "Anabaptists and the Civil Authority of Strasbourg, 1526–1548," *Church History,* 24, 1955.

Lang, August, *Der Evangelienkommentar Martin Butzers und die Grundzüge seiner Theologie,* Studien zur Geschichte der Theologie und der Kirche, Zweite Band, Heft 2, Leipzig, Dietrich, 1900.

Langsdorff von, Karl Georg Wilhelm, *Die deutsche-protestantische Politik Jacob Sturms von Strassburg,* Inaugural-Dissertation der Universität Heidelberg, Leipzig, Sturm und Koppe, 1904.

Lecerf, A., *Etudes Calvinistes,* Paris, Delachaux et Niestlé, 1949.

Lévy-Mertz, Georges, "Le Commerce Strasbourgeois au XVe siècle," *Revue d'Alsace,* 97, 1958.

Littell, Franklin Hamlin, *The Anabaptist View of the Church,* Boston, Starr King Press, 1958.

———, ed., *Reformation Studies,* Richmond, Va., John Knox Press, 1962.

Locher, Gottfried W., "The Change in the Understanding of Zwingli in Recent Research," *Church History,* 34, 1965.

Mann, Julius, *Die Kirchenpolitik der Stadt Strassburg am Ausgang des Mittelalters,* Inaugural-Dissertation, Kaiser-Wilhelms Universität, Strassburg, 1914.

Maus, Theodor, *Brant, Geiler und Mürner, Inaugural-Dissertation,* Marburg, 1914.

Mentz, F., "Bibliographische Zusammenstellung der gedruckten Schriften Butzers," in *Zur 400 jahrigen Geburtsfeier Martin Butzers,* Strassburg, J. H. Ed. Heitz, 1891.

Mesnard, P., "Bucer et la réforme religieuse," *Bulletin de la Societé de l'histoire du protestantisme française,* 102, 1956.

———, L'Evangélisme politique de Martin Bucer: état politique et culturel de l'Alsace à la veille de la réforme," *Bulletin de la Societé de l'histoire du protestantisme française,* 102, 1956.

Meyer, Sebastian, *Doctor Sebastian Mayers etwann Predicant zur Barfussen zu Strassburg Widerrüffung, an ain Löblichen Freystatt Strassburg,* Strassburg, 1524.

Mieg, Philippe, "Note sur les négociants Strasbourgeois Muege au XVe siècle," *Revue d'Alsace,* 98, 1959.

Bibliography

Mitchell, Charles B., "Martin Bucer and Sectarian Dissent," Unpublished Ph.D. thesis, Yale University, New Haven, Conn., 1960.

Moeller, Bernd, "Die deutschen Humanisten und die Anfänge der Reformation," *Zeitschrift für Kirchengeschichte*, 70, 1959.

——, *Reichstadt und Reformation*, Schriften des Vereins für Reformationsgeschichte, 180, Jahrgang 69, Gütersloh, Verlaghaus Gerd Mohn, 1962.

Mueller, William A., *Church and State in Luther and Calvin*, Nashville, Tenn., Broadman Press, 1954.

Needon, Kurt Ossian, *Jacob Wimphelings Pädogogische Ansichten*, Inaugural-Dissertation, Universität zu Leipzig, Naumburg a, S., Gottfried Patz, n.d.

Neu, D. Heinrich, *Pfarrerbuch der Evangelische Kirche Badens von der Reformation bis zur Gegenwart*, Lahr (Schwarzwald), M. Schauenburg, 1939.

Neue Deutsche Biographie, 5 vols. Berlin, Duncker und Humblot, 1952–60.

Otther, Jacob, *Die Epistel Sancti Pauli an Titu, geprediget und ausgelegt*, Strassburg, Johann Grüniger, 1524.

Pannier, Jacques, *Calvin à Strasbourg*, Cahiers de la Revue d'histoire et de philosophie religieuses publiés par la Faculté de Théologie protestante de l'Université de Strasbourg, 12, Strasbourg, Imprimerie Strasbourgeoise, 1925.

——, *Recherches sur la formation intellectuelle de Calvin*, Cahiers de la Revue d'histoire et de philosophie religieuses publiés par la Faculté de Théologie protestante de l'Université de Strasbourg, 24, Paris, Librairie Alcan, 1931.

Panofsky, Erwin, "Renaissance and Renascences," *Kenyon Review*, 6, 1944.

Pascal, R., *The Social Basis of the German Reformation*, London, Watts and Co., 1933.

Peter, Rodolphe, "Le Jardinier Clement Ziegler, l'homme et son oeuvre," Unpublished thèse de baccalaureate en théologie, l'Université de Strasbourg, 1954.

Pfleger, Luzian, *Kirchengeschichte der Stadt Strassburg in Mittelalter*, Forschungen zur Kirchengeschichte des Elsass, 6, Colmar, Alsatia Verlag, 1941.

Pollet, J. V., ed., *Martin Bucer, études sur la correspondance*, 2 vols. Paris, Presses Universitaires de France, 1959–62.

Raeuber, Eugène, *Inventaire des archives de la ville de Strasbourg antérieures à 1790*, Série IV, Strasbourg, 1949.
Série III, Strasbourg, 1950.

Rajewski, Sister Mary Alvarita, *Sebastian Brant*, Catholic University of America, Studies in German, 20, Washington, D.C., Catholic University of America Press, 1944.

Rapp, Francis, "Ce qu'il en coûtait d'argent et de démarches pour obtenir de Rome la confirmation d'une élection épiscopale. Le cas de Guillaume de Honstein, évêque de Strasbourg en 1506," *Revue d'Alsace, 101,* 1962.

Rathgeber, Julius, *Strassburg im sechzehnten Jahrhundert, 1500–1598,* Stuttgart, J. F. Steinkopf, 1871.

Reuss, Rodolphe, *Histoire d'Alsace,* Paris, Boivin et Cie, 1920.

———, *Histoire de Strasbourg,* Paris, Fischbacher, 1922.

Ritter, François, *Catalogue des incunables et livres du XVIᵉ siecle de la Bibliothèque municipale de Strasbourg,* Strasbourg, P. H. Heitz, 1948.

———, *Catalogue des livres du XVIᵉ siècle ne figurant pas à la Bibliothèque nationale universitaire de Strasbourg,* Heitz, 1960.

———, *Répertoire bibliographique des livres imprimés en Alsace au 16me siècle de la Bibliothèque nationale et universitaire de Strasbourg,* 3 parts, Strasbourg, Heitz et cie, 1932–45.

Ritter, Gerhard, *Die Heidelberger Universität,* Heidelberg, C. Winter, 1936.

Röhrich, Timotheus Wilhelm, *Geschichte der Reformation im Elsass und besonders in Strassburg,* 3 vols. Strassburg, Friederich Carl Heitz, 1830–32.

———, *Mittheilungen aus der Geschichte der Evangelischen Kirche des Elsasses,* 3 vols. Strassburg, Treuttel und Würtz, 1855.

Rott, Jean, "Artisanat et mouvements sociaux à Strasbourg," in *Artisans et ouvriers d'Alsace,* Publications de la Societé savante d'Alsace et des régions de l'Est, 9, Strasbourg, Librairie Istra, 1965.

———, "Documents Strasbourgeois concernant Calvin," *Revue d'histoire et de philosophie religieuses, 44,* 1964.

———, "L'Humanisme et la réforme pédagogique en Alsace," in *L'Humanisme en Alsace,* Etudes de l'Association Guillaume Budé, Paris, Societé d'édition, "Les Belles Lettres," 1939.

———, "L'Humaniste Strasbourgeois Nicholas Gerbel et son Diaire (1522–1529)," Extrait du Bulletin philologique et historique (jusqu'à 1715), 1946–47, Paris, Imprimerie Nationale, 1950.

Rupprich, Hans, *Humanismus und Renaissance in den deutschen Städten und an den Universitäten,* Deutsche Literatur, Sammlung literarischer Kunst-und Kulturdenkmäler, 2, Leipzig, P. Reclam, 1935.

Schmidt, Charles, *Histoire du Chapitre de St. Thomas,* Strasbourg, C. F. Schmidt, 1860.

———, *Histoire littéraire de l'Alsace,* 2 vols. Paris, Sandoz et Fischbacher, 1879.

———, *Répertoire bibliographique Strasbourgeois jusqu'à vers 1530,* 6 vols. Strasbourg, J. H. Ed. Heitz (Heitz und Mündel), 1893–96.

Bibliography

Schmoller, Gustav, *Die Strassburger Tucher-und Weberzunft*, Strassburg, K. J. Trübner, 1879.

——, *Strassburg zur Zeit der Zunftkämpfe und die Reform seiner Verfassung und Verwaltung*, Quellen und Forschungen zur Sprach und Kulturgeschichte der Germanische Völker, 11, Strassburg, Trübner, 1875.

Sittler, Lucien, "Les Associations artisanales en Alsace au moyen âge et sous l'ancien régime," *Revue d'Alsace*, 97, 1958.

——, "Les Mouvements sociaux à Colmar du XIVe au XVIe siècle," *Revue d'Alsace*, 95, 1956.

Sohm, Walter, *Die Schule Johann Sturms und die Kirche Strassburgs in ihrem gegenseitigen Verhältnis, 1530–1581*, Historische Bibliothek, 27, München und Berlin, R. Oldenbourg, 1912.

Specklin, Daniel, *Les Collectanées*, Fragments recueillis par Rodolphe Reuss, Fragments des anciennes chroniques d'Alsace, 4 vols. Strasbourg, Librairie J. Noiriel, 1892–1901, vol. 2. Also published in: *Bulletin de la Societé pour la conservation des monuments historiques d'Alsace*, deuxième série, 14, 1889.

Staehelin, Ernest, "Bâle et l'Alsace," in *L'Humanisme en Alsace*, Etudes de l'Association Guillaume Budé, Paris, Societé d'édition, "Les Belles Lettres," 1939.

Stenzel, Karl, *Die Politik der Stadt Strassburg am Ausgang der Mittelalters*, Inaugural-Dissertation, Strassburg, 1914.

Strasser, Otto, "Un Chrétien humaniste: Wolfgang Capiton," *Revue d'histoire et de philosophie religieuses*, 20, 1940.

Strohl, Henri, "Un aspect de l'humanisme chrétien de Bucer," *Revue d'histoire et de philosophie religieuses*, 18, 1938.

——, "Bucer interprète de Luther," *Revue d'histoire et de philosophie religieuses*, 19, 1939.

——, "La Notion d'église chez Bucer dans son développement historique," *Revue d'histoire et de philosophie religieuses*, 13, 1933.

——, "La Théorie et la pratique de quatre ministères à Strasbourg avant l'arrivée de Calvin," *Bulletin de la Societé de l'histoire du protestantisme français*, 84, 1935.

Stupperich, Robert, *Bibliographia Bucerana*, Schriften des Vereins für Reformationsgeschichte, 169, Jahrgang 58, Heft 2, C. Bertelsmann Verlag, Gütersloh, 1952.

——, ed., *Martin Bucers Deutsche Schriften*, 2 vols. Gütersloh, Verlaghaus Gerd Mohn, 1960–62.

Thiriet, Freddy, "Sur les relations commerciales entre Strasbourg et l'Italie du Nord à la fin du moyen âge," *Revue d'Alsace*, 100, 1961.

Thompson, James Westfall, *Literacy of the Laity*, Burt Franklin Research and Source Works Series, 2, New York, B. Franklin, 1960.

Thomson, Bard, "Bucer Study Since 1918," *Church History*, 25, 1956.

Trausch, Jacques and Wencker, Jean, *Les Chroniques Strasbourgeoises de Jacques Trausch et de Jean Wencker,* Fragments recueillis par l'Abbé L. Dacheux, Fragments des anciennes chroniques d'Alsace, 4 vols. Strasbourg, Imprimerie Strasbourgeoise, 1892–1901. Also published in: *Bulletin de la Societé pour la conservation des monuments historiques d'Alsace,* deuxième série, 15, Strasbourg, 1892.

Ungerer, Jacques, *Le pont du Rhin à Strasbourg du XIVᵉ siècle à la revolution,* Publications de l'Institut des Hautes Etudes Alsaciennes, 7, Strasbourg, F. X. Le Roux, 1952.

Vansteenberghe, M., "Influences Rhénanes," in *L'Humanisme en Alsace,* Etudes de l'Association Guillaume Budé, Paris, Societé d'édition, "Les Belles Lettres," 1939.

Vermeulen, Adeodatus, O.E.S.A., *Der Augustiner Konrad Treger, Die Jahre seines Provinzialates, 1518–1542,* Rome, Institutum Historicum Ord. Erem. S. Augustini, 1962.

Die vertütschen Text aus den Bebstlichen Rechten, und vil anderen glaubwirdigen geschrifften daraus sich meniklich allerley mag erkunden wie erbahrlich bis her mit ein gemeine Christenheyt ist gehandelt worden, Strassburg, J. Knobloch, 1521.

Vierling, Josef Fridolin, *Das Ringen um die letzten dem Katholizismus treuen Kloster Strassburgs zur Zeit der Reformation und Gegenreformation,* Inaugural-Dissertation, Kaiser-Wilhelms Universität, Strassburg, Herdersche Buchhandlung, 1913.

Virck, Hans, ed., *Politische Correspondenz der Stadt Strassburg im Zeitalter der Reformation,* Urkunden und Akten der Stadt Strassburg, 5 vols. Strassburg, Karl J. Trübner, 1882–98.

Vogt, Jean, "A propos de la propriété bourgeoise en Alsace, XVIᵉ–XVIIIᵉ siècles," *Revue d'Alsace, 100,* 1961.

Voss, E. K. J. H., ed., *Jacob Wympfflingers Tütschland,* Reprinted from Transactions of the Wisconsin Academy of Sciences, Arts and Letters, 15, Part 2, December 1907.

Wackernagel, Hans Georg, *Die Matrikel der Universität Basel,* 2 vols. Basel, Verlag der Universitätsbibliothek, 1951–56.

Wendel, François, *Calvin, sources et evolution de sa pensée religieuse,* L'Université de Strasbourg, série B, 40, Paris, Presses Universitaires de France, 1950.

——, *L'Eglise de Strasbourg, sa constitution et son organization, 1532–1535,* Etudes d'histoire et de philosophie religieuses publiés par la Faculté de Théologie protestante de l'Université de Strasbourg, 38, Paris, Presses Universitaires de France, 1942.

——, *Le Mariage à Strasbourg à l'époque de la réforme, 1520–1692,* Collection d'études sur l'histoire du droit et des institutions de l'Alsace, 4, Strasbourg, Imprimerie Alsacienne, 1928.

Bibliography

Williams, George H., *The Radical Reformation*, London, Weidenfeld and Nicolson, 1962.

Wimphelingii, Jacobus, *Adolescentia*, Strassburg, Martin Flach, 1500.

[Wimpheling, Jacobus]

——, *Epithoma Rerum Germanicum usque ad Nostra Tempora*, Strassburg, J. Preuss, 1505.

[Wympflinger von Slettstatt, Jacob]

——, *Tütschland zu ere der Statt Strassburg*, Strassburg, Johann Philip Mülben und Josias Städeln, 1648.

Winckelmann, Otto, *Das Fürsorgewesen der Stadt Strassburg vor und nach der Reformation bis zum Ausgang der sechzehnten Jahrhunderts*, Quellen und Forschungen zur Reformationsgeschichte, 5, two parts in one volume, Leipzig, Vermittlungsverlag von M. Heinsius Nachfolger, 1922.

——, "Strassburgs Verfassung und Verwaltung in 16ten Jahrhundert," *Zeitschrift für die Geschichte des Oberrheins*, N. F. 18, 1903.

Wittmer, Charles and Meyer, J. Charles, *Le livre de bourgeoisie de la ville de Strasbourg, 1440–1530*, 3 vols. Strasbourg, P. H. Heitz/ Mairie de Strasbourg, 1948–1961.

Zell, Matthäus, *Christliche Verantwortung über Artickel in vom Bischofflichen Fiscal dasselbs entgegen gesetzt und in rechten übergeben*, Strassburg, Köpfel, 1523.

INDEX

Abolition of the Mass, in the parish churches (1525), 150; petition of the six burghers (1525), 148–49

Agricola, Rudolf, 48

Agriculture: conditions (1480–1520), 11; prices, 12

Albrecht, Archbishop of Mainz, 88, 89

Albrecht, Duke of Bavaria, Bishop of Strasbourg (1478–1506), 41, 70; Geiler urges him to reform church, 68

Almsgiving: decline during Reform, 280; reformers concept of, 279

Almosenherren, 279, 297

Almosenpfleger, 279

Alsace, 3, 244, 285; Hapsburg claim to, 30; influence of French in, 30

Alsatian cities, confer on control of Journeymen, 9

Altbiesser, Symphorian (Symphorius), 50, 113; assures Rat of his support, 151; marriage of, 138

Altorf, convent of, 150

Amerbach, Bonifacius, 88

Ammeister, 18, 24, 25, 265; social origins of, 26

Anabaptism, 177–200; concept of the church, 179; doctrine, 178; practices, 183, 193; social origins, 178

Anabaptists, 155, 177–200, 206, 215, 220, 290; cities and territories closed to them, 189; concept of the ministry, 206; first congregation of, 183; irenicism of reformers toward, 188; Marbeck's attempt to establish a church, 195; ordered to leave the city (1527), 186; reformers ask Rat to treat them with clemency, 198

Anchor, guild, 307, 308. *See also* Boatmen

Anthony, Duke of Lorraine, 151

Antwerp, 5

Apprentices, 286; conditions of, 7

Archbishop of Mainz, 195

Articles of Faith: Basel, 207; Strasbourg, 211–15, 217–18 n.

Augsburg, 98, 191, 192, 197, 251 n., 284, 285

Augustana, 201–02, 221

Augustine, St., 225

Augustine convent, 33, 292

Augustine order, 139, 235, 264; riot at, 142

Ausbürgertum, 19–20

Bahlenheim, 247

Bakers, guild, 169, 308

Ban: invoked against married clergy by bishop, 137; threatened against Firn, 135

Baptism, German service used (1524), 143

Basel, 88, 92, 98, 212, 228; Magistrat of, 207; transportation to, 4; University of, 48, 49, 88

Bavaria, 285

Bedrot, Jacob, 265, 270, 273

Belfort gap, 4

Betscholt, Martin, 95, 171

Biberach, 269

Biel, Gabriel, 131

Bishop of Strasbourg, 25, 155; appeals to pope and emperor, 172; asks Magistrat to discuss issue of the Mass with him, 162;

Index

Gross, Jacob, 183

Guerber, Erasmus, 150

Guilds, 6–8, 25, 286, 292; ammeister chosen from, 19; apprentice shops, 7; autonomy of, 8; book of guild ordinances, 7; clothmakers and weavers, 7; constitutional position of after *1400*, 24; constitutions of, 7; domination of city government, 19; gardeners guild, 113; growth of autocracy in, 8; levied taxes, 19; loss of democratic forms, 8; loyalty to Magistrat, 152; Lucern, 24; masters, 7; Mörlin, 24; organization of, 7; petition for abolition of the Mass, 168; polled by Magistrat with regard to policy toward clergy and clerical property, 151-52; political power of workers, 26; reformers ask Magistrat to supervise guild rooms, 151; reorganization of, 24; roster lists of, 307–08; tribunals, 7

Hackfurt, Lucas, 82, 136, 278, 280; administrator of poor relief, 278; and Anabaptism, 193; opens private Latin school, 265; renounces Anabaptism, 196. *See also* Welfare

Haguenau, 83, 198, 240; meeting of *1540*, 257

Han, Jacob, 46, 47, 50

Handwerksgemeinde, position of, 8

Hapsburg, house of, 62, 143; attacked by Sebastian Franck, 195; policy toward Alsace, 28, 30; rivalry with Valois, 30–31; territories of, 189

Hausbergen, battle of, 16

Hedio, Caspar, 83, 92, 113, 153, 196, 212, 221, 232, 258, 265, 270; appointed scholarchen, 265; assures Rat of his support, 151; friendship with Capito, 92; lectures on theology and history, 267; marriage of, 138; preaches sermon at installation of Bishop Erasmus, 257; sermons criticizing tithing, 125–27; sermon on the duties of the Magistrat, 220

Heidelberg, University of, 48

Held, Cüntz, 165

Herlin, Martin, 94, 137, 196, 211, 218, 258, 313

Hermann, Sixt, 46

Hesse, organization of church, 226

Hetzer, Ludwig, 185

Hildesheim, Bishop of, 174

Hirt, Assmus, 192, 312

Historical studies. *See* Humanists

Hofmann, Melchior, 189–90, 218, 220

Hohenstaufen family, 28

Holland, 220

Holy Roman Empire, 3, 30; Emperor Maximilian's plan for restoration, 31; and Strasbourg, see Municipal–imperial relations

Holy Roman Emperor, 172

Horb, the armorer, 193

Horb, city, 194

Hubmaier, Balthazar, 183

Hugonis, Johann, 46

Humanism, 45–67; Christian emphasis of, 49; and Christian symbolism, 54; and Geiler, 73; in German universities, 48; and national consciousness, 49, 59, 61

Humanists, 266; arrival of, 50; at-

Index

tempts to establish new educational institutions, 65; classical style of, 52; educational background of, 48; educational treatises by, 63, 64; form a *sodalitas literaria*, 51; historical studies by, 58–61; Latin translations by, 65; literary work, 51; and Marian controversy, 54; panegyrics to Hapsburgs, 62; social origins of, 46–48

Hutten, Ulrich von, 82, 90

Iconoclasm, 144
Ill river, 139; Strasbourg's position on, 4
Immaculate Conception. *See* Marian controversy
Imperial Chapters to the city (*1205, 1219, 1260*), 16
Imperial Free City, 3; new privileges granted by Emperor Sigismund, 29; privileges of, 16
Incarnation, Ziegler on, 182
Indulgences, authorities remove sums of money for local alms, 143; preached in Lent (*1524*), 142
Infant baptism: Bucer's view, 180; Capito's view, 187
Ingolt family, 10, 311
Ingolstadt, University of, 88
Interim of *1548*, 273; effect of on financial leaders, 10; interim religion, 96
Isny, 269
Italy, 285; trade routes from, 4

Jacob, Heinrich, wife of, 193
Joham, Conrad, 96
Journeymen, 286; limitations on activities, 9; passivity after *1525*, 10; and Peasants War, 9; position of, 8; prohibited from

forming associations, 9; strike of *1495*, 9; subordination to masters, 9; unrest of, 9; as wage workers, 11

Karcher, Diebold, 247
Kautz, Jacob, 188, 196, 206
Kaysersberg, 83
Kempten, 251 n.
Kenlin, Christman, 149
Kentzingen, 244
Kieffer, Diebolt, 165
Kirchenpfleger, 209, 211, 212–13, 216, 223, 229
Klosterherrin (convent supervisors), 147, 237, 297; appointment of, 141; inventory of Franciscan and Dominican property, 142; powers of, 145
Kniebis, Klaus (Nicolaus), 94, 171, 265
Knightly orders, not supervised by Klosterpfleger, 141
Knights of the Order of St. John, 33, 139, 264; lectures in Latin literature, 66; untouched by Reform, 238
Konvent, 205, 210, 212, 223, 229
Krutenau, 181
Kuno, Bishop of Strasbourg (*1105*), 42
Kursthans, 108 n.

Landau, 251 n.
Landstuhl, 84
Latomus, Johann, 193, 196, 231
Leipzig, 6
Lenglin, Johannes, 231
Leonardspital, 42; immune from taxation, 43
Lindau, 269
Locher, Jacob, controversy with Wimpfeling, 55
Lorraine: duchy of Holy Roman

343

Index

Index

Marian controversy, 54
Marriage of the clergy, 254. *See also* Clerical celibacy
Mary of Burgundy, 30
Masons guild, 169, 308
Mass: abolition of in the parish churches, 150; alternative services proposal, 161; bishop's defense of, 158; continued in convents, 238; first German, 114, 142; opposed by guilds, 168; reformers attitude toward, 156–58; Schöffen vote for abolition, 172; use of German for, 162. *See also* Abolition of Mass
Maximilian, Holy Roman Emperor, 30, 70
Medieval city: aims of civil government, 28; concepts of political authority, 27
Meffert, Jörge, 194
Melanchthon, Philip, 201
Mellisopolitanus, Conrad, 66
Memmingen, 251 n.
Menschen, Jacob der Jung, 149
Meyer, Jacob, 95, 265, 277
Milan, 4
Möhrin guild, 24, 169, 307–08
Mölsheim, conference of (1541), 258
Monastic orders: closing of, 140, 235–37; convents and monasteries, 33; curbing of legacies to, 35; Rat's authority over, 35; right of monks to inherit property, 36; schools, 45; use of revenues for schools, 264–65; voluntary closing, 147
Money, changes in the market, 284
Mueg, Andreas, 196, 211
Mueg, Daniel, 93, 135, 162
Munich, 285
Municipal–imperial relations:

friendship of the Emperor Maximilian, 30; new balance of power after 1480, 30; privileges granted by Emperor Sigismund, 29; provisions of Golden Bull, 29; city's recognition of Robert of Wittelsbach, 29
Murner, Thomas, 46, 47, 48, 50
Musculus, Wolfgang, 225

National council of the German church, 143, 174
Nigri, Theobold, 231
Nobility of Strasbourg. *See* Constoffler
Northofer, Georg, 92
Nuremberg, 98, 186
Nuremberg Mandate of 1523, 107, 133, 134, 144

Offenburg, 240
Oecolampadius, Johannes, 90, 187, 207–08
Old St. Peter, chapter, 32, 242, 290; Lutheran preacher appointed, 99; oath of loyalty to city, 40; school, 263; voluntary exile, 239
Old St. Peter, parish, 32; requests evangelical preacher, 114

Paedogogium, 270
Palatinate, 189
Paner, Anndres, 194
Paris, 271
Parishes: choose men to preach the Gospel, 113; parish registers, 138–40; petition Magistrat for evangelical preachers (1524), 115; responsibility divided between Magistrat and chapters, 240–41; schools provided for

345

Southern Methodist Univ.   fond
BR 848.S7C45
Strasbourg and the Reform;

3 2177 00460 8657